21st Century Dem
the Americas

This volume examines the promotion and defense of democracy in the Americas. Taking the Inter-American Democratic Charter (IADC) of 2001 as a baseline, it charts the evolution of the issue over the past decade. Although it considers historical antecedents, the main focus of the book is on key instances of promotion and defense of democracy in the Western hemisphere since the adoption of the IADC. It analyzes democratic norms, norm enforcement mechanisms and how they work in practice. Special attention is paid to the 2009 Honduras coup, the issues raised by it and the debates that surrounded it, as this was the first instance in which a member state was suspended in accordance with the IADC. Three central themes guide the analysis: the nature of challenges to democracy in Latin America; the role of regional organizations as democracy promoters; and the transformation of inter-American relations.

The book unveils the key achievements and limitations of the Organization of American States (OAS) in the field and will be of great interest to students and scholars of democratization, US–Latin American relations, international relations of Latin America and international organizations.

Jorge Heine is CIGI Professor of Global Governance at the Balsillie School of International Affairs, Wilfrid Laurier University, and a Wilson Center Global Fellow.

Brigitte Weiffen is a Lecturer in the Department of Politics and Public Administration at the University of Konstanz and a Visiting Professor at the Institute of International Relations, University of São Paulo.

Routledge Global Institutions Series

Edited by Thomas G. Weiss

The CUNY Graduate Center, New York, USA

and Rorden Wilkinson

University of Sussex, UK

About the series

The "Global Institutions Series" provides cutting-edge books about many aspects of what we know as "global governance." It emerges from our shared frustrations with the state of available knowledge—electronic and print-wise, for research and teaching—in the area. The series is designed as a resource for those interested in exploring issues of international organization and global governance. Since the first volumes appeared in 2005, we have taken significant strides toward filling conceptual gaps.

The series consists of three related "streams" distinguished by their blue, red, and green covers. The blue volumes, comprising the majority of the books in the series, provide user-friendly and short (usually no more than 50,000 words) but authoritative guides to major global and regional organizations, as well as key issues in the global governance of security, the environment, human rights, poverty, and humanitarian action among others. The books with red covers are designed to present original research and serve as extended and more specialized treatments of issues pertinent for advancing understanding about global governance. The volumes with green covers—the most recent departure in the series—are comprehensive and accessible accounts of the major theoretical approaches to global governance and international organization.

The books in each of the streams are written by experts in the field, ranging from the most senior and respected authors to first-rate scholars at the beginning of their careers. In combination, the three components of the series—blue, red, and green—serve as key resources for faculty, students, and practitioners alike. The works in the blue and green streams have value as core and complementary readings in courses on, among other things, international organization, global governance, international law, international relations, and international political economy; the red volumes allow further reflection and investigation in these and related areas.

The books in the series also provide a segue to the foundation volume that offers the most comprehensive textbook treatment available dealing with all the major issues, approaches, institutions, and actors in contemporary global governance—our edited work *International Organization and Global Governance* (2014)—a volume to which many of the authors in the series have contributed essays.

Understanding global governance—past, present, and future—is far from a finished journey. The books in this series nonetheless represent significant steps toward a better way of conceiving contemporary problems and issues as well as, hopefully, doing something to improve world order. We value the feedback from our readers and their role in helping shape the ongoing development of the series.

A complete list of titles appears at the end of this book. The most recent titles in the series are:

The BRICS and Coexistence (2014)
Edited by Cedric de Coning, Thomas Mandrup, and Liselotte Odgaard

India-Brazil-South Africa Dialogue Forum (IBSA) (2014)
Oliver Stuenkel

Making Global Institutions Work (2014)
Edited by Kate Brennan

Post-2015 UN Development (2014)
edited by Stephen Browne and Thomas G. Weiss

Who Participates in Global Governance? (2014)
Molly A. Ruhlman

The Security Council as Global Legislator (2014)
Edited by Vesselin Popovski and Trudy Fraser

UNICEF (2014)
Richard Jolly

21st Century Democracy Promotion in the Americas

Standing up for the polity

Jorge Heine and Brigitte Weiffen

Routledge
Taylor & Francis Group

LONDON AND NEW YORK

First published 2015
Routledge
2 Park Square, Milton Park, Abingdon, Oxon OX14 4RN

and by Routledge
711 Third Avenue, New York, NY 10017

Routledge is an imprint of the Taylor & Francis Group, an informa business

© 2015 Jorge Heine and Brigitte Weiffen

British Library Cataloguing in Publication Data
A catalogue record for this book is available from the British Library

Library of Congress Cataloging in Publication Data
Heine, Jorge.
21st century democracy promotion in the Americas : standing up for the polity / Jorge Heine and Brigitte Weiffen.
    pages cm. – (Routledge global institutions series ; 91)
Includes bibliographical references and index.
    1. Democratization–Latin America. 2. Democracy–Latin America. 3. Inter-American Democratic Charter (2001) 4. Organization of American States. I. Weiffen, Brigitte. II. Title. III. Title: Twenty-first century democracy promotion in the Americas.
    JL966.H455 2014
    341.24'5–dc23
                                2014010133

ISBN: 978-0-415-62636-1 (hbk)
ISBN: 978-0-415-62637-8 (pbk)
ISBN: 978-1-315-75513-7 (ebk)

Typeset in Times New Roman
by Taylor & Francis Books

Contents

Illustrations

Tables

Acknowledgments

This book is the result of the longstanding interest of the authors in democracy in the Americas. It is also the product of their dual commitments to the study of both international relations and comparative politics within political science. As in few other issue areas in the discipline, it is in the international promotion and defense of democracy that these two subfields merge and interact in challenging and unexpected ways, which we have found especially illuminating to understand the changing nature of politics in the new century. Over the past five years we have collaborated across the Atlantic on a variety of projects. In the summer of 2012 a visiting professorship in the Department of Politics and Public Administration at the University of Konstanz allowed Jorge Heine to spend three months in that beautiful city on the Rhine (where Britta Weiffen has been based since 2008) and made it possible for us to lay the foundations for the book. Another of Jorge's visiting appointments, this time at the Institut des Hautes Etudes de l'Amérique Latine (IHEAL) at the University of Paris in the fall of 2012–13, allowed us additional time in Europe to work together and further develop our ideas on the subject.

Extended interviews with Kevin Casas-Zamora, Luigi Einaudi, Peter Hakim, José Miguel Insulza, Rubén Perina, Ted Piccone, Carlos Portales and María Fernanda Trigo in Washington, DC, provided us with valuable insights into the many challenges posited by the protection of democracy in the Western hemisphere. Karen Bozicovic facilitated additional material. We are also indebted to Dirk Leuffen, Wolfgang Merkel, Michael Shifter and Laurence Whitehead, who commented on individual chapters, as well as to participants at several conferences where parts of the project were presented throughout 2013. Kevin Heyer, Nadine Petermann, Nora Schütze and Joseph Turcotte provided invaluable research assistance. Chilean artist Ximena Mandiola has kindly allowed us to use her painting 'Estudio de campo I' (2011) for the cover. The authors gratefully acknowledge funding and institutional support from the Center of Excellence "Cultural Foundations of Social Integration" and its Institute for Advanced Study, the Young Scholar Fund, and the Zukunftskolleg, all at the University of Konstanz. Jorge Heine is indebted to the Balsillie School of International Affairs and the Department of Political Science at Wilfrid Laurier University, in Waterloo, Ontario, his home institution for a number of years now, for providing him with the time, the flexibility, and the supportive and stimulating environment any project such as this one demands. Our final thanks go to Thomas Weiss and Rorden Wilkinson, the editors of Routledge's Global Institutions Series, for their invaluable support and unfailing patience throughout the writing of this book. They believed in it from the word go.

Jorge Heine and Britta Weiffen
Santiago, Chile, and Konstanz, Germany
March 2014

Abbreviations

ALBA	Alianza Bolivariana para los Pueblos de Nuestra América (Bolivarian Alliance for the Peoples of Our America)
APEC	Asia-Pacific Economic Cooperation
ASEAN	Association of Southeast Asian Nations
AU	African Union
BRICS	Brazil, Russia, India, China, South Africa
BTI	Bertelsmann Transformation Index
CAFTA-DR	Dominican Republic-Central America-United States Free Trade Agreement
CAN	Comunidad Andina de Naciones (Andean Community)
CARICOM	Caribbean Community
CELAC	Comunidad de Estados Latinoamericanos y Caribeños (Community of Latin American and Caribbean States)
DECO	Department of Electoral Cooperation and Observation
ECOWAS	Economic Community of West African States
EU	European Union
FDI	foreign direct investment
FTAA	Free Trade Area of the Americas
IACHR	Inter-American Commission on Human Rights
IADC	Inter-American Democratic Charter
IAJC	Inter-American Juridical Committee
IBSA	India, Brazil, South Africa
IMF	International Monetary Fund
IO	international organization
MERCOSUR	Mercado Común del Sur (Common Market of the South)
MICIVIH	International Civilian Mission in Haiti
MINUSTAH	United Nations Stabilization Mission in Haiti
NAFTA	North American Free Trade Agreement

NATO	North Atlantic Treaty Organization
NGO	nongovernmental organization
OAS	Organization of American States
OECD	Organisation for Economic Co-operation and Development
SADC	Southern African Development Community
SELA	Sistema Económico Latinoamericano y del Caribe (Latin American and Caribbean Economic System)
SG	Secretary-General
SICA	Sistema de la Integración Centroamericana (Central American Integration System)
UN	United Nations
UNASUR	Unión de Naciones Suramericanas (Union of South American Nations)
UNDP	United Nations Development Programme
UPD	Unit for the Promotion of Democracy

Introduction

On 11 September 2001, in a special session of the Organization of American States (OAS) General Assembly, the foreign ministers of the Americas approved in Lima, Peru, the Inter-American Democratic Charter (IADC). Over the course of the next decade, Latin America was to enter a highly fruitful and productive period, marked by strong economic growth and democratic stability—one that has signaled a real regional turnaround. This volume examines the promotion and defense of democracy in the Americas, and the role it has played in this veritable regional renaissance. Although it considers historical antecedents, the main focus of the book is on key instances of promotion and defense of democracy in the Western hemisphere since the adoption of the IADC. Taking the latter as a baseline, it describes the evolution of the issue over the past decade. It analyzes democratic norms, norm enforcement mechanisms and how they work in practice. Special attention is paid to the 2009 Honduras coup, the issues raised by it and the debates that surrounded it, as this was the first instance in which a member state was suspended in accordance with the IADC. Three central themes guide our analysis: the nature of challenges to democracy in Latin America; the role of regional organizations as democracy promoters; and the transformation of inter-American relations.

Since the 1980s, Latin America went through a long and protracted struggle to construct and consolidate democracy.[1] Although much progress has been made over the past few decades, many of the region's countries have not yet escaped from their condition as "low-intensity democracies." In the past, threats to democracy emanated from unelected actors such as the military that challenged elected governments by means of *coups d'état*. More recently, however, democratic crises arose when incumbent presidents overreached in their efforts to accumulate political power at the expense of democratic accountability and the rule of law. The relative fragility of the region's democratic institutions was described in a recent United Nations Development Programme (UNDP) study. The democratic deficits identified include that of representation and the growing gap between elected representatives and those they purport to represent, illustrated by the growing disaffection of large sectors of the population with the electoral process and politics in general; that of the balance between the various government branches, with ever more powerful executives with little horizontal accountability; and, last but not least, state capacity, with a state facing ever larger demands for services, but unable to provide them, for budgetary and other reasons.[2] In a context of widespread poverty and income inequality, it should come as no surprise that these huge deficits trigger political discontent. They also sow the seeds of political instability. Imperfect and fragile political institutions are unable to process the demands for change these conditions instill.

For a snapshot overview, Table I.1 displays the status of democratic transformation in Latin America in 2011 and disaggregates it

Table I.1 Status of democracy in Latin America

	Democracy status	Electoral regime	Political liberties	Civil rights	Horizontal accountability	Effective power to govern
Uruguay	9.95	10	10	10	10	10
Costa Rica	9.40	10	9.5	10	9	10
Chile	9.20	10	9.5	9	9.5	9
Brazil	8.15	10	8.5	7	8	9
Panama	7.70	9	7.5	6	6	9
Argentina	7.55	9	9	6.5	5	8
El Salvador	7.45	8	8	6	6.5	9
Dominican Rep.	7.40	8	8.5	6.5	6	9
Paraguay	7.00	8	7.5	6	6.5	7
Mexico	6.95	8	7	5.5	6	7
Bolivia	6.85	9	8	5.5	5.5	8
Peru	6.70	9	8	6	6	7
Honduras	6.40	7	7	6	5.5	6
Colombia	6.05	6	6.5	5.5	5.5	6
Nicaragua	5.75	6	7	4.5	3.5	8
Ecuador	5.70	7	7	5.5	4.5	7
Guatemala	5.55	7	6	5	5.5	5
Venezuela	4.40	6	5	3.5	2	2
Haiti	3.67	4	6	4	3.5	2
Cuba	3.42	1	2	2.5	3	1

Source: Authors' elaboration based on Bertelsmann Transformation Index 2012 (www.bti-project.org/index/). The Index "Status of Political Transformation" and each of its components range from 1 (=low) to 10 (=high).

according to various dimensions, drawing on the Bertelsmann Transformation Index (BTI) 2012.[3] In line with an intermediate concept of democracy (situated between minimalist and maximalist notions), the overall status of democracy is not only based on elections, but also on other crucial components of a democratic political regime, such as political rights, civil liberties, horizontal accountability and elected officeholders' effective power to govern.[4] Accordingly, Table I.1 illustrates the overall "democracy status" score as well as specific institutional deficits in Latin American democracies.[5] A categorical assessment based on those scores rates Uruguay, Costa Rica, Chile and Brazil as democracies in consolidation. Panama, Argentina, El Salvador, Dominican Republic, Paraguay, Mexico, Bolivia, Peru, Honduras and Colombia are termed defective democracies, in which civil liberties are limited by deficiencies in the rule of law, or in which the separation of powers is curtailed by the executive. Nicaragua, Ecuador and Guatemala are highly defective democracies, while Venezuela is classified as moderate autocracy. In addition to grave deficits in civil rights and horizontal accountability, they also suffer from the development of parastatal structures that curtail state institutions' effective power to govern. Haiti and Cuba are the only countries in the region currently classified as hard-line autocracies according to the BTI categorization.[6]

In the age of globalization, respect for democracy has ceased to be a merely internal matter. Hence, democratization studies must account for the role of external factors in democratic transition and consolidation. In an interdependent world, in which countries can obtain significant benefits from international trade, foreign direct investment (FDI) and tourism (to mention only a few items), the international community demands that certain conditions be met. Democracy promotion as a strand of foreign policy adopted by governments and international organizations is an expanding field, relevant both to scholars and to practitioners in the fields of comparative politics, international relations and development studies. Recent research suggests that regional intergovernmental organizations play an important role in the promotion and reinforcement of democracy by means of socialization, conditionality and enforcement. Yet most of the more comprehensive comparative studies on regional organizations as "norm entrepreneurs" in the area of democracy promotion concentrate on Europe, although a few studies have included other world regions from a comparative perspective.[7]

The OAS has not received as much attention. Recent publications examine its institutional structure, its role in regional security and the construction of the democratic paradigm. Mônica Herz's book on the

OAS contains one chapter on the democratic paradigm where she offers a brief historical summary and a tabular overview of OAS reactions to democratic crises.[8] Most of the few books and articles that focus on the democracy promotion regime in the Americas mainly reconstruct the development of the 1990s[9] or cover the adoption of the IADC and its first applications in the early 2000s, at most.[10] A few studies undertake an in-depth examination of specific cases, in particular the defense of democracy in Peru (1992–2000) and Venezuela (2002–04).[11] Most recently, Thomas Legler has offered an account on the performance of the OAS defense of democracy regime in the Honduran crisis.[12]

Democracy promotion in the Americas has been dependent on the dynamics of US–Latin American relations. The literature on US–Latin American relations, while often addressing the issue of democracy on the US foreign policy agenda, usually pays little attention to the role of the OAS. During the Cold War, the fight against communism overshadowed other foreign policy goals. The US government backed anti-communist authoritarian regimes in the region and supported the overthrow of democratically elected governments. In the post-Cold War era, US-Latin American relations experienced a multilateral moment. In the 1990s, countries in the hemisphere unanimously pushed for a renewal of the inter-American system and US administrations committed more seriously to the promotion and defense of democracy. US influence also remained largely uncontested in the economic sphere. The region provided the ground for the most ambitious attempt to establish a regional economic governance framework, the Free Trade Area of the Americas (FTAA). When the hemispheric heads of state signed the FTAA at the 1994 Miami Summit of the Americas, there was a widespread acceptance of US leadership in the post-Cold War world and of the deregulation and liberalization policies known as the Washington Consensus. The sub-regional economic integration schemes that were founded or revitalized during this period, such as the Common Market of the South (MERCOSUR) or the Andean Community (CAN), likewise subscribed to the principles of trade liberalization and open regionalism.

However, this did not last long. As a result of the terrorist attacks on the United States on 11 September 2001 (9/11), and the ensuing "War on Terror," US foreign and security policy focused on the Middle East and Central Asia almost to the exclusion of everything else. Latin America dropped from sight.[13] In the economic sphere, the US ambition to lead a continent-wide project faced growing regional pushback. Disillusioned with neoliberal reforms, new governments came to power, turned away from the Washington Consensus and withdrew their support to the FTAA.[14] At the same time, Brazil and Venezuela raised their foreign policy profile, and promoted South American unity. A number of new international institutions have been founded to strengthen Latin or South American cooperation to the exclusion of the United States. In order to bolster its claim for regional leadership, Brazil created the South American Community of Nations which came into existence in 2004 and was renamed Union of South American Nations (UNASUR) in 2007.[15] The Bolivarian Alliance for the Peoples of Our America (ALBA) was promoted by President Hugo Chávez of Venezuela reaching out to Cuba, the Caribbean, Bolivia, and Ecuador. Founded in 2004, ALBA promotes a socially oriented trade bloc rather than one strictly based on market incentives. The Community of Latin American and Caribbean States (CELAC), established in 2010, encompasses all Latin American and Caribbean states.

Thus, in the new millennium, hemispheric cooperation came under pressure from North and South. Washington increasingly lost interest in developments south of the Rio Grande. Latin American governments went for the creation of their own spheres of influence. UNASUR has emerged as the main contender to the OAS. As far as the defense of democracy is concerned, UNASUR, as well as other sub-regional organizations like MERCOSUR, CAN and CELAC, have followed the example of the OAS and have adopted mechanisms for the protection of democracy, creating significant overlap and, potentially, competition between the different regional institutions.[16] The book therefore also addresses the question whether the United States still acts as a regional hegemon, and studies the role of emerging regional powers such as Brazil and Venezuela which challenge the existing international order. The question whether OAS policies merely reflect the underlying balance of power within the international system or can be regarded as reflection of a normative consensus shared by member states also links the subject of the book to competing theories of international relations.

This book thus aims at a more comprehensive examination of the promotion and defense of democracy in the Western hemisphere in the course of the past decade. It takes into consideration the specific nature of the challenges to democracy in the Americas and power shifts in the Western hemisphere. It adds to research on the evolution of the OAS democratic paradigm by examining more recent applications of the democratic charter, in particular OAS actions responding to the 2009 coup in Honduras.

Chapter 1 provides the theoretical background to the debate on democracy promotion by regional organizations. It includes a short account of the forms of democracy support that these organizations apply and a survey of democratic commitments, monitoring and enforcement across different world regions. The two subsequent chapters describe the evolution of the OAS democratic paradigm. Chapter 2 provides an overview of the history and development of the concept of representative democracy in the OAS. It summarizes the emergence of the democracy promotion regime after the end of the Cold War, related legal and institutional changes of the organization, and the first applications of the provisions in the 1990s in Haiti, Peru, Guatemala, and Paraguay. Chapter 3 analyzes the creation and contents of the IADC. It makes reference to key moments in its conception and approval as well as to how it built on and improved upon the democracy promotion regime of the 1990s, but also points to some of the IADC's shortcomings.

Chapters 4 and 5 explore how the democratic principles have been put into practice. Chapter 4 reviews the democratic crises in the Americas after the approval of the IADC and the instances where it was invoked. The chapter provides a comparison of democratic crises, analyzing them in line with our three central themes: origin and type of democratic crisis, action taken by the OAS to defend and promote democracy (and, if applicable, action taken by other regional organizations), and implications for inter-American relations. The cases include the 2002 coup in Venezuela, the 2004 presidential resignation in Haiti, the 2005 constitutional crisis in Nicaragua, repeated institutional crises, forced presidential resignations and allegations of a coup in Bolivia and Ecuador, and the contested impeachment proceedings in Paraguay in 2012. Chapter 5 reconstructs the events following the ouster of Honduran President Manuel Zelaya in June 2009, which challenged the democratic consensus attained in the 1990s and codified in the IADC. The widely shared diagnosis that the forced removal of the president was an illegal and unconstitutional coup and the fact that Honduras is one of the poorest and smallest states in the region would have led us to expect forceful and ultimately successful OAS actions in defense of democracy. However, in spite of the initial unanimous repudiation of the coup and the involvement of the OAS in efforts to return to democracy, Zelaya was not restored to power. The chapter dissects the reasons for this seemingly counterintuitive outcome and discusses whether this has to be considered a failure of the common defense of democracy regime.

Building on the overall picture presented in the case studies, Chapter 6 reflects on the implications of the Honduran crisis for the defense of democracy in the Americas and inter-American relations. One of the most significant trends in the Americas over the past two decades has been the reestablishment of democracy and the eradication of military coups. The Honduras coup of June 2009 broke that trend and set a dangerous precedent for the hemisphere. Implications for the inter-American system include a potential reform of the IADC. Suggested changes relate to the OAS' difficulty in dealing with different variants of authoritarian regression, the possibility of taking action in early stages of a democratic crisis, and the concept of democracy that the organization is supposed to spread. The Honduras imbroglio also underlines the need to rethink inter-American relations at a time when Latin America is an ever more marginal issue in US foreign policy, new regional actors emerge and the launch of new entities like UNASUR and CELAC challenges the role of the OAS in the Americas. The concluding chapter summarizes the achievements and limitations of the OAS in the sphere of democracy promotion, reflects upon potential scenarios for the future of the inter-American system, and charts avenues for further research.

Notes

1 The literature on democratic transitions and democratic consolidation in Latin America and on challenges that democracies in the region face today mainly stems from the field of comparative politics. See for example, Frances Hagopian and Scott Mainwaring, eds, *The Third Wave of Democratization in Latin America: Advances and Setbacks* (Cambridge: Cambridge University Press, 2005); Larry Diamond, Marc F. Plattner and Diego Abente Brun, eds, *Latin America's Struggle for Democracy* (Baltimore, Md.: Johns Hopkins University Press, 2008); Jorge I. Domínguez and Michael Shifter, *Constructing Democratic Governance in Latin America* (Baltimore, Md.: Johns Hopkins University Press, third edn, 2008); Daniel C. Hellinger, *Comparative Politics of Latin America: Democracy at Last?* (New York and London: Routledge, 2011); Daniel H. Levine and José E. Molina, eds, *The Quality of Democracy in Latin America* (Boulder, Colo.: Lynne Rienner, 2011).
2 UNDP and OAS, *Nuestra Democracia* (Mexico City: Fondo de Cultura Económica, United Nations Development Programme and Organization of American States, 2010), 99–157.
3 The BTI 2012 refers to the year 2011. Information on the project, the scores, the coding rules and related publications are available at: www.bti-project.org/index/ and in Bertelsmann-Stiftung, ed., *Bertelsmann Transformation Index 2012. Political Management in International Comparison* (Gütersloh, Germany: Verlag Bertelsmann-Stiftung, 2012).
4 Wolfgang Merkel, "Embedded and Defective Democracies," *Democratization* 11, no. 5 (2004): 33–58.
5 The partial regimes are measured by the following BTI items (in case of two relevant items, the mean was calculated): (A) "Free and fair elections"; (B) "Association/assembly rights" and "Freedom of expression"; (C) "Independent judiciary" and "Civil rights ensured"; (D) "Separation of

powers" and "Abuse of office prosecuted"; (E) "Effective power to govern."
The calculations in the table follow Peter Thiery, "Intakte und defekte
Demokratien: Wohin bewegt sich Lateinamerika?" *Lateinamerika Analysen*
20 (2008): 55–75.

6 This categorization is taken from the BTI dataset, available at: www.bti-
project.org/index/.

7 See, for example, Jon C. Pevehouse, *Democracy from Above: Regional
Organizations and Democratization* (Cambridge: Cambridge University
Press, 2005), who examines the role of regional organizations in Europe
and South America in the 1990s; and more recently, Thomas Legler and
Thomas Kwasi Tieku, "What Difference can a Path Make? Regional
Democracy Promotion Regimes in the Americas and Africa," *Democrati-
zation* 17, no. 3 (2010): 465–91; Daniela Donno, *Defending Democratic
Norms: International Actors and the Politics of Electoral Misconduct* (New
York: Oxford University Press, 2013). Donno's study undertakes a global
survey of norm enforcement by regional organizations, but concentrates on
their reactions to electoral irregularities.

8 Mônica Herz, *The Organization of American States (OAS)* (London and
New York: Routledge, 2011), Chapter 3.

9 See Viron P. Vaky and Heraldo Muñoz, *The Future of the Organization of
American States* (New York: Twentieth Century Fund, 1993); Tom Farer,
ed., *Beyond Sovereignty: Collectively Defending Democracy in the Americas*
(Baltimore, Md. and London: Johns Hopkins University Press, 1996);
Andrew F. Cooper and Thomas Legler, "The OAS Democratic Solidarity
Paradigm: Questions of Collective and National Leadership," *Latin Amer-
ican Politics and Society* 43, no. 1 (2001): 103–26; Dexter S. Boniface, "Is
There a Democratic Norm in the Americas? An Analysis of the Organiza-
tion of American States," *Global Governance* 8, no. 3 (2002): 365–81; Ran-
dall Parish and Mark Peceny, "Kantian Liberalism and the Collective
Defense of Democracy in Latin America," *Journal of Peace Research* 39,
no. 2 (2002): 229–50.

10 See Andrew F. Cooper, "The Making of the Inter-American Democratic
Charter: A Case of Complex Multilateralism," *International Studies Per-
spectives* 5, no. 1 (2004): 92–113; Barry S. Levitt, "A Desultory Defense of
Democracy: OAS Resolution 1080 and the Inter-American Democratic
Charter," *Latin American Politics and Society* 48, no. 3 (2006): 93–123;
Craig Arceneaux and David Pion-Berlin, "Issues, Threats, and Institutions:
Explaining OAS Responses to Democratic Dilemmas in Latin America,"
Latin American Politics and Society 49, no. 2 (2007): 1–31; Thomas Legler,
Sharon F. Lean, and Dexter S. Boniface, eds, *Promoting Democracy in the
Americas* (Baltimore, Md.: Johns Hopkins University Press, 2007); Thomas
Legler, "The Inter-American Democratic Charter: Rhetoric or Reality?" in
Governing the Americas: Assessing Multilateral Institutions, ed. Gordon
Mace, Jean-Philippe Thérien and Paul Haslam (Boulder, Colo.: Lynne
Rienner, 2007), 113–30; Darren Hawkins and Carolyn M. Shaw, "Legalis-
ing Norms of Democracy in the Americas," *Review of International Studies*
34, no. 3 (2008): 459–80. See also Dexter S. Boniface, "Dealing with
Threats to Democracy," and Sharon F. Lean, "Monitoring Elections," in
Which Way Latin America? Hemispheric Politics Meets Globalization, ed.

Andrew F. Cooper and Jorge Heine (Tokyo: United Nations University Press, 2009).

11 See Andrew F. Cooper and Thomas Legler, "The OAS in Peru. A Model for the Future?" *Journal of Democracy* 12, no. 4 (2001): 123–36; Cynthia McClintock, "The OAS in Peru: Room for Improvement," *Journal of Democracy* 12, no. 4 (2001): 137–40; Andrew F. Cooper and Thomas Legler, "A Tale of Two Mesas: The OAS Defense of Democracy in Peru and Venezuela," *Global Governance* 11, no. 4 (2005): 425–44; Andrew F. Cooper and Thomas Legler, *Intervention Without Intervening? The OAS Defense and Promotion of Democracy in the Americas* (New York: Palgrave Macmillan, 2006); Randall R. Parish Jr, Mark Peceny and Justin Delacour, "Venezuela and the Collective Defence of Democracy Regime in the Americas," *Democratization* 14, no. 2 (2007): 207–31.

12 Thomas Legler, "The Democratic Charter in Action: Reflections on the Honduran Crisis," *Latin American Policy* 3, no. 1 (2012): 74–87; Thomas Legler, "Learning the Hard Way. Defending Democracy in Honduras," *International Journal* 65, no. 3 (2010): 601–18.

13 Peter Hakim, "Is Washington Losing Latin America?" *Foreign Affairs* 85, no. 1 (2006): 39–53.

14 Paul Kellogg, "Regional Integration in Latin America: Dawn of an Alternative to Neoliberalism?" *New Political Science* 29, no. 2 (2007): 187–209; Diana Tussie, "Latin America: Contrasting Motivations for Regional Projects," *Review of International Studies* 35, no. S1 (2009): 169–88.

15 José Briceño-Ruiz, "From the South American Free Trade Area to the Union of South American Nations: The Transformations of a Rising Regional Process," *Latin American Policy* 1, no. 2 (2010): 208–29.

16 On the concept of overlapping institutions and the case of OAS and UNASUR in the area of security, see Brigitte Weiffen, Leslie Wehner and Detlef Nolte, "Overlapping Regional Security Institutions in South America: The Case of OAS and UNASUR," *International Area Studies Review* 16, no. 4 (2013): 370–89.

1 The challenges of regional democracy promotion

- The trend towards regional democracy promotion
- Mechanisms for regional promotion and defense of democracy
- Regional democracy promotion in comparative perspective
- Limitations and challenges
- Conclusion

For a long time, democratic transition and consolidation were regarded as driven predominantly by domestic factors. As late as 2006, when introducing the topic of defense and promotion of democracy by the OAS, Cooper and Legler felt impelled to justify why multilateralism should be considered a relevant influence on democracy. According to them, international influences on democratization had by then mainly been accounted for in terms of structures, if at all.[1] By now, the role of international actors attempting to foster democracy across the globe has attained high visibility. Governments, government agencies, international organizations (IOs) and internationally active nongovernmental organizations (NGOs) engage in democracy assistance and democracy promotion abroad. Along the same line, regional instruments to promote and protect democracy are created. Most regional organizations such as the European Union (EU), OAS, and the African Union (AU) have adopted multilateral frameworks to help strengthen democracy and human rights norms and practices in their member states. Sub-regional organizations such as MERCOSUR, CAN, UNASUR, the Economic Community of West African States (ECOWAS), the Southern African Development Community (SADC), and even the Association of Southeast Asian Nations (ASEAN) have followed suit.

Democracy promotion is also an expanding field of research, relevant to scholars in comparative politics, international relations, and development studies. The creation of multilateral mechanisms for the promotion and defense of democracy within regional organizations is studied mainly by scholars in the field of international relations. They discuss the new phenomenon under different labels, including broader ones like regional organizations as democratizers or regional democracy promotion regimes,[2] and more specific ones like the legalization of international norms promoting domestic democracy, the commitment to democratic norms, norm enforcement, or democracy clauses.[3] The focus of this book is on multilateral mechanisms for the protection and defense of democracy when it is unconstitutionally interrupted or threatened. Yet, this chapter takes a more general look at the role of regional organizations as promoters of democracy in order to set the stage for an exploration of the OAS collective defense of democracy regime, its genesis and key features, and its application in situations of democratic crisis in Latin America. The first section reviews rival theoretical explanations for the emergence of regional democracy promotion regimes. The second makes some terminological clarifications and explores how and by what means regional organizations contribute to democratization. The third provides a global overview of the adherence to democratic norms and multilateral mechanisms for norm enforcement. The fourth section then examines the problems and pitfalls of regional democracy promotion regimes.

The trend towards regional democracy promotion

Proponents of liberal peace theory have long argued that membership in IOs promotes and strengthens democracy. Recent evidence suggests that regional organizations play an important intermediary role between the nation-state and global institutions. One should expect more effective influence on the domestic governance structure from a regional entity, as regional organizations tend to operate with fewer actors and higher levels of interaction than global organizations. In addition, since the vast majority of economic and military agreements are made under the auspices of regional organizations, they are more likely to be able to wield leverage to influence the democratic development of their member states.[4]

To explain the proliferation of regional multilateral democracy promotion regimes and the fact that some regional organizations have advanced more than others in their attempts to bolster democracy, structural and agency-centered explanations have been offered. According to structural explanations, the trend towards regional democracy promotion is an offshoot of a profound, historic diffusion of democracy and human rights norms across the globe.[5] The end of the Cold War lifted the obstacles to democracy promotion as a foreign policy objective. The diffusion of democracy and human rights was also helped by globalization with its increased trans-border flows of goods, services, capital, knowledge and ideas, and the growing trans-nationalization of civil society organizations and protest campaigns resulting from the information technology and telecommunications revolutions.

The global diffusion of democratic norms is most likely to lead to regional democracy promotion regimes when those norms have spread equally across a particular region and when regional actors unanimously subscribe to the same values. Thus, the adherence of more and more member states to democratic norms will result in a normative change within regional organizations. Hawkins and Shaw have pointed out that multilateral institutions are typically built around robust norms.[6] Norms are considered robust when they have been in effect for some time, have been upheld even in times of crises, and ultimately are taken for granted and are not challenged. Thus, it usually takes an evolutionary process until norms can be considered robust. Several regional organizations rhetorically endorsed democracy long before they actually established monitoring and enforcement mechanisms.

According to Pevehouse, the promotion of democratic transition and consolidation is strongest in regional organizations with a higher democratic "density," that is, with the highest share of permanent members that are democratic.[7] Hence, homogenously democratic organizations reflect existent democratic norms in their member states. Building on those explanations, Hawkins argues that the diffusion of democratic norms is also reflected in the openness of regional organizations to civil society actors. He argues that "institutional permeability"—defined as the extent to which regional organizations are accessible to non-state and civil society actors—helps explain differences in multilateral provisions for democracy promotion: "The higher the level of institutional permeability, the more likely it is that the institution's policies and practices will seek to constrain state behavior through increasing levels of precision and obligation."[8]

Agency-centered explanations look at the impact of individual states' preferences on the development of democracy clauses. By creating international standards, states may want to protect their own fledgling democratic regime. They may also want to exert pressure on other states to become democratic, either because the promotion of democracy is declared a foreign policy priority for reasons of domestic legitimacy, or because states hope that expanding the number of democracies will bring economic and political advantages, such as an expansion of interaction opportunities for trade and cooperation.

In times of political transition, there is often a functional demand by governments of member states to expand an organization's mandate to democracy promotion or to improve the organization's democracy promotion instruments. In a study on the evolution of human rights regimes in post-war Europe, Moravcsik found out that the membership in binding international regimes might be in the domestic political self-interest of national governments when the benefits of reducing future domestic uncertainty outweigh the sovereignty costs of membership.[9] This "lock-in effect" denotes the aim to embed newly attained norms in a binding regional regime as a means to stabilize the domestic status quo. Following this logic, countries that have recently experienced a democratic transition are expected to be the most active in constructing regional democracy promotion regimes that are meant to prevent returns to authoritarian rule and seek to bind the hands of future leaders.[10]

Apart from the democratic status of member states and the organization as a whole, the distribution of power within the region also influences the crafting of democracy promotion regimes. A crucial factor is whether the dominant mode of decision making is unilateral or multilateral. Following a realist understanding of world politics, the interests and preferences of powerful states determine the shape of international institutions. New programmatic initiatives within these institutions are launched by powerful states to serve their interests: "The most powerful states in the system create and shape institutions so that they can maintain their share of world power, or even increase it."[11] This might imply that powerful states inject their ideologies into international institutions in an effort to project their political system and values on weaker states. For regional organizations, this perspective would expect that a regional hegemonic power drives organizational development and leaves its imprint on the organization.[12] A countervailing explanation suggests that the adoption of democracy clauses is more likely in a multilateral setting. According to this view, states are more willing to commit to rules and accept constraints on their behavior under conditions where they do not fear an abuse of the established norm for unilateral intervention into internal affairs. The lower the threat that powerful states use legalized rules in unwanted ways, the greater the likelihood of strong democratic norms.[13]

The decision to institutionalize democratic norms might also result from crucial events or "shocks." One such challenge is a process of enlargement. In the face of applications for membership, an organization has to clarify whether political conditions should be set for accession. Another challenge is posed by acute political crises. When democratic norms are under attack in a particular member state, regional organizations might decide to establish mechanisms for the defense of democracy in response to the crisis.[14]

While each of the approaches contributes a piece to the puzzle, it is difficult to distil generalizable explanatory factors. First, some of the approaches focus on particular regions—often, Europe and the Americas—and neglect others. Legler and Tieku thus highlight the importance of path dependency. They propose that the unique constellation of actors and processes that initially created the regional regimes continues to shape their operation and reinforces distinct modes of democracy promotion and defense.[15] Second, the approaches do not always seek to explain the same phenomenon. While some of them look at the general propensity to establish a common democracy norm in the region, others explore the intensity of commitments, the progress and stagnation of such regimes over time, or the existence of particular instruments, such as accession requirements or monitoring. The following section will thus dissect in more detail what is meant by democracy promotion and how it works on the regional level.

Mechanisms for regional promotion and defense of democracy

Democracy promotion has different meanings. It has become a catch-all term that refers to any effort by international actors to encourage or facilitate the creation and consolidation of democratic institutions.[16] The term is increasingly perceived as denoting a field of scholarship at the intersection between comparative politics, international relations and development studies, related to a field of practice on how to support democratization from the outside.[17] At the same time, democracy promotion is a particular type of external support for democracy that needs to be kept apart from the defense of democracy. The terms refer to different phases and challenges in the process of democratization. Democracy promotion is any attempt to foster and support democratic transition, i.e. the retreat of a non-democratic regime, the holding of elections and the establishment of democratic institutions. However, democracy promotion does not end with democratic institutionalization. It might also contribute to what Pridham termed "positive" consolidation. This is the attitudinal shift in society towards democratic values at both elite and mass levels. It entails the remaking of the political culture towards systemic support for a new democracy.[18] In contrast, defense of democracy deals with "negative" consolidation, involving "the solution of any problems remaining from the transition process and, in general, the containment or reduction, if not removal, of any serious challenges to democratization."[19] It denotes measures to prevent democratic backsliding as well as reactions to democratic backsliding, and, in the most extreme case, reactions to democratic breakdown. Put differently, the promotion of democracy fosters a movement towards more democracy, while the defense of democracy is meant to hinder or halt democratic decline.

Promotion and defense of democracy in regional organizations can further be differentiated according to their target. Typically, democracy promotion is outward-oriented. It targets third countries and employs various instruments to persuade or pressure them to adopt democratic reforms. In some cases, the externally induced democratization process opens the path to accession to the organization. The example of democratic socialization of Eastern Europe (and currently, Southeast Europe) in order to prepare them for accession to the EU is a case in point.[20] However, democracy promotion might also be directed towards member states. Börzel and her coauthors speak of "governance transfer" if regional organizations explicitly demand and/or intentionally and actively promote standards for legitimate governance institutions like democracy, human rights, the rule of law and good governance in member states.[21] Democracy promotion in its inward-oriented version fosters "positive" consolidation. Measures like election supervision support the institutionalization of the democratic system and the adherence to the democratic rules of the game.

The defense of democracy is typically inward-oriented, codifies the democratic consensus of the member states and applies enforcement measures when members deviate from the mutually agreed-upon norms. However, there are also a few cases of defense of democracy by regional organizations in non-member countries, usually confined to diplomatic measures, such as the condemnation of a coup attempt in a third country. In very few instances have regional organizations gone beyond that and carried out enforcement measures to defend or restore democracy in non-member states.[22]

Mechanisms to promote democracy vary in their degree of coerciveness. Soft instruments, like consultation, socialization and persuasion, are used for information only and without obligation. Target states will be convinced of the benefits of democracy by dialogue and exchange. The most common and most analyzed variant of democracy promotion is democracy assistance. It is usually based on consent of the target country and therefore employed when domestic actors have already embarked on the process of democratization.[23] According to Carothers, democracy assistance occurs when international supporters allocate resources (i.e., money and/or expertise) to governments or civil society actors for specific tasks. These can involve training judges, rewriting municipal laws, or providing electoral support and supervision.[24] Dimitrova and Pridham further distinguish top-down procedures that target the national level from bottom-up practices that build on local participation. They also differentiate between different addressees of democracy assistance, like capacity building for the national or local governments, training for political elites, political parties or civil society organizations, or measures of political education of the wider public.[25]

Democracy promotion furthermore refers to activities that do not presuppose consent, but offer tangible or intangible rewards to the target state. In line with Schmitter, democratization might be fostered by convergence or by positive conditionality.[26] Convergence happens when the attainment of certain democratic standards is a prerequisite for membership in an association of countries. While states face certain constraints, they embark on the process voluntarily in the first place, following a drive to join an international organization in order to protect domestic democracy and to reap the associated macroeconomic benefits, security protection, and desirable political status. Democratization by conditionality—where democratic reforms are a condition for the allocation of foreign aid or the approval of a loan—is more coercive.[27] Both variants are usually accompanied by monitoring and institutional tools such as regular reports or impact evaluations. The most coercive mechanism is democratization by control, as Whitehead and Schmitter have called it,[28] when economic sanctions or military force are used to pressure states to democratize.

Scholars who analyzed democratization processes in Southern Europe in an early phase of transition studies pointed to the importance of European regional organizations in democracy promotion. In what is to our knowledge the first attempt to study the influence of regional organizations on democratization going beyond anecdotal case evidence, Jon Pevehouse mapped out how regional organizations influence the transition to democracy and the long-term survival of democracy.[29] The mechanisms he describes refer to democracy promotion, i.e. the support of democratic transition and positive consolidation.[30] Pevehouse hypothesizes three distinct causal mechanisms through which membership in a democratic regional organization may further democratic transition. The first is called pressure. Regional organizations are the mechanisms of choice for pressure against authoritarian regimes, as they are an accessible forum for public condemnation, diplomatic pressure and economic sanctions. Multilateral efforts are considered more legitimate than unilateral ones. External pressure can help to weaken an authoritarian regime's grip on power.

Through open verbal condemnation and threats of sanctions, a regional organization may hurt or at least threaten to hurt the international reputation and the economy of an authoritarian regime. If allies and institutional partners treat the regime as a pariah state, this can impact on public and elite perceptions within the state and help to delegitimize it domestically.[31] The second mechanism is the acquiescence effect. Involvement in a regional organization that adheres to democratic norms may dampen fears of democracy among elite groups supporting the authoritarian regime and may thereby help them acquiesce to a democratic transition. The first variant of how this mechanism may operate is a preference lock-in through membership in regional economic agreements. These agreements create credible guarantees, such as the protection of property rights, which are crucial for business elites in order to assuage their fears of democracy. The second variant is socialization of the military by cooperation in regional security arrangements. When interacting with military elites from more democratic countries, the military may be persuaded that its role is not that of an internal police force involved in domestic politics, but rather that of protecting the state from external enemies.[32]

The third mechanism sets in when regional organizations promote democratization by legitimizing interim governments during the time span between the breakdown of autocracy and the holding of founding elections. Membership in democratic regional organizations may help these fragile governments to signal to internal and external actors that they mean what they say when they talk about holding free and fair elections in the not-too-distant future.[33]

According to Pevehouse, regional organizations may also help to remove major obstacles to democratic consolidation arising on the side of the winners and the losers of the democratic transition. The winners, the new democratic rulers, might have to cope with distrust and a lack of democratic commitment among elites or dissatisfaction on the part of the masses. They might also be tempted to turn their new-found power into a permanent political advantage. At the same time, the distributional losers of the democratic transition, the former authoritarian rulers which often consist of the military and business elites, may face a temptation to undermine or overthrow the democratic regime.

Regional organizations can counteract those dangers by binding winners and by binding and bribing losers.[34] For the winners, membership in a regional organization or the prospect of accession functions as an external commitment device through which winners bind themselves to political liberalization. Membership (or the prospect thereof) is also a highly visible external validation of the new regime, which increases the probability that the masses will commit to the new democracy. Both winners and losers are deterred from violating membership conditions, as any elite group that moves to overturn the regime faces high costs, such as the threat of economic isolation, the denial of accession or suspension/expulsion from the organization. Regional organizations may also provide positive incentives to "bribe" losers into complying with democratic institutions. They can provide direct material resources to groups or can help to implement certain policies that benefit disaffected groups.

While there is by now an extensive literature categorizing mechanisms to encourage movement toward democracy, there are hardly any attempts to assess systematically mechanisms for the defense of democracy. In his comparative study of international mechanisms for protecting democracy, Piccone lists a number of showcase multilateral responses in defense of democracy, including the condemnation of an illegitimate act, the threat to suspend a government's membership or to cut economic benefits, and the application of increasingly tough measures. These range from the recall of ambassadors, the appointment of special envoys and other diplomatic tools, to visa restrictions on coup plotters, arms embargoes and freezing of assets.[35]

The most sophisticated attempt at systematization is Donno's work on regional organizations' reactions to electoral misconduct.[36] Donno uses enforcement as a catch-all term for all kinds of international organizations' reactions that impose material, political, or reputational costs on a norm-violating government. A number of specific enforcement tools which vary in coerciveness are employed by international actors. The first is shaming: official declarations, resolutions, or statements that criticize the norm-violating government impose reputational costs on governments. Second, international organizations may employ mediation and diplomatic missions. High-ranking international organization officials are sent to the target country to exert pressure for adherence to democratic norms or to resolve conflicts between adversary domestic actors. Diplomatic and mediation missions impose political and reputational costs, but are less overtly punitive than the third tool, conditionality. Conditionality in Donno's understanding is in fact negative conditionality, where the threat or the application of sanctions is used in response to violations of democratic norms. Sanctions can be economic, political or, in exceptional cases, military, and impose severe material or political costs on the government in order to punish it and to attempt to change its behavior.

It comes as no surprise that the promotion of democracy is much more common and much more intensively studied than the defense of democracy. The defense of democracy is costlier and more difficult to achieve than democracy promotion because it requires high levels of coordination among an organization's member states on matters that have traditionally been considered internal affairs. Penalties are more difficult to implement than rewards as they appear to infringe on state sovereignty, incur costs in terms of decreased goodwill, and may engender negative reciprocity from sanctioned states and their supporters.[37]

Moreover, there is a tension between defense of democracy regimes that legitimize intervention in internal affairs, and state sovereignty and its corollary, the principle of non-intervention. Instruments for defending democracy are often adopted with reservations, stipulating the ultimate precedence of state sovereignty. Therefore, the strength of the norm of state sovereignty in the particular region or regional organization may be an important constraint on the establishment of instruments to defend democracy. Nevertheless, some regional organizations have adopted provisions with the goal to protect and defend democracy against the danger of democratic regression and breakdown.

Regional democracy promotion in comparative perspective

To make the promotion and defense of democracy by regional organizations work, these organizations must have at least three features.[38] First, regional organizations have to adhere formally to democratic norms. To put into place a democracy promotion regime, governments start by building consensus among the participating states in favor of defining democracy as a core norm. Thus, the formal adherence to democracy is an expression of the political will to set conditions on membership resulting from ideological elite support for democracy. Second, the tipping point from mere formal adherence to putting the conditions into practice is reached when member governments exhibit sufficient political will to adopt enforcement provisions. Third, the actual application of enforcement mechanisms in reaction to democratic crises presupposes the existence of sufficient means to enforce political conditionality.

The comparative overview in Table 1.1 covers the first two characteristics and reviews the formal adherence to democratic norms and the establishment of enforcement mechanisms by well-known regional organizations. The table displays the organizations sorted by region and the date of their foundation (and, if applicable, the foundation of their precursor). The first category, formal adherence to democratic

Table 1.1 Comparing regional democracy promotion

Region	Organization	Year of foundation (precursor)	Years of advances in democracy promotion			
			Formal adherence		Enforcement mechanisms	
			Endorsement	Commitment	Facilitation	Sanctions
Americas	OAS	1948 (1889)	1948	1985	1991	1992
	CAN	1996 (1969)	1969	1980	2000	2000
	MERCOSUR	1991	1992	1996	1996	1996
	UNASUR	2008 (2004)	2008	2010	2010	2010
Europe	EU	1993 (1951)	1986	1993	1997	1997
	NATO	1949	1949	1991	–	–
Africa	AU	2000 (1963)	2000	2000	2000	2000
	ECOWAS	1975	1991	1993	1999	2001
	SADC	1992 (1980)	1992	2001	–	–
Asia	ASEAN	1967	2007	2009	–	–

Source: Authors' elaboration.

norms, is subdivided into two variants: endorsement means that in its founding charter—typically in the preamble or an enumeration of principles—or in other key documents an organization expresses its adherence to the principle of (representative) democracy. Commitment is more demanding, in that democracy is not only referred to as an important principle, but as an actual objective of the organization, and that its active promotion and/or defense are stated as essential purposes. This may include a democratic membership requirement, i.e. that aspiring members need to reach a certain standard to be admitted and that the membership of existent member states might be subject to scrutiny in the case of an interruption of the democratic order. However, formal adherence alone runs the risk of remaining merely rhetorical. Therefore the second category, enforcement mechanisms, captures whether the organization disposes of concrete measures to defend democracy. Facilitation encompasses cooperative tools used in reaction to a democratic crisis, such as mediation, diplomatic missions, or "good offices" of the secretary-general. In turn, sanctions refer to coercive tools such as membership suspension, economic sanctions, or military intervention.

The table illustrates that the OAS is at the forefront in terms of international mechanisms for the promotion and defense of democracy. Most of the mechanisms for protecting democracy surveyed here were first established in the Western hemisphere. The OAS is one of the few organizations that formally endorsed democracy already in its founding document, and, along with the CAN, it is the only one that before the end of the Cold War already included a more far-reaching commitment stipulating democracy as an objective of the organization. Especially with respect to enforcement mechanisms, the OAS was a pioneer, as will be described in detail in Chapter 2.

Some caveats are in order when comparing across regions. The table only captures mechanisms that have been formally established by a treaty or agreement. This approach has its limits, as informal practices are not taken into account, nor is it always clear whether formal mechanisms exist on paper only or are actually applied. More importantly, regional organizations were founded at different points in time, with a very different geographical scope, and with different original purposes. These factors are reflected in the variation in time regarding the establishment of democracy promotion provisions as well as in their binding force. For example, continental organizations such as the OAS and the AU for the Americas and Africa, or the League of Arab States as a pan-Arab organization, bring together all countries within a geographically or culturally defined region for the sake of political cooperation. Sub-regional organizations, in turn, frequently focus on economic and/or security integration among a smaller group of member states. The various regions experienced different waves of regional integration and different records of success: while the European organizations founded in the wake of World War II still exist, most economic integration schemes founded in Latin America in the 1960s and 1970s against the background of import substitution industrialization have fallen into oblivion, and even some of the organizations founded or revitalized in the 1990s, driven by the paradigms of open regionalism and world market integration, are now obsolete. One might suspect that organizations concentrating on economic integration or a specific security threat might be less inclined to formulate a common democratic norm. The trajectory of the EU and the North Atlantic Treaty Organization (NATO), both of which established an explicit commitment to democracy in the 1990s only, supports that claim.

By focusing on enforcement mechanisms the table captures defense of democracy provisions and hence does not cover a range of mechanisms of democracy promotion that contribute to democratic transition and positive consolidation. This does not do justice to those organizations whose main record of success has been pre-accession democracy promotion. The EU and NATO are considered very successful in the democratic socialization of prospective member states in the course of their stepwise association and accession procedures. These virtues are not recognized in an analysis focusing on post-accession defense of democracy. Apparently, those organizations that possess the most leverage during the pre-accession stage have a disproportionately reduced amount of leverage after accession. A reason for them paying less attention to democratic backsliding might be the fact that these organizations are the most demanding in terms of pre-accession requirements and the democratic bona fides of most member states. For example, in the case of the EU, it was not before the Amsterdam Treaty of 1997 that mechanisms to handle threats to democracy were incorporated. The Treaty of the European Union in its Article 7 now stipulates mechanisms to handle a breach of the *acquis communautaire*—respect for human dignity, freedom, democracy, equality, the rule of law and respect for human rights, which Article 2 of the EU Treaty defines as common values of the member states on which the EU is founded. A "serious and persistent" breach of these values may lead to a Council decision to suspend certain rights of the member states, including voting rights. So far this provision has never been invoked.

In line with Moravcsik, one might assume that the defense of democracy is more important for organizations made up of emerging democracies than for organizations composed of established democracies. Regional organizations with such post-accession leverage—mechanisms in place to assure the adherence to democratic principles—do not possess the same amount of leverage during the pre-accession stage.[39] Overall, when regional organizations with post-accession leverage engage in the institutionalization of mechanisms beyond the mere adherence to democratic norms, it looks like they are much stronger in protecting the status quo against unconstitutional change than actively promoting its improvement. This might also be the case for historical-evolutionary reasons: The explicit formulation of democratic member-ship criteria in the EU and NATO happened in response to demands for accession, in particular after the end of the Cold War. In contrast, the membership of the other organizations was largely complete when they adopted their democracy promotion regimes, so that there was no need to set up membership criteria with a view to potential candidate countries.

Limitations and challenges

As we have seen, in spite of some caveats, the formal adherence to democratic norms and the existence of enforcement mechanisms are relatively straightforward. But while it is an important symbolic achievement to have provisions for the defense of democracy in place, they must also be applicable and operational. However, the third component of an effective democracy promotion regime, the capacity to put democratic norms into practice and actually to apply the stipulated mechanisms, is much more difficult to assess. The majority of democratic commitments are political declarations rather than for-mally binding obligations under international law, and even if legally binding, the application of enforcement measures still hinges on poli-tical decisions. This makes enforcement problematic almost by design. An assessment of enforcement mechanisms is even more challenging when the claim is not only to check for application as such, but also to measure its success.

Some authors have started to study the conditions that affect the strength of regional organizations' defense of democracy regimes—the capacity to enforce norms—and have singled out a number of factors that determine whether enforcement is likely in a given case. One set of factors is convergence or divergence of interests among member states as well as between the bureaucracy of the regional organization and its member states. In her analysis of election monitoring and reactions to electoral misconduct in Europe and the Americas, Donno looks at the strategic importance of a country, its economic and military power and its resources, concluding that enforcement is less likely in countries of high geopolitical importance.[40] Enforcement can also be hindered by divergence of interests among member states resulting from mistrust vis-à-vis an overly interventionist hegemonic power, or from an ongoing competition for regional power status. Another impediment mentioned before is the extent to which member states uphold the principles of state sovereignty and non-intervention and whether they are willing to subordinate them to the aim of supporting the "noble" goal of norm enforcement.

The second set of factors that determine external reaction to democratic crises are the very features of those crises. It might play a role whether the agents of change are democratically legitimized or unelected actors, as well as which strategies of change they employ. While outright illegal strategies such as military coups elicit a response, the situation is much more complicated when a democratic regime is challenged by legal or quasi-legal means, such as violent street protests or inter-branch conflicts.[41] In other words, ambiguity or uncertainty about the nature and scope of norm violations are an obstacle to enforcement.[42]

The question of success of regional organizations' reactions is yet a separate issue. Most studies so far have focused on the policies and practices of international organizations, the enforcement mechanisms that they have at their disposition and whether these are used or not. The outcomes in the country where democracy is being defended have not been scrutinized to the same extent. Assessing the success of democracy promotion might already be tricky, but it is an even more challenging task to evaluate the success of measures to defend democracy. The logic of democracy promotion implies that "the only way is up." Provided that democracy promoters have a clear idea what, for them, constitutes a democracy, they can set goals that shall be achieved, and success is rather straightforward to assess by looking at the extent to which these "benchmarks" have been reached.

In contrast, the defense of democracy is a much more unwieldy concept. Questions like what type of action constitutes a violation of democratic norms, what kind of impairments represent a threat to democracy or an instance of democratic backsliding, how to weigh different "defects" of democracy against each other, and at what point democratic backsliding is serious enough to trigger a reaction, are all hotly contested. The influence of regional organizations on the deterrence or reversal of a violation of democratic principles is difficult to identify because of omitted variable bias, conditional effects, and the indirect nature of the effect. A deterrent effect of enforcement provisions is difficult to prove when countries—in anticipation of punishment—refrain from violating democratic norms. The effect of enforcement measures on halting or reversing a democratic crisis is hard to disentangle from parallel domestic or other international forces working to preserve democracy. In addition, the success of enforcement measures depends partly on properties of the target state, such as its vulnerability to specific types of sanctions. Regional organizations' actions such as a symbolic condemnation might not have a direct measurable impact, but might encourage and support other international institutions, governments or business actors to take measures that are costlier to the norm-violating government. Evaluating the success of an intervention also presents practical challenges, since most enforcement mechanisms are "one-shot" events in reaction to past behavior and not equipped with follow-up tools to monitor future behavior and to continue supporting shaky governments even when the imminent crisis is over. While a symbolic upholding of democratic principles is certainly important, disappointment might ensue if international action does not lead to a clear-cut solution of the crisis or a visible improvement of democratic institutions.

Conclusion

As has been shown above, regional organizations have a role to play in democracy promotion. Regional organizations can pressure post-authoritarian governments to implement democratic reforms. A lot of research has concentrated on how the EU prescribes and promotes standards for national governance beyond rather than within its borders, targeting accession candidates, neighboring countries, and third states. However, some regional organizations also dispose of policies and instruments explicitly aiming to protect and defend democratic norms within their member states. Remarkably, it was not the European regional organizations, but non-Western organizations composed of troubled or fledgling democracies that have been at the forefront of establishing such provisions for the defense of democracy. The mechanisms for the promotion and defense of democracy outlined above, but also many of the limitations and challenges, will become apparent in the following chapters which trace the emergence of the OAS democratic paradigm and review its application.

Notes

1 Andrew F. Cooper and Thomas Legler, *Intervention Without Intervening? The OAS Defense and Promotion of Democracy in the Americas* (New York: Palgrave Macmillan, 2006), Chapter 1.
2 In comparative politics, regime denotes a form of government (e.g. democratic, authoritarian and totalitarian regimes). In contrast, in international relations, regimes are multilateral arrangements with the aim to resolve international problems through collective efforts. International regimes often form in response to a need to coordinate behavior among countries around an issue. They typically take the form of treaties or international organizations. For an overview, see Stephan Haggard and Beth A. Simmons, "Theories of International Regimes," *International Organization* 41, no. 3 (1987): 491–517; Andreas Hasenclever, Peter Mayer and Volker Rittberger, *Theories of International Regimes* (Cambridge: Cambridge University Press, 1997).
3 The different terms were introduced into the debate by Jon C. Pevehouse, *Democracy from Above: Regional Organizations and Democratization* (Cambridge: Cambridge University Press, 2005); Edward R. McMahon and Scott H. Baker, *Piecing a Democratic Quilt: Regional Organizations and Universal Norms* (Bloomfield, Conn.: Kumarian, 2006); Darren Hawkins and Carolyn M. Shaw, "Legalising Norms of Democracy in the Americas," *Review of International Studies* 34, no. 3 (2008): 459–80; Daniela Donno, "Who is Punished? Regional Intergovernmental Organizations and the Enforcement of Democratic Norms," *International Organization* 64, no. 4 (2010): 593–625; Thomas Legler and Thomas Kwasi Tieku, "What Difference Can a Path Make? Regional Democracy Promotion Regimes in the Americas and Africa," *Democratization* 17, no. 3 (2010): 465–91.
4 Laurence Whitehead, "Democratic Regions, Ostracism, and Pariahs," in *The International Dimensions of Democratization: Europe and the Americas,* ed. Laurence Whitehead (Oxford: Oxford University Press, 2001), 395–412; Pevehouse, *Democracy from Above.*
5 Martha Finnemore and Kathryn Sikkink, "International Norm Dynamics and Political Change," *International Organization* 52, no. 4 (1998): 887–917; Michael McFaul, "Democracy Promotion as a World Value," *Washington Quarterly* 28, no. 1 (2005): 147–63; McMahon and Baker, *Piecing a Democratic Quilt.*
6 Hawkins and Shaw, "Legalising Norms of Democracy in the Americas"; Darren Hawkins and Carolyn M. Shaw, "The OAS and Legalizing Norms of Democracy," in *Promoting Democracy in the Americas,* ed. Thomas Legler, Sharon F. Lean and Dexter S. Boniface (Baltimore, Md.: Johns Hopkins University Press, 2007), 21–39.
7 Pevehouse, *Democracy from Above.*
8 Darren Hawkins, "Protecting Democracy in Europe and the Americas," *International Organization* 62, no. 3 (2008): 373–403 (383).
9 Andrew Moravcsik, "The Origins of Human Rights Regimes: Democratic Delegation in Postwar Europe," *International Organization* 54, no. 2 (2000): 217–52.
10 Pevehouse's "democratic density" argument and Moravcsik's "lock-in effect" complement each other when looking at the development over time.

When members of a regional organization transition to democracy (or when democratizing states join or found regional organizations), the organization's democratic density increases. Empirical studies suggest that both democratizing states and stable democracies are more likely to intensify their involvement in international organizations than non-democratic countries. Additionally, it has been shown that in order to commit to democratic reform more credibly, democratizing states purposefully tend to join organizations with a highly democratic membership. See Edward D. Mansfield and Jon C. Pevehouse, "Democratization and International Organizations," *International Organization* 60, no. 1 (2006): 137–67; Edward D. Mansfield and Jon C. Pevehouse, "Democratization and the Varieties of International Organizations," *Journal of Conflict Resolution* 52, no. 2 (2008): 269–94.

11 John J. Mearsheimer, "The False Promise of International Institutions," *International Security* 19, no. 3 (1994–95): 5–49 (13).

12 The influence of powerful states in regional democracy promotion has been discussed, among others, by Hawkins, "Protecting Democracy in Europe and the Americas," and Hawkins and Shaw, "Legalising Norms of Democracy in the Americas."

13 Hawkins and Shaw, "Legalising Norms of Democracy in the Americas," 465–66.

14 Andrea Ribeiro Hoffmann, "Political Conditionality and Democratic Clauses in the EU and Mercosur," in *Closing or Widening the Gap? Legitimacy and Democracy in Regional Integration Organizations*, ed. Andrea Ribeiro Hoffmann and Anna van der Vleuten (Aldershot: Ashgate, 2007), 173–89.

15 Legler and Tieku, "What Difference Can a Path Make?"

16 Thomas Carothers, *Aiding Democracy Abroad: The Learning Curve* (Washington, DC: Carnegie Endowment for International Peace, 1999).

17 Important works mapping the field of democracy promotion include: Peter Burnell, ed., *Democracy Assistance: International Co-operation for Democratization* (London: Frank Cass, 2000); Thomas Carothers, *Aiding Democracy Abroad*; Thomas Carothers, "Democracy Assistance: Political vs. Developmental?" *Journal of Democracy* 20, no. 1 (2009): 5–19; Steven E. Finkel, Aníbal Pérez-Liñán and Mitchell A. Seligson, "The Effects of U.S. Foreign Assistance on Democracy Building, 1990–2003," *World Politics* 59, no. 3 (2007): 404–39; Jonas Wolff and Iris Wurm, "Towards a Theory of External Democracy Promotion: A Proposal for Theoretical Classification," *Security Dialogue* 42, no. 1 (2011): 77–96.

18 Geoffrey Pridham, "The International Context of Democratic Consolidation: Southern Europe in Comparative Perspective," in *The Politics of Democratic Consolidation: Southern Europe in Comparative Perspective*, ed. Richard Gunther, P. Nikiforos Diamandouros and Hans-Jürgen Puhle (Baltimore, Md. and London: Johns Hopkins University Press, 1995), 166–203.

19 Pridham, "The International Context of Democratic Consolidation," 169.

20 Frank Schimmelfennig, Stefan Engert and Heiko Knobel, *International Socialization in the New Europe: European Organizations, Political Conditionality, and Democratic Change* (Basingstoke: Palgrave Macmillan, 2006).

21 Tanja A. Börzel, Vera van Hüllen and Mathis Lohaus, *Governance Transfer by Regional Organizations: Following a Global Script?* SFB Governance

Working Paper Series no. 42 (Berlin, Germany: Freie Universität Berlin, DFG Collaborative Research Center 700, 2013), www.sfb-governance.de/publikationen/sfbgov_wp/wp42_en/index.html.

22 One example is the EU-led mission in Mali initiated in 2013.

23 Philippe Schmitter, "The Influence of the International Context upon the Choice of National Institutions and Policies in Neo-Democracies," in *The International Dimensions of Democratization: Europe and the Americas*, ed. Laurence Whitehead (Oxford: Oxford University Press, 2001), 26–54.

24 Carothers, *Aiding Democracy Abroad*.

25 Antoaneta Dimitrova and Geoffrey Pridham, "International Actors and Democracy Promotion in Central and Eastern Europe: The Integration Model and its Limits," *Democratization* 11, no. 5 (2004): 91–112.

26 Schmitter, "The Influence of the International Context upon the Choice of National Institutions and Policies in Neo-Democracies."

27 Conditionality has also been described as "external incentives model"; see Frank Schimmelfennig and Ulrich Sedelmeier, "Governance by Conditionality: EU Rule Transfer to the Candidate Countries of Central and Eastern Europe," *Journal of European Public Policy* 11, no. 4 (2004): 661–79.

28 Laurence Whitehead, "Three International Dimensions of Democratization," in *The International Dimensions of Democratization: Europe and the Americas*, ed. Laurence Whitehead (Oxford: Oxford University Press, 2001), 3–25; Schmitter, "The Influence of the International Context upon the Choice of National Institutions and Policies in Neo-Democracies."

29 See Jon C. Pevehouse, "With a Little Help from My Friends? Regional Organizations and the Consolidation of Democracy," *American Journal of Political Science* 46, no. 3 (2002): 611–26; Jon C. Pevehouse, "Democracy from the Outside-In? International Organization and Democratization," *International Organization* 56, no. 3 (2002): 515–49; Pevehouse, *Democracy from Above*.

30 Although Pevehouse in chapters 5 and 7 introduces some cases where regional organizations contributed to negative consolidation, i.e. responded to attempts to overthrow democracy, his theoretical framework does not explicitly address defense of democracy. See Pevehouse, *Democracy from Above*.

31 Ibid., 16–20.

32 Ibid., 20–25.

33 Ibid., 25–27.

34 Ibid., 38–45.

35 Theodore J. Piccone, "International Mechanisms for Protecting Democracy," in *Protecting Democracy: International Responses*, ed. Morton H. Halperin and Mirna Galic (Lanham, Md.: Lexington Books, 2005), 101–26.

36 Donno, "Who is Punished?"; Daniela Donno, *Defending Democratic Norms: International Actors and the Politics of Electoral Misconduct* (New York: Oxford University Press, 2013).

37 See Hawkins, "Protecting Democracy in Europe and the Americas."

38 See Pevehouse, "With a Little Help from My Friends?," 615.

39 McMahon and Baker, *Piecing a Democratic Quilt*, Chapter 10.

40 Donno, "Who is Punished?"

41 For the importance of strategies and agents of change, see Chapter 4 of this book and Dexter S. Boniface, "Dealing with Threats to Democracy," in

Which Way Latin America? Hemispheric Politics Meets Globalization, ed. Andrew F. Cooper and Jorge Heine (Tokyo: United Nations University Press, 2009), 182–201; Craig Arceneaux and David Pion-Berlin, "Issues, Threats, and Institutions: Explaining OAS Responses to Democratic Dilemmas in Latin America," *Latin American Politics and Society* 49, no. 2 (2007): 1–31.

42 Donno, "Who is Punished?"

2 The emergence of the OAS democratic paradigm

- From the International Union of American Republics to the OAS
- The Cold War: representative democracy between rhetoric and reality
- The end of the Cold War and Latin America's transition
- Resolution 1080 and the Washington Protocol
- Collective diplomacy and the defense of democracy
- Conclusion

Few instances reflect as well the sea change that has taken place in the Americas on the defense of democracy in the second half of the twentieth century than the trajectory of Chile. In 1970, free and fair presidential elections had given power to Salvador Allende, leader of the Unidad Popular movement with backing from both socialists and communists. That a socialist government could be elected and rule through democratic means was anathema to Cold War ideology, and the "Chilean road to socialism" was considered a major threat to the existing geopolitical arrangements in the hemisphere. On 11 September 1973, when the military seized power in a brutal coup, the US government greeted Allende's overthrow with enthusiasm. Meanwhile, the OAS kept silent and stayed on the sidelines. Barely 18 years later, in June 1991, the newly elected democratic government of Chile hosted the twenty-first regular session of the OAS General Assembly (a body formed by the foreign ministers of the member states) and spearheaded the initiative to adopt the Santiago Commitment and Resolution 1080. The latter commits the American states to take action when the democratic institutional order is violated. A few years later, in January 2000, the second socialist after Allende won Chile's presidential elections in the *ballotage*. Barely a ripple moved, and Ricardo Lagos's election was accepted with remarkable equanimity, if not downright enthusiasm, from Washington, DC, to Buenos Aires.

How did this sea change come about? The purpose of this chapter is to examine the origins and evolution of the OAS democratic paradigm, i.e. the notion that democratic institutions need to be promoted and defended throughout the Western hemisphere, and that this be a collective responsibility of all member states. This paradigm did not come out of the blue. Rather, it originated in the long and complex history of the inter-American system, going back all the way to the nineteenth century.

From the International Union of American Republics to the OAS

It could well be argued that a democratic form of government was a goal of the peoples of the Americas since their independence. Admittedly, south of the Rio Grande that aspiration was for a long time honored more in the breach than in its actual practice. Beyond its application and implementation in national political systems, the recognition of democracy as a guiding principle of all American states was a long and difficult process. A key starting point for it took place in 1889, when the first of nine International Conferences of American States created the International Union of American Republics. This was renamed the Pan American Union in 1910 and served as an intergovernmental discussion forum on trade, international disputes resolution and key international legal issues.[1]

In 1907, the General Treaty of Peace and Friendship negotiated at the Washington Conference by officials from the United States and Central America agreed to withhold recognition of any government arising out of a rebellion rather than of free elections. Under the label of "missionary diplomacy," the notion of denying recognition to unconstitutional governments in Latin America was reinforced by the Woodrow Wilson Administration (1913–21). At another conference, in 1922–23, the nations of the Americas banned the recognition of any government installed by the use of force, even if subsequently legitimated by free elections. This went hand in hand with a US activist policy in favor of democracy in the region, particularly in Central America and the Caribbean, until the Great Depression halted that campaign.[2]

Within the inter-American system proper, the first official statement of the "existence of democracy as a common cause" in the Americas was made in Buenos Aires in 1936 when the Inter-American Conference on the Consolidation of Peace adopted the Declaration of Principles of Inter-American Solidarity and Cooperation. In 1945 Uruguay's foreign minister, Eduardo Rodríguez Larreta, proposed for the first time a multilateral cooperation in defense of democratic processes and human rights. Although never approved, this proposal indicated the continuing hemispheric interest in the defense of democracy.[3] After World War II, the Ninth Inter-American Conference in Bogotá in 1948 supported essential individual rights and freedoms and condemned the methods of any political regime that proposes to suppress political and civil rights and freedoms. The conference culminated with the signing of the OAS Charter and the American Declaration of Rights and Duties of Man, which predated the Universal Declaration of Human Rights by seven months.[4]

Unlike the founding documents of other regional organizations, the OAS Charter included clear references to democracy. The Preamble refers to the human rights declaration, stating "that the true significance of American solidarity and good neighborliness can only mean the consolidation on this continent, within the framework of democratic institutions, of a system of individual liberty and social justice based on respect for the essential rights of man." When enumerating its principles, the charter also states that "The solidarity of the American States and the high aims which are sought through it require the political organization of those States on the basis of the effective exercise of representative democracy."[5] On this basis, it could be argued that any coup or illegal interruption of the democratic process posed a challenge to one of the essential bases of the organization and that the presence of nondemocratic governments in the organization was incompatible with its goals.[6]

The Cold War: representative democracy between rhetoric and reality

Yet, for all the hopes that might have been raised by such commendable aspirations, the OAS did not live up to the expectations it created. Despite repeated expressions of their allegiance to representative democracy,[7] in practice democratic governments in the region were often toppled by *coups d'état*, and many countries lived for years under oppressive authoritarian regimes. It was considered compatible that a state with an autocratic or dictorial government could continue to be a full-fledged member of the OAS. Domestic constraints stood in the way of implementing the principle of representative democracy across Latin America. First, despite the clear references to democracy in the founding documents of the OAS, none of the member states envisaged granting the OAS a mandate actually to act in defense of democracy, because most of them continued to uphold the validity of national sovereignty and the principle of non-intervention. Second, the emergence of dictatorships froze any progress in furthering representative democracy. Throughout the twentieth century, social mobilization and claims for political participation in combination with insufficient economic development repeatedly led to authoritarian backlash. Threatened by the rise of new societal actors, both conservative elites and the middle classes frequently resorted to an alliance with the military to overthrow governments perceived as too reformist and progressive.[8]

US interests were another obstacle. Unilateral US intervention in the region persisted despite some initial success in multilateral cooperation in the 1940s and 1950s.[9] Headquartered in an ornate white marble building on Constitution Avenue, in the very heart of Washington, DC, the OAS was immediately caught up in the ideological struggles of the Cold War. During that time, a key purpose of the OAS's focus on collective defense against external threats, at least from the point of view of the United States, was to serve as a bulwark against communism and Soviet foreign policy aims. This it did hand in hand with the Rio Treaty of 1947, designed to fend off any extra-continental threats, supplemented by the Inter-American Defense Board, founded in 1942, and, in particular, the Inter-American Defense College (1962).

In 1954, the United States backed the military overthrow of a democratically elected president in Guatemala. Following the Cuban Revolution in 1959, Latin America turned "into both a battleground and a prize in the conflict between communism and capitalism."[10] Henceforward, the United States repeatedly attempted to topple and ostracize the Fidel Castro regime. Between 1970 and 1973, it made strenuous efforts to undermine the Allende regime in Chile. The OAS could do little to restrain US unilateral actions. Especially the 1965 Dominican crisis seriously damaged the organization's reputation: a US unilateral invasion supporting conservative politicians against the rise of Juan Bosch, an advocate of social reform, was turned into a collective operation by converting foreign military forces in Dominican territory into an "Inter-American Peace Force." Since then, governments in the region perceived the organization as an entity hijacked by the United States to advance its national interests and buttress its hegemony—"The Ministry of Colonies of the United States," as it became known throughout *la América morena*.

In such cases, the clash between the principle of representative democracy and the need to stand up for it, on the one hand, and national sovereignty and the principle of non-intervention, on the other, became especially apparent, as it did for much of the first four decades of the OAS's history. Almost every major crisis in the hemisphere—civil wars, farcical elections, human rights abuses—involved a clash of these principles, and the OAS was left with its hands tied as these problems festered or the United States intervened.[11] The US national security doctrine pre-empted other considerations, including democratic ones, as Washington's support for anti-communist dictatorships and its complicity in toppling freely elected democratic governments became the rule.[12] In an extraordinary sleight of hand, Washington would even refer to the principle of non-intervention as it did so, arguing that it was all done to defend the target state's sovereignty against the intrusion of international communism.[13]

Still, in the best Spanish tradition of *"se acata, pero no se cumple"* (accept, but do not comply), several inter-American meetings continued to reiterate, at least in theory, the concepts of freedom and representative democracy set forth in the OAS Charter.[14] Triggered by the Cuban Revolution and the specter of communism, the scope and reach of the organization's democratic commitment came under intense discussion from 1959 on. The Declaration of Santiago of 1959, adopted at the Fifth Meeting of Consultation of Ministers of Foreign Affairs, spelled out a list of specific attributes of "representative democracy" and made clear that "the existence of antidemocratic regimes constitutes a violation of the principles on which the Organization of American States is founded, and a danger to united and peaceful relationships in the hemisphere."[15] The meeting also created the Inter-American Commission on Human Rights (IACHR) and resolved that the Inter-American Juridical Committee (IAJC) should study the relationship between the respect for human rights and the exercise of representative democracy and to draft a document on the effective exercise of representative democracy.[16] The IAJC's report affirmed the linkage between human rights and democratic governance and upheld the binding nature of the charter's principles, but considered collective action to defend or restore democracy to be inadmissible.

When the bureaucratic-authoritarian regimes of the Southern Cone and other military regimes elsewhere came to the fore in the 1960s and 1970s, the OAS kept mum. As recently as 1979, only three elected governments were in place in all of South America. Perhaps the OAS's darkest moment in that regard came in 1976, when it held a General Assembly in Santiago de Chile, at the height of Augusto Pinochet's iron-fisted military rule. Secretary of State Henry Kissinger decided to attend personally and meet with General Pinochet to provide an international platform to the Chilean junta and burnish its credentials as a trustworthy hemispheric partner at a time of the country's growing international isolation for human rights violations.[17]

This only reinforced the perception that the principle of democratic solidarity was not one the organization was willing to stand up for. The only entity in the OAS at that point that can be credited for having done something in defense of democracy was the inter-American human rights system.[18] The signing of the American Convention on Human Rights in 1969 (entering into force in 1978) buttressed the IACHR and created the Inter-American Court of Human Rights. The Jimmy Carter Administration in the United States increased the budget of the commission, appointed a forceful chair to run it and otherwise enhanced its hitherto meager role. The commission contributed to the defense of human rights by means of inspection visits to the many countries under military rule at the time, and called international attention to human rights violations by these dictatorships, in particular to the dirty war in Argentina. In many ways, it started a regional trend in which the collective defense of human rights began to be regarded as a legitimate topic and such collective action was not considered a violation of the principle of non-intervention.[19]

The end of the Cold War and Latin America's transition

A key moment in the evolution of the inter-American system's defense of democracy was the 1979 fall of the Somoza regime in Nicaragua. Until then, on grounds of national sovereignty, member states had been unwilling to discuss the state of internal democratic arrangements in any given country, but the Somoza regime was subject to severe criticism in November 1978 when the IACHR published a report charging the National Guard with numerous human rights violations. The report was followed by a United Nations (UN) declaration condemning the Nicaraguan government. In late June 1979, on the eve of the Sandinista victory, the OAS voted to condemn the Somoza government and demand Anastasio "Tachito" Somoza Debayle's resignation, and while a number of countries abstained and Paraguay voted against the resolution, there was for the first time "the presumption ... that the words of the charter about America being a land of liberty might have some real meaning."[20]

At the same time, an informal US proposal to revive the Inter-American Peace Force in order to intervene and manage the transition from the Somoza regime to a putatively democratic government was rejected by the foreign ministers.[21] The Central American wars followed and the OAS was once again marginalized when the United

States supported the government of El Salvador in its struggle against Marxist Farabundo Martí National Liberation Front (FMLN) rebels and the Contra rebels' attempts to topple the leftist Sandinista National Liberation Front (FSLN) government in Nicaragua. Latin America responded to those unilateralist and partisan US endeavors by starting ad hoc conflict resolution entities such as the Contadora Group and the Esquipulas Group. These Latin American initiatives in the Central American peace processes marked a turning point in US–Latin American relations in times of crisis. Unilateral interventionism was on the wane.

In the 1980s, with Latin America's transition to democracy, democratic governance once again became a focal point of inter-American interest. OAS provisions to promote and protect democracy were expanded and strengthened.[22] Reforms to the OAS Charter, enshrined in the Cartagena Protocol of 1985, provided new language emphasizing the centrality of representative democracy as a mode of governance and added the following preamble to the charter: "Representative democracy is an indispensable condition for stability, peace, and development of the region."[23] Even more important, the following phrase was included in Chapter 1 as one of the organization's essential purposes: "to promote and consolidate representative democracy, with due respect for the principle of non-intervention."[24] By being declared an essential purpose, representative democracy became one of the *raisons d'être* of the OAS. Thus, the organization changed its pro forma adherence to representative democracy from mere endorsement to actual commitment to it (see Table 1.1).

A first step to put that commitment into practice was taken in 1989. The General Assembly passed Resolution 991, which authorized the OAS to undertake election observation missions in member countries upon an invitation by the host country. Efforts to promote democracy acquired a special impetus with the end of the Cold War as well as from Canada's joining of the organization in 1990, as the country added substantial human and budgetary resources to this endeavor. Already in 1990 Ottawa provided the leadership for the creation of a Unit for the Promotion of Democracy (UPD). Initially, the UPD focused on electoral observation. Later on, its mandate was expanded to the strengthening of political institutions and democratic procedures, educational activities, and electoral technical assistance.[25]

Events in Panama buttressed the claim that the OAS should be equipped with additional means to strengthen and defend democracy. In May 1989, Manuel Noriega blatantly stole Panama's elections. In response, the hemisphere's countries, through the OAS, appointed a mission headed by Colombia's foreign minister and tasked it with negotiating a solution, which failed to budge Noriega. In December 1989, the United States intervened militarily, removed Noriega, and installed the winners of the election. This sequence of events led leaders such as Venezuelan President Carlos Andrés Pérez to kick-start the initiative resulting in the first institutionalized mechanism for the defense of democracy, Resolution 1080. Pérez argued that US military intervention in Panama could have been avoided had the OAS disposed of the means to defend democracy. In an article in *Foreign Policy* in 1990, he made the case for the OAS as a meeting place to work out hemispheric problems collectively, after containing communism was rendered obsolete.[26]

Resolution 1080 and the Washington Protocol

The early 1990s saw the end of the Cold War, the return of democracy in South America, and the end of civil wars and external interventions in Central America. Washington's fears of communist regimes in the hemisphere abated and the United States finally accepted the idea of democracy as a norm for the region. In turn, Latin American countries that had gone through military rule and now had elected rulers were keen to find ways to anchor their fragile and unconsolidated democratic systems. For the first time all governments had some claim to be democratic and perceived anything that was done in defense of democracy as in their own defense. It was then that politicians and diplomats working as their governments' permanent representatives to the OAS grasped that more should be done to "lock in" the recently attained democratic achievements.

The adoption of mechanisms against coup attempts began in May 1991 at the meeting of the Presidential Council of the Andean Pact hosted by President Pérez in Caracas.[27] In the final declaration, the presidents of Bolivia, Colombia, Ecuador, Peru, and Venezuela agreed that the OAS Charter should be amended to provide for the non-recognition of any government that comes to power by force. Until then, the foreign ministers when meeting at the annual OAS General Assembly had subscribed to the principle of non-intervention, implying that any government in control of the national territory should be recognized. The presidents' final communiqué took the foreign ministers by surprise, but they soon accepted it as new official policy.[28]

As the ground for the democracy clause was being laid, it was helpful that the secretary-general (SG) of the OAS at the time, the Brazilian João Clemente Baena Soares, was a person whom no one would have suspected of being an interventionist bent on using the defense of democracy as an excuse to pursue individual states' foreign policy preferences. Additionally, with the 1991 OAS General Assembly scheduled to take place in Santiago, the newly elected Chilean government seized the opportunity to show the world its commitment to the protection of democracy in the Western hemisphere. The chief authors of a draft resolution to enable the OAS to react to democratic interruptions were Chilean Permanent Representative to the OAS Heraldo Muñoz, Brazilian Permanent Representative Bernardo Pericas, and US Permanent Representative Luigi Einaudi.[29]

On 4 June 1991, the General Assembly passed the Santiago Commitment to Democracy and the Renewal of the Inter-American System. Member states declared their "inescapable commitment to the defense and promotion of representative democracy and human rights in the region"[30] and resolved to respond collectively to threats to the constitutional order of OAS countries. The Santiago Commitment was joined by Resolution 1080, adopted on 5 June 1991, and characteristically entitled "Representative Democracy," which stipulated that "in the event of any occurrences giving rise to the sudden or irregular interruption of the democratic political institutional process or of the legitimate exercise of power by the democratically elected government in any of the Organization's member states," the SG was mandated to call a meeting of the Permanent Council. The council would examine the situation and decide on convening an ad hoc Meeting of the Ministers of Foreign Affairs or a special session of the General Assembly within 10 days of the interruption of the constitutional order, "to look into the events collectively and adopt any decisions deemed appropriate" to protect or defend the integrity of the democratic government.[31]

A number of debates preceded the adoption of the resolution at the General Assembly meeting. One was procedural, on the role of the 14 Caribbean countries in the OAS which, due to their British parliamentary tradition, were distrustful of a democracy clause in the spirit of the Spanish American tradition.[32] The more substantial issue was how to specify the anti-democratic events that would trigger a reaction and how to do this without pointing fingers. Many governments were hesitant about agreeing to anything that used the term "coup," given that coup, or *golpe*, by definition and historical practice in the region was a military coup. Because many civilian governments at that time still felt threatened by their military establishments, nobody wanted to adopt a resolution that would make it seem as though they were criticizing the military in their own countries. Thus the phrase, "any occurrences giving rise to the sudden or irregular interruption of the democratic political institutional process" was proposed, and a consensus emerged around this as a way of referring to any challenge to an elected government.[33] A second substantial issue on the table was what would happen in reaction to the interruption of the democratic process. Many participants of the General Assembly, including the majority of the US delegation, favored the automatic non-recognition of the government, in line with the final communiqué of the Andean Pact presidential summit, adopted a few weeks before. Others advocated a more flexible response on the grounds that a "one-size-fits-all" approach might not do justice to all kinds of potential circumstances. The issue was resolved by saying that there would be an automatic concerted response to an interruption of the democratic order: a meeting of the Permanent Council "to examine the situation, decide on and convene an ad hoc Meeting of the Ministers of Foreign Affairs, or a special session of the General Assembly, all of which must take place within a ten-day period."[34] The credibility of this reaction was provided by its automaticity.

In order to circumvent the reluctance of states to interfere with neighboring countries' domestic affairs, the first paragraph of Resolution 1080 resolved "To instruct the Secretary General to call for the immediate convocation of a meeting." This provision relieves the SG of having to vindicate his actions: on the one hand, he cannot decide not to do something; on the other hand, others cannot criticize the SG for doing something that they think he should not do. In addition, the expectation was that an automatic meeting would inevitably create pressure to do something, independently of which country has experienced the sudden or irregular interruption of the democratic order.[35] According to its second paragraph, Resolution 1080 did not foresee any specific consequences, but leaves it at the discretion of the Meeting of the Ministers of Foreign Affairs or the special session of the General Assembly to adopt "any decisions deemed appropriate."[36]

Resolution 1080 was a turning point in the history of the OAS. It reflected both Latin America's trend towards democratization and the US Administration's new multilateral approach regarding Latin America. For the first time, Resolution 1080 provided the OAS with an automatic, rapid-response collective mechanism against democratic breakdown. It set the stage for the establishment of legal parameters for the collective promotion and defense of democracy in the hemisphere, enabled the organization to react collectively in the case of democratic breakdown, defined the character of the defense of democracy and kick-started the construction of a new hemispheric norm whereby democracy should be actively protected and stimulated.

Yet, Resolution 1080 had limitations. As a mere resolution of the General Assembly, it carried little obligatory force. It did not specify the possible sanctions to any interruptions of the democratic process. Thus, in 1992 the OAS signed the Washington Protocol, which allowed the organization to suspend a member state. The Protocol, which took effect in September 1997, added a new article to the OAS Charter providing for the suspension of OAS membership by a two-thirds majority if a forceful, extra-constitutional overthrow of a democratically constituted government occurred.[37] Article 9 effectively made democracy a requirement for participation in any OAS body. This was also the first time that in a legally binding document, a regional organization set up a penalty mechanism for member states whose democratically elected government is overthrown by force. In addition, the Washington Protocol listed the elimination of extreme poverty among the organization's principles and purposes, and emphasized this as an essential contribution to the promotion and consolidation of representative democracy.[38]

The Declaration of Managua for the Promotion of Democracy and Development, adopted at the 1993 General Assembly, further underscored the importance of democracy in the new hemispheric context of the 1990s. Its main thrust was to expand the definition of democracy beyond the mere fact of holding elections. It recognized the need for further refinement of the OAS's approach to situations of democratic crisis, calling for "ongoing and creative work to consolidate democracy as well as a continuing effort to prevent and anticipate the very causes of the problems that work against democratic rule."[39] It also emphasized a range of topics related to democratic governance and democratic consolidation, such as the need to modernize administrative and political structures and to improve public administration, the protection of minorities and political opposition groups, the provision of basic human needs safeguards, the achievement of national reconciliation, and the subordination of the armed forces to the legitimately constituted civilian authority.

Collective diplomacy and the defense of democracy

During the 1990s, Resolution 1080 was invoked in reaction to four situations: a *coup d'état* which took place in Haiti in 1991, two "self-staged coups" (*autogolpes*) in Peru in 1992 and Guatemala in 1993, and an attempt to overthrow the president of Paraguay in 1996. In all four cases, the Permanent Council convened in an emergency session, adopted a resolution condemning the breach of the democratic

Table 2.1 Key OAS documents on democracy

Date	Document
1948	OAS Charter
1959	Declaration of Santiago
1985	Cartagena Protocol
1991	Santiago Commitment and Resolution 1080
1992	Washington Protocol
1993	Declaration of Managua
2001	Inter-American Democratic Charter

Source: Authors' elaboration.

institutional order and convoked an ad hoc Meeting of the Ministers of Foreign Affairs. The foreign ministers then decided what measures to take.

In the case of Haiti, where the first democratically elected leader in the country's history, Jean-Bertrand Aristide, was overthrown on 29 September 1991, the Meeting of the Ministers of Foreign Affairs demanded the immediate reinstatement of President Aristide and proposed specific sanctions, including the diplomatic isolation of the de facto government and the imposition of a commercial blockade.[40] However, the economic boycott was ignored by several member states and did not have much of an effect. A long diplomatic seesaw followed, and the UN soon became involved in the crisis. In coordination with the OAS and the US government, the UN helped to force the de facto government to sign the Governor's Island agreement on 3 July 1993, which would have restored Aristide to power. After the military junta failed to comply with the agreement, in July 1994 the UN authorized the use of "all necessary means" to achieve the restoration of democracy in Haiti under Chapter VII of the UN Charter. When a US military force was sent to Haiti, the Haitian military finally accepted Aristide's return. While coercive political and economic measures had not intimidated Haiti's leaders, the imminent use of force solved the crisis.[41] The Haitian case was crucial because it put paid to the established OAS practice of accepting coups quietly. It also embodied the first experience of the reinstallation of a democratically elected president ousted by a coup. Still, the long time it took to reinstate Aristide and the need to draw on UN and US support revealed the limits of OAS actions.

In the cases of Peru and Guatemala, the threat to democracy originated from democratically elected incumbents. On 5 April 1992 President Alberto Fujimori staged a self-coup. On 25 May 1993 President

Jorge Serrano Elías of Guatemala followed suit. Both presidents dissolved congress, closed the courts, suspended the constitution and a number of fundamental rights, and instituted rule by decree. They also detained journalists, human rights advocates, and other opponents to their regimes and instituted censorship of the press and electronic media. In both cases, the OAS reacted swiftly.[42] The Meeting of the Ministers of Foreign Affairs, convoked by the Permanent Council, called for the immediate restoration of constitutional government and for an end of all actions impairing human rights. A mission of foreign ministers, accompanied by the OAS SG in the Guatemalan case, was dispatched to each of the two countries.

A decisive difference between the two cases was that Fujimori's cause did have popular approval. To justify his actions, Fujimori had cited the need to respond to the attacks of the Maoist Shining Path guerrilla group, the weakness of political institutions and corruption in Peruvian congress and the courts. In turn, Serrano's actions triggered immediate domestic opposition. Accordingly, their projects suffered a divergent fate: giving in to the pressure from the OAS, Fujimori addressed the subsequent session of the ad hoc Meeting of the Ministers of Foreign Affairs and announced that he would convoke a constitutional congress through an election. Once the elections were held, on 22 November 1992, the foreign ministers resolved that an important step in restoring democracy had been taken and declared the matter closed. The further decline of democracy in Peru in subsequent years could not be halted. Fujimori remained in power until 2000 when the OAS once again intervened in the face of blatant electoral fraud and when he finally had to resign following corruption charges. In contrast, Serrano of Guatemala was forced from office by the military only one week after he seized power, with strong support from the political parties, the business community, and civil society groups. The former human rights ombudsman, Ramiro de León Carpio, later became president. While domestic dynamics were important, the OAS's quick response was essential to aborting the Guatemalan *autogolpe*. The presence of the OAS high-level mission buttressed the message that the president's unconstitutional actions would not be tolerated.

In all three cases, the constitutional order had been interrupted. This was not the case in Paraguay in 1996, where democratic institutions were not dismantled, but the country's nascent democracy was threatened by the insubordination of the army chief. After decades of military dictatorship, the civilian Juan Carlos Wasmosy had been elected president in 1993. However, the head of the army, Lino Oviedo, became ever more powerful, to the point that, on 22 April 1996, President

Wasmosy decided to dismiss him. The refusal of Oviedo to obey this order precipitated a major political crisis. Yet, the emergency meeting of the OAS Permanent Council in Washington was marked by confusion. Some delegations questioned whether Resolution 1080 was applicable, given that there had been no interruption of the constitutional order. The Permanent Council ultimately condemned General Oviedo's refusal to submit to civilian authority and called an ad hoc meeting as per Resolution 1080.[43] OAS SG César Gaviria travelled to Asunción to offer his support to President Wasmosy. Further actions were not necessary, though, as a wide range of international actors, including the embassies of Brazil and Argentina, MERCOSUR, the EU, and US President Bill Clinton, as well as loyalist sectors from the armed forces and the people of Paraguay supported Wasmosy, insisting that the president hold his ground. On the morning of 24 April Oviedo was forced to resign as army commander.[44]

Resolution 1080 is also said to have had a deterrent effect, in that the prospect of its invocation stopped looming threats to democratic rule. One example is the situation in Ecuador in 2000, where military leaders staged a coup, but stepped down after threats of punishment from the OAS and the international community.[45]

The cases of Haiti, Guatemala, Peru and Paraguay proved the need for international action to protect democracy. The OAS's almost immediate reactions to those crises sent a strong signal in favor of democracy. It reinforced the established precedent that the interruption of the democratic process was not a matter of domestic jurisdiction, but that international organizations had a right and responsibility to address internal political issues. However, in none of the four cases where Resolution 1080 was invoked is it possible to claim that the OAS intervention was the decisive factor. There were always other domestic and international factors at play, and it is difficult to assess their respective share of explanatory power in absolute terms. However, in Haiti and Peru, OAS action had a positive effect in preventing an even worse outcome, while in Guatemala and Paraguay OAS condemnations of the threats to democracy supported the sectors of society standing up for democracy.

Resolution 1080 represented a significant step forward. Yet, its limitations were also apparent. First, with its focus on avoiding or repairing disruptions in constitutional government, the role of the OAS and its Resolution 1080 was restricted to reactive measures. The "firefighter approach"[46] of Resolution 1080 was a valuable mechanism for bringing members of the international community together to consider possible responses to the interruption of the democratic process in any country of the hemisphere. One may speculate that it also deterred those tempted to launch a coup, but Resolution 1080 did not have any tools to prevent democratic decline. The OAS did not monitor the state of democracy in the Americas. Furthermore, continuity of constitutional government was not a sufficient condition for respect for democracy and human rights to persist. Structural impediments, like vast inequalities of wealth and income, reduced the likelihood of democracy's long-term survival, but the OAS did not remedy the underlying social and economic causes of political instability. The subsequent trajectory of Guatemala, Haiti, Paraguay and Peru presents ample evidence of these difficulties, as it was largely determined by domestic and structural factors beyond control of the OAS. In spite of its prior involvement, the organization was unable to prevent these countries from plunging back into democratic crises several years later.

Second, what the framers of Resolution 1080 had in mind was clear, unambiguous, abrupt reversals of the constitutional order, such as sudden overthrow of a democratic government by force, typically a military coup. However, events rarely evolved in such clear-cut fashion, and Resolution 1080's supporters came to realize that "creeping coups," governments engaging in constitutional backsliding, and other more subtle threats to the democratic process (such as constitutional irregularities or electoral fraud) would have to be addressed. In short, definitional issues of what constituted a threat to the constitutional order required some refinement. The fact that threats to democracy were not limited to unambiguous coups and overthrows of sitting governments was addressed in the Managua Declaration, which noted that less overt threats to democracy also needed tackling.

The third problem was that while Resolution 1080 took the initial step of setting up a mechanism for the investigation of cases in which democratic governments had been overthrown, there was no effective enforcement mechanism. Even the new Article 9 of the OAS Charter created by the Washington Protocol only threatened members with suspension from all activities, but did not contain any expulsion mechanism. It was never invoked anyway, as it entered into force in 1997 only and was then soon to be displaced by the IADC. In addition, it was clear that the implementation of these mechanisms to a large extent would be subject to political will. The punitive measures foreseen were still hampered by the lingering contradiction between the mission to promote and consolidate democracy, on the one hand, and the principle of non-intervention, on the other. The fact that Resolution 1080 emphasized "due respect" for national sovereignty and that Article 9 required exercising "the powers referred to in this article ... in accordance with this Charter"—which repeatedly stipulates the respect for national sovereignty—minimized the democratic clause's deterrent effect. Moreover, in his far-sighted analysis of the cases of Haiti and Peru, Schnably emphasized that the promise of greater enforcement of the norms of democracy and human rights through the direct involvement of states in the diplomatic dealings of the OAS Permanent Council and the Meeting of the Ministers of Foreign Affairs is undermined by the tendency of governments to press only half-heartedly for the restoration of elected governments whose policies they dislike.[47]

Conclusion

The establishment of the OAS defense of democracy regime is remarkable because there are no precedents. Resolution 1080 and the Washington Protocol are evidence of an emerging "right to democracy"[48] and of a corresponding weakening of the OAS's ban on intervention in states' domestic affairs. The 1948 OAS Charter had a number of references to democracy as the preferred choice for its member states, and established it as the common norm. Yet, during the phase prior to Resolution 1080 and the Washington Protocol, these were seen as declaratory, pro-forma statements and not as a collective commitment. It was only in the 1980s that the promotion and defense of democracy became an explicit aim of the organization. In the early 1990s, enforcement measures were established. The basic concern then was the protection against "interruptions" of the democratic order. In Resolution 1080 of 1991 and the Washington Protocol of 1992 this was done through an anti-coup norm, i.e. the sanctioning of coups and coup attempts. Provisions for the defense of democracy are key instruments to secure the realization of democratic values of a regional organization's member states. If implemented with suitable tools and harnessed to domestic support, they may help to foster democratic consolidation.

These tools were to come in handy in a decade that saw a not insignificant number of attempts (some successful, some not) to unseat elected governments. Yet, their weaknesses became apparent in the course of the first applications: they are reactive measures, tailored to clear and abrupt interruptions of the constitutional order, and effective application of punitive measures is hampered by the clash between the idea of intervening on behalf of democracy and states' insistence on national sovereignty. Clearly, the OAS had to do more to protect democracy in the Western hemisphere. An attempt to remedy those flaws was made with the IADC, whose genesis and contents will be the focus of the next chapter.

Notes

1 For an overview of the history of the OAS, see M. Margaret Ball, *The OAS in Transition* (Durham, N.C.: Duke University Press, 1969); Gordon Connell-Smith, *The Inter-American System* (London: Oxford University Press, 1966); Samuel Guy Inman, *Inter-American Conferences, 1826–1954: History and Problems* (Washington, DC: University Press of Washington, 1965).
2 Paul W. Drake, "From Good Men to Good Neighbors, 1912–32," in *Exporting Democracy: The United States and Latin America: Case Studies*, ed. Abraham F. Lowenthal (Baltimore, Md. and London: Johns Hopkins University Press, 1991), 3–40; Peter H. Smith, *Talons of the Eagle: Latin America, the United States, and the World* (New York and Oxford: Oxford University Press, 2008), chapter 2.
3 Heraldo Muñoz, "The Right to Democracy in the Americas," *Journal of Interamerican Studies and World Affairs* 40, no. 1 (1998): 1–18; Michael Shifter, "The United States, the Organization of American States, and the Origins of the Inter-American System," in *The Globalization of U.S.-Latin American Relations: Democracy, Intervention, and Human Rights*, ed. Virginia M. Bouvier (Westport, Conn. and London: Praeger, 2002), 85–104.
4 For an overview of the emergence and the activities of the OAS, see Viron P. Vaky and Heraldo Muñoz, *The Future of the Organization of American States* (New York: Twentieth Century Fund, 1993); Christopher R. Thomas and Juliana T. Magloire, *Regionalism Versus Multilateralism: The Organization of American States in a Global Changing Environment* (Boston, Mass., Dordrecht and London: Kluwer Academic Publishers, 2000); Betty Horwitz, *The Transformation of the Organization of American States: A Multilateral Framework for Regional Governance* (London: Anthem Press, 2010); Mônica Herz, *The Organization of American States (OAS)* (London and New York: Routledge, 2011).
5 Charter of the OAS, Chapter II, Article 5(d) in its original version from 1948, avalon.law.yale.edu/20th_century/decad062.asp. In the current version of the Charter, this provision is found in Chapter II, Article 3(d), www.oas.org/juridico/english/charter.html.
6 Muñoz, "The Right to Democracy in the Americas," 4.
7 Ball, *The OAS in Transition*, 485–98.
8 Guillermo O'Donnell, *Modernization and Bureaucratic-Authoritarianism: Studies in South American Politics* (Berkeley, Calif.: Institute of International Studies, University of California, 1973); Dietrich Rueschemeyer, Evelyne Huber Stephens and John D. Stephens, *Capitalist Development and Democracy* (Chicago, Ill.: University of Chicago Press, 1992), Chapters 5 and 6; Peter H. Smith, *Democracy in Latin America: Political Change in Comparative Perspective* (New York and Oxford: Oxford University Press, 2005), 53–62.
9 See Carolyn M. Shaw, *Cooperation, Conflict, and Consensus in the Organization of American States* (New York: Palgrave Macmillan, 2004).
10 Smith, *Talons of the Eagle*, 5.

11 See Robert A. Pastor, *Whirlpool: U.S. Foreign Policy toward Latin America and the Caribbean* (Princeton, N.J.: Princeton University Press, 1992), 287–88.
12 Carolyn M. Shaw, "The United States: Rhetoric and Reality," in *Promoting Democracy in the Americas*, ed. Thomas Legler, Sharon F. Lean and Dexter S. Boniface (Baltimore, Md.: Johns Hopkins University Press, 2007), 63–84; Smith, *Talons of the Eagle*, chapter 5.
13 Lothar Brock, "Die Funktion der OAS für die Rechtfertigung der Lateinamerika-Politik der USA," *Politische Vierteljahresschrift* 19, no. 1 (1978): 3–22. That the defense of representative democracy did not rank very high on the OAS agenda during the Cold War era is also reflected in numerous publications on the inter-American system from that period. Early analyses focused on the organization's institutional structure and its record on peace and security, and the most vividly debated topic was that of US–Latin American relations. See Ball, *The OAS in Transition*: this book at least does have a short chapter on representative democracy under the heading "Other Political Questions" (485–98); O. Carlos Stoetzer, *The Organization of American States: An Introduction* (New York: Praeger, 1965); Gordon Connell-Smith, *The United States and Latin America: An Historical Analysis of Inter-American Relations* (London: Heinemann, 1974); Jerome Slater, *The OAS and United States Foreign Policy* (Columbus: Ohio State University Press, 1967); Lothar Brock, *Entwicklungsnationalismus und Kompradorenpolitik: Die Gründung der OAS und die Entwicklung der Abhängigkeit Lateinamerikas von den USA* (Meisenheim am Glan, Germany: Verlag Anton Hain, 1975); Henry H. Han, *Problems and Prospects of the Organization of American States: Perceptions of the Member States' Leaders* (New York: Peter Lang, 1987); V. Shiv Kumar, *US Interventionism in Latin America: Dominican Crisis and the OAS* (London: Sangam Books, 1987).
14 Muñoz, "The Right to Democracy in the Americas."
15 Declaration of Santiago, General Secretariat of the Organization of American States, Fifth Meeting of Consultation of Ministers of Foreign Affairs, Santiago, Chile, 12–18 August 1959, Final Act, www.oas.org/consejo/MEETINGS%20OF%20CONSULTATION/minutes.asp.
16 Ibid.; also see Muñoz, "The Right to Democracy in the Americas," 5.
17 Lucy Komisar, "Kissinger Declassified," *The Progressive Magazine* 63, no. 5 (1999): 24–26.
18 For an overview and the relation of human rights and democracy, see Tom Farer, "The Rise of the Inter-American Human Rights Regime: No Longer a Unicorn, Not Yet an Ox," *Human Rights Quarterly* 19, no. 3 (1997): 510–46; Robert K. Goldman, "History and Action: The Inter-American Human Rights System and the Role of the Inter-American Commission on Human Rights," *Human Rights Quarterly* 31, no. 4 (2009): 856–87.
19 Hugo de Zela Martínez, "The Organization of American States (OAS) and its Quest for Democracy in the Americas," *Yale Journal of International Affairs* 8, no. 3 (2013): 23–36.
20 Personal interview with Luigi Einaudi, former US Permanent Representative to the OAS, former Acting Secretary-General (2004–05), Washington, DC, 23 May 2013.
21 Ibid.
22 See, for example, Vaky and Muñoz, *The Future of the Organization of American States*; Tom Farer, ed., *Beyond Sovereignty: Collectively*

Defending Democracy in the Americas (Baltimore, Md. and London: Johns Hopkins University Press, 1996); Andrew F. Cooper and Thomas Legler, "The OAS Democratic Solidarity Paradigm: Questions of Collective and National Leadership," *Latin American Politics and Society* 43, no. 1 (2001): 103–26; Dexter S. Boniface, "Is There a Democratic Norm in the Americas? An Analysis of the Organization of American States," *Global Governance* 8, no. 3 (2002): 365–81; Randall Parish and Mark Peceny, "Kantian Liberalism and the Collective Defense of Democracy in Latin America," *Journal of Peace Research* 39, no. 2 (2002): 229–50.

23 Charter of the OAS, Preamble.

24 Charter of the OAS, Chapter I, Article 2(b).

25 Guy Gosselin and Jean-Philippe Thérien, "The Organization of American States and Regionalism in the Americas," in *The Americas in Transition: The Contours of Regionalism*, ed. Gordon Mace and Louis Bélanger (Boulder, Colo.: Lynne Rienner, 1999), 175–93. In the course of the 2005 reform of the OAS General Secretariat, the UPD was turned into what is now called the Department for Electoral Cooperation and Observation (DECO) under the roof of the Secretariat for Political Affairs (see www.oas.org/en/spa/deco/).

26 Personal interview with Luigi Einaudi; also see Carlos Andrés Pérez, "OAS Opportunities," *Foreign Policy* 80 (1990): 52–55.

27 Today's Andean Community was called Andean Pact until 1996.

28 Personal interview with Luigi Einaudi; also see Muñoz, "The Right to Democracy in the Americas," 9.

29 Personal interview with Luigi Einaudi.

30 Santiago Commitment to Democracy and the Renewal of the Inter-American System, 4 June 1991, General Assembly Declaration, www.oas.org/consejo/GENERAL%20ASSEMBLY/Resoluciones-Declaraciones.asp.

31 OAS General Assembly Resolution 1080, 5 June 1991, www.oas.org/juridic o/english/agres1080.htm.

32 Interesting insights on the role of the Caribbean countries in the OAS are presented in Thomas and Magloire, *Regionalism Versus Multilateralism*.

33 Personal interview with Luigi Einaudi.

34 OAS General Assembly Resolution 1080.

35 Personal interview with Luigi Einaudi.

36 Another aspect of this resolution that has often been ignored is the provision mentioned in the third paragraph, which instructs the Permanent Council to develop "incentives to preserve and strengthen democratic systems" in order to prevent future democratic interruptions.

37 Charter of the OAS, Chapter III, Article 9.

38 Charter of the OAS, Chapter I, Articles 2(g) and Chapter II, Article 3(f).

39 All declarations and resolutions of the regular sessions of the General Assembly from 1971 to date are accessible via: www.oas.org/consejo/GENE RAL%20ASSEMBLY/Resoluciones-Declaraciones.asp.

40 OAS Meeting of Consultation of Ministers of Foreign Affairs Resolution 1/91, 2 October 1991, and Resolution 2/91, 8 October 1991.

41 A detailed account of the case of Haiti is given by Stephen J. Schnably, "The Santiago Commitment as a Call to Democracy in the United States: Evaluating the OAS Role in Haiti, Peru, and Guatemala," *University of Miami Inter-American Law Review* 25, no. 3 (1994): 393–587; also see Domingo E. Acevedo and Claudio Grossman, "The Organization of

American States and the Protection of Democracy," in *Beyond Sovereignty: Collectively Defending Democracy in the Americas*, ed. Tom Farer (Baltimore, Md. and London: Johns Hopkins University Press, 1996), 132–49.

42 In the case of Peru, the OAS Permanent Council adopted Resolution 579 in April 1992; in the Guatemalan case, the Permanent Council reacted on the day of the coup with the adoption of Resolution 605.

43 OAS Permanent Council Resolution 681 (1971/96), 23 April 1996.

44 For a detailed assessment of the Paraguayan crisis, see Arturo Valenzuela, "Paraguay: The Coup that Didn't Happen," *Journal of Democracy* 8, no. 1 (1997): 43–55.

45 The Permanent Council issued Resolution 763 and 764 to express support for the constitutional government and condemn the attempted *coup d'état*. Also see Dexter S. Boniface, "The OAS's Mixed Record," in *Promoting Democracy in the Americas*, ed. Thomas Legler, Sharon F. Lean and Dexter S. Boniface (Baltimore, Md.: Johns Hopkins University Press, 2007), 40–62.

46 See Acevedo and Grossman, "The Organization of American States and the Protection of Democracy," 148.

47 Schnably, "The Santiago Commitment as a Call to Democracy in the United States."

48 Thomas M. Franck, "The Emerging Right to Democratic Governance," *American Journal of International Law* 86, no. 1 (1992): 46–91; Muñoz, "The Right to Democracy in the Americas."

3 The Inter-American Democratic Charter

Entering the new millennium, OAS member states faced a number of challenges in strengthening democracy in the region. In the 1990s, for a brief moment, Latin American transitions to democracy and the US switch to a seemingly genuine support for democratic rule in the Americas opened a window of opportunity for putting the defense and promotion of democracy front and center on the hemispheric agenda. The 1990s were thus the "golden decade" of democracy promotion in the Americas, with the adoption of a collective defense of democracy regime. The highly professional work in technical assistance for elections as well as in electoral observation established the practice of externally validating electoral processes. For these purposes, the OAS brought together representatives from almost all governments throughout the Western hemisphere. Latin America's low-intensity democracies were keen to obtain outside support for their fledgling institutions, and looked anxiously for external sources to buttress their still young, elected governments. In this context, the somewhat sorry past record of the OAS during the Cold War was easily overlooked. What mattered was this new opportunity to be able to count on the organization and on the United States to stand up for democracy and not for dictatorships, as had so often been the case before.

By the turn of the century, however, the OAS efforts to defend democracy had achieved only mixed success. While Resolution 1080 and the Washington Protocol had been designed to counter *coups d'état*, in the course of the 1990s the threat of coups was replaced by a new one: authoritarian regression or "backsliding" by democratically elected incumbent presidents. This chapter analyzes the creation and contents of the IADC. The first section makes reference to key moments of change and leadership in the process of its creation. The two subsequent sections review the contents of the democratic charter, highlight its innovations and examine the collective mechanisms for the defense of democracy stipulated in its Chapter IV. The fourth section examines some of the shortcomings and unresolved issues that emerged soon after the charter's creation, as well as the challenges posed by changes in the nature of democratic threats and by the geopolitical context.

Origins and antecedents

The charter was the product of the confluence of a unique set of factors at the beginning of the new century. This was a time of remarkable consensus on what democracy, democratic values and democratic institutions were all about. After the end of the Cold War, Latin America's transition to democracy, a decade-long Washington Consensus as the one and only economic program, and the FTAA as the dominant pan-hemispheric project (targeted to come into effect in 2005), there was widespread agreement on democracy and free markets as the prevailing paradigms of the era. Much as the FTAA was designed to formalize that commitment to a certain type of market economy (as open as possible, with a minimal role for the state, and explicitly friendly to "deep globalization"), the IADC arose as a framework and a set of principles committed to a certain type of democracy. This was representative democracy in its classical, liberal expression, with its emphasis on separation of powers, free elections and freedom of the press. While the OAS from its inception had endorsed representative democracy, this principle was not put into practice during the long, dark night of military rule which engulfed much of Latin America from the 1960s to the 1980s.

Once Cold War tensions were left behind and the military was back in its barracks, collective diplomacy in the hemisphere focused on eradicating once and for all the possibility of military coups. With Augusto Pinochet still commander-in-chief of the Chilean army and a number of uprisings of provincial garrisons in Argentina, this was by no means an unwarranted concern. The 1991 military coup in Haiti against President Jean-Bertrand Aristide, the 1996 failed coup in Paraguay against President Juan Carlos Wasmosy, and the 2000 short-lived military coup against President Jamil Mahuad in Ecuador were all instances in which this collective commitment to the democratic rules of the game was tested, and did not do too badly. It showed that the newly elected leaders meant what they said, and acted accordingly, and although the Latin American military remained a force to be reckoned with, impunity for their *golpismo* was no longer on. This made it much more difficult to re-enact the recurring vicious cycle of alternation between civilian and military regimes that has been such a prominent feature of the region's history. The Haitian armed forces, after one coup too many, were dissolved by an Aristide triumphantly returned to office, and have not been re-established. General Pinochet, a scant seven months after having left his position as commander-in-chief of the Chilean army, was arrested in London, and spent 18 months under detention in the United Kingdom.[1]

However, if the re-enactment of military dictatorships in the region became an increasingly distant possibility as the 1990s wore on, a different threat emerged that did not come from the barracks, but from the civilian leadership itself. Newly elected presidents such as Fernando Collor de Mello in Brazil (1989–92), Carlos Menem in Argentina (1989–99), and, most significantly, Alberto Fujimori in Peru (1990–2000) embodied a new version of yesteryear's "man on horseback." Portraying themselves as the *salvadores de la patria* (saviors of the fatherland), they each came to power in the midst of severe economic crises. Once in office, and in the long tradition of Latin American *caudillos*, they sought to elevate themselves beyond the mundane limitations of working democracies, eliminate, as far as possible, horizontal accountability for their actions to other government branches, and amass in their hands as much power as they could. A classic feature in these three cases was the imposition of "austerity packages" which, reneging on promises made on the campaign trail, imposed much of the adjustment burden of the economies on the popular sectors. Their preferred mode of government was through executive decrees, the famous *decretismo* that allowed them to skip the messy and cumbersome logrolling and compromise involved in legislating through congress. They were, in short, delegative democracies, in the expression of Guillermo O'Donnell.[2] In hindsight, they all ended badly: with the impeachment and ouster of Collor de Mello in Brazil; with Argentina's default, not long after Menem had left office; and with Fujimori's resignation and his later trial and sentence to prison (a place where he still finds himself today). However, this is not to say that at the time they did not wreak much havoc, triggering impassioned responses among their respective countries' democratic forces, and imperiling transitions from authoritarianism that had raised so much hope among the citizenry.

The most extreme form of delegative democracy took place in Peru. In 1992, scarcely two years after his election, Fujimori closed the congress, established a state of emergency, and in the name of fighting terrorism, suspended many civil liberties and freedoms. Peruvians experienced first-hand that the main threat to their democratic rights did not come from a military *junta*, but from an elected leader who decided to concentrate power in his own hands.[3] It is thus not a coincidence that it was in Peru where the efforts to enlist a regional response to this type of authoritarian regression took off and stayed the course for much of the decade.

The trigger for the creation of the IADC was the denouement of the Peruvian presidential elections of 2000. Peruvian strongman Alberto Fujimori was re-elected for a controversial third term, despite what some considered serious irregularities in the second-round elections on 28 May. As a result, the OAS electoral observation mission led by Guatemalan Eduardo Stein withdrew from the country, triggering extensive deliberations within the OAS as to what to do about Peru. Although reservations were expressed by some member states (notably Brazil and Mexico) about interfering in Peru's internal affairs, at the June 2000 OAS General Assembly held in Windsor, Canada, a working solution was hammered out in conjunction with Peruvian government representatives. Before the month was out, OAS SG César Gaviria and Canadian Foreign Minister Lloyd Axworthy found themselves in Lima, heading the organization's special delegation mandated to deal with Peru's post-election impasse.[4]

The delegation demanded that the Peruvian government kick-start an ambitious reform program, proposed an elaborate Dialogue Table (*Mesa de Diálogo*) process with government, opposition and civil society representatives to broker a deal between government and opposition, and otherwise exerted pressure on the incumbent government to clean up its act and roll back the creeping authoritarianism that had become a hallmark of Peru under Fujimori ever since the 1992 *autogolpe*. This was a milestone in the process that eventually led to Fujimori's resignation, and on 20 November 2000, Alberto Fujimori became the first head of state to turn in his resignation by fax—from Tokyo, where he was on a state visit. With remarkable smoothness, and through the good offices of an enlightened provisional government, Peru made the transition to a respected, fully democratic government, elected in free and fair elections in 2001. In this context, the OAS and the international community played a not insignificant role in facilitating the passage from Alberto Fujimori's delegative democracy to Alejandro Toledo's representative one. With its emphasis on dialogue and the program of gradual change it fostered, the OAS mission also helped to bring together the elites of a highly divided society.[5]

It was as a result of that protracted struggle for their democratic rights that Peruvian leaders and intellectuals came up with the idea of a democratic charter for the hemisphere. The rationale for it was to state explicitly that serious threats to and disruptions of the democratic institutional system are more than just *coups d'état*. Codifying this in a document would help others in the future avoid a similar predicament to the one they faced as they took on *fujimorismo*. The idea was to leave behind the bedrock components of the Cold War-era inter-American system, state sovereignty and the principle of non-intervention, or at least make them more permeable to concerns about democratic norms, much as they had been made more permeable to human rights concerns before.

The leaders of the interim government that succeeded that of Alberto Fujimori, President Valentín Paniagua and Foreign Minister Javier Pérez de Cuéllar, took the lead in this and introduced the initial proposal for a democratic charter shortly before the Third Summit of the Americas, which took place in April 2001 in Quebec City. Much as it did at the OAS General Assembly in Windsor in 2000, Canada as the host of the conference once again played an important role.[6] In what became known as the democracy clause of the Declaration of Quebec City, the hemispheric heads of state stated that a shared commitment to democracy and the rule of law was an essential condition for participation in the summit process, thus emphasizing the need to strengthen the capacity of the American nations to respond to situations that threaten democracy.[7]

The OAS General Assembly held in San José, Costa Rica two months later reiterated the consensus on the subject, to be found in the Resolution of San José.[8] The final text of the document was formally adopted as the IADC at a special session of the General Assembly held in Lima, Peru, on the same day on which the terrorist attacks in the United States took place, 11 September 2001.

A new charter for the new century

The IADC is the most significant document on democracy as a form of government in the Western hemisphere.[9] The core and main innovative potential of the charter resides in Chapters I and IV. They put forth certain concepts that, while reflecting already existing procedures, are new insofar as they represent an effort to achieve greater precision in the concepts and organization of said procedures and their gradual application (see Table 3.1). By contrast, other conceptual and procedural areas covered in the democratic charter, such as Chapters II and III, already were a part of ordinary OAS activity.

The conceptual baseline regarding the meaning of democracy in the inter-American system is drawn in Chapter I. In its very first article, the IADC identifies the "right to democracy"—a notion that had been developed by Thomas Franck—as a key right of the peoples of the Americas, and defines democracy as a prerequisite for the "social, political and economic development" of those living in the continent.[10] The charter then proceeds to define what representative democracy is all about, distinguishes between "essential elements" (Art. 3) and "essential components of the exercise" (Art. 4) of representative democracy, and highlights other ingredients of the political system whose development and strengthening are necessary for democratic institutions to flourish.[11]

The essential elements of representative democracy include standard features such as respect for fundamental freedoms and human rights, the holding of periodic elections that are free, fair, and based on universal and secret suffrage as an expression of the sovereignty of the people, access to power and its exercise subject to the rule of law, separation of powers and independence of the branches of government, and a pluralistic party system. Along the same lines, the fundamental components of the exercise of democracy are defined as the transparency of governmental activities, integrity, the responsibility of governments in public administration, respect for social rights and for freedom of expression and of the press, the constitutional subordination of all state institutions to the legally constituted civil authority, and respect for the rule of law on the part of all agencies and sectors of society. Contrary to what is sometimes said, the IADC also stresses that citizen participation not only strengthens democracy, but is a "necessary condition" for the full exercise of democracy (Art. 2 and 6).

As befits any such document, it includes full sections on human rights (Chapter II, Art. 7–10) and on integral development and combating poverty (Chapter III, Art. 11–16). For their part, Chapters II and III are geared toward reaffirming, in general terms, the commitment of the OAS and its member states to human rights and the struggle against poverty and inequality, and provide a crucial linkage between the consolidation of democracy and socioeconomic development (Art. 11–16), as well as the defense, oversight and guarantee of human rights (Art. 7–10).

Yet, the most innovative part of the charter comes in its operational sections—the one on the promotion and defense of democracy (Chapter IV, Art. 17–22, the longest section of the document) and, to a lesser extent, the one on electoral observation (Chapter V, Art. 23–25). This is where the difficult balancing act between standing up for democracy,

Table 3.1 Key principles of democracy promotion in the IADC

	Reaffirmation	*Innovation*
Conceptual	Anti-coup norm ("unconstitutional interruption of the democratic order")	Anti-authoritarian backsliding norm ("unconstitutional alteration of the constitutional regime that seriously impairs the democratic order")
	Democracy as a membership requirement	Right to democracy
	Membership suspension	Definition of representative democracy
	Electoral (in)validation	
Procedural	Executive sovereignty ("by invitation only")	Graduated, proportionate response

Source: Authors' elaboration based on Thomas Legler, "The Shifting Sands of Regional Governance: The Case of Inter-American Democracy Promotion," *Politics & Policy* 40, no. 5 (2012): 848–70.

on the one hand, and not violating the OAS's quasi-sacred principles of state sovereignty and non-intervention, on the other, takes place. If democracy is a right of the peoples of the Americas (Art. 1) and is at the foundation of the rule of law and constitutional regimes of OAS member states (Art. 2), then their governments are obliged to promote it, and it is necessary to establish collective mechanisms for the protection and defense of democracy, and charge the OAS with this responsibility. Accordingly, Chapter IV lays out procedures for collective response to the various possible situations in which democracy in any of the OAS member states is threatened, seriously affected or destroyed.

Chapter V offers a new institutional framework for the already established OAS practice of electoral observation, originally carried out by the Unit for the Promotion of Democracy and now managed by the Department of Electoral Cooperation and Observation (DECO) within the Secretariat for Political Affairs. Finally, Chapter VI defines general guidelines to be adopted by the OAS and its member states to strengthen a democratic culture and promote democratic principles and practices. While particular emphasis is laid on education (Art. 27) and the participation of women (Art. 28), no specific plans of action were defined at this point.

Collective mechanisms for the defense of democracy

As shown above, the creation of the IADC was driven by two factors: first, the persistence of occasional political instability in the region throughout the 1990s, despite the considerable progress made on the region's transition to democracy; and second, the fact that threats to democracy were taking new forms, different from the classical military coup. Resolution 1080 and the Washington Protocol were tailored exclusively to interruptions of the democratic institutional order. In a carefully crafted effort to respond to new challenges, Chapter IV distinguishes between different situations and establishes specific action mechanisms for each one in a scaling exercise nonexistent in the concise Resolution 1080 (see Table 3.2 for an overview). It provides four modalities in which the OAS can stand up for democracy, wherever the latter is deemed to be under threat. The hierarchical nature of Articles 17–21 thus seeks to implement the principle of graduated and proportionate response. The options available through the IADC can be reduced to two approaches. The first approach, preventive in nature, makes use of the mechanisms provided by diplomacy and international cooperation to help overcome and reverse an ongoing democratic crisis. Consent from the government concerned—in varying forms and degrees—is necessary for it. The second approach, clearly punitive, consists of the threat or application of sanctions to a state in which the democratic order has broken down.[12]

In line with the first approach, Article 17 allows for the government of any member state to request help from the OAS SG or the Permanent Council if its democratic political institutional process is at risk. This is a relatively straightforward proposition that should not lend itself to any interpretive difficulties. If a government asks for help from the OAS, it can hardly contend later that its sovereignty was violated or that the principle of non-intervention was not applied. On the other hand, it is true that this article is unlikely to be widely used, for two reasons. If one of the most acute threats to democracy in the region from 1990 onwards has been what, for want of a better word, has been termed "democratic backsliding"—i.e. an encroaching of authoritarian tendencies from within the executive branch—it is improbable that those guilty of that very behavior would reach out to the OAS to denounce themselves. In turn, if that is not the case, and it is the executive branch that finds itself under assault from other branches of government, or by, say, an unarmed insurrection of civil society members, making a formal call for help on the OAS (by definition a public act) signals institutional weakness, and may further embolden the opposition forces determined to bring down that particular government. Thus, to rely on Article 17 puts governments in a bit of a quandary, as invoking it means to admit that the own government is "at risk." As we shall see in Chapter 5, President Manuel Zelaya of Honduras resorted to Article

17 in June 2009, only a few days before the 28 June coup that deposed him. When he did so, it was too late, and the wheels turning towards his ouster had acquired too much speed to be stopped. Yet, arguably, an earlier resort to this particular mechanism might have avoided the breakdown of Honduran democracy and the ensuing imbroglio.[13] There is also the danger that the executive calling on the OAS for help might be interpreted by the opposition as undue interference in domestic political dynamics that are taking their own course, and that the OAS might henceforth be perceived as partisan by the president's opponents, which might limit the organization's room for maneuver in later mediation efforts.[14]

A second weapon in the arsenal of the IADC is its Article 18, which calls for the OAS SG or the Permanent Council to take the initiative in cases where democracy is in peril. Ayala sees another distinction between Articles 17 and 18: one of timing. Whereas the use of the term "risk" in Article 17 implies that the problem has not yet occurred, Article 18 speaks of a situation already in place that may affect the democratic process or the legitimate exercise of power.[15] In such cases, inspection visits may be arranged, reports prepared, situations assessed, and decisions made on how to deal with such threats. Once again, a critical issue becomes that of the required consent of the government in question. This may turn out to be an obstacle that makes it impossible for the OAS to adopt actions to protect democracy, especially if it is the actions of the very government which are weakening democratic institutions. According to some, this is a critical deficiency in the democratic charter, one that needs to be remedied to allow the SG greater leeway to send delegations and establish what is happening on the ground. Interestingly, there are differences on this issue between current SG José Miguel Insulza and former SG César Gaviria, with the former arguing for greater powers for the Secretariat, and the latter affirming that this would be unnecessary, as current rules would provide plenty of room for doing the needful.[16]

The real "teeth" in the charter, though, are provided in Articles 19–22, which specify the sanctions to member states in cases of transgression of democratic standards. Article 19 is the core democracy clause of the IADC and has a special status as a principle that is connected to the provisions of Articles 20 and 21 (see Table 3.2). It stipulates that an "unconstitutional interruption of the democratic order" (Art. 21) or an "unconstitutional alteration of the constitutional regime that seriously impairs the democratic order" (Art. 20) are, while they persist, an "insurmountable obstacle" to a member state's participation in OAS bodies. According to Article 20, an unconstitutional alteration would

Table 3.2 Collective mechanisms for the defense of democracy in Chapter IV, IADC

Article	Situation	Initiative	Action
17	Democratic institutional process or government's legitimate exercise of power is at risk	Government of the affected member state	Assistance of the Secretary General or Permanent Council
18	Situations that may affect democratic institutional process or legitimate exercise of power	Secretary-General or Permanent Council, with prior consent of the government concerned	Visits or other action, and report to the Permanent Council
19	Unconstitutional interruption of the democratic order or an unconstitutional alteration of the constitutional regime that seriously impairs the democratic order	Defined as insurmountable obstacles for participation of a member state in OAS organs	
20	Unconstitutional alteration of the constitutional regime that seriously impairs the democratic order	Step 1: Any other member state or Secretary-General Step 2: Permanent Council	Convocation of Permanent Council to undertake collective assessment and diplomatic initiatives Special session of General Assembly, continuation of diplomatic initiatives
21	Unconstitutional interruption of the democratic order	Special session of General Assembly	Suspension of member state with two-thirds vote, continuation of diplomatic initiatives
22	Situation that led to suspension has been resolved	Any member state or the Secretary-General	Special session of General Assembly lifts suspension with two-thirds vote

Source: Authors' elaboration based on OAS Secretariat for Political Affairs, IADC worksheet prepared for OAS Democracy Workshop "The State of Democracy in the Americas: The Inter-American Democratic Charter in Review," Washington, DC, 15–16 July 2013; and Pedro Nikken Bellshaw-Hógg, "Analysis of the Basic Conceptual Definitions for the Application of Mechanisms for the Collective Defense of Democracy Provided for in the Inter-American Democratic Charter," in Collective Defense of Democracy: Concepts and Procedures, ed. Carlos Ayala Corao and Pedro Nikken Bellshaw-Hógg (Lima, Peru: Andean Commission of Jurists, 2006), 29–85.

trigger the calling of the Permanent Council and diplomatic initiatives to restore the situation. If diplomatic efforts fail to reach the objective of normalizing democratic institutionality, a special session of the General Assembly is to be convened and must decide if the seriousness of the situation has crossed the threshold to an unconstitutional interruption and thus for the application of Article 21.[17] If so, the General Assembly is empowered to suspend the membership of the state in question, with a required majority of two thirds of the member states. Yet, Article 21 also stipulates that a suspension does not preclude the continuation of diplomatic initiatives. Finally, Article 22 contains instructions on how to proceed once the situation that led to the suspension has been resolved.

The first (and only) time Article 21 has been applied so far was in 2009. On that occasion, a unanimous vote of the General Assembly supported the suspension of Honduras after the 28 June ouster of President Zelaya. It took a full two years for Honduras to be readmitted to the OAS. This happened in June 2011, after a deal brokered between Presidents Juan Manuel Santos of Colombia and Hugo Chávez of Venezuela removed the main obstacle for such a step, i.e. the issue of the return of Zelaya to Honduras from his exile in the Dominican Republic.[18]

It is easy to underestimate the significance of the IADC. Comparing the number of democratic crises in Latin America in the decade before the approval of the IADC and in the one after it, no significant decline is discernible.[19] In the face of these manifold crises, the apparent scarcity of IADC invocations could be taken to mean that it has not performed a valuable function. Yet, Graham, for example, observes that the charter has a value as a diplomatic tool to stigmatize recalcitrant states and hence might be a credible deterrent halting the escalation of mounting threats to democracy.[20] In addition, from the point of view of OAS SG Insulza, the IADC has two dimensions: on the one hand, it provides a set of rules on how to defend and promote democracy in the Americas; on the other, it constitutes a declaration of intent, a program for moving forward and getting closer to the democratic ideal.[21] In a similar vein, Peter Hakim of the Inter-American Dialogue has characterized the IADC as an "aspirational document."[22] It is in this dual capacity, both as a handbook and as a manifesto, that the IADC has to be judged.

The charter has thus established new, more stringent democractic norms to which countries in the Americas must adhere.[23] It has also set forth the notion that the international community, and particularly the hemispheric community, has a greater role in enforcing those norms than had been the case before. In terms of the mechanics of enforcing those norms, the key idea by which it is inspired is that of a graduated response to complex developments. In other words, diplomatic initiatives and good offices play a key role in dealing with the often subtle authoritarian encroachments into democratic institutions. These are very different from old-style military coups, and thus demand more nuanced responses and tools to confront them. In finding the right balance between firm responses that convey the concerns of the hemispheric community about impending threats to the integrity of democratic institutions in any given member state, on the one hand, and interventions that are too blunt and heavy handed, on the other, lies much of the art and science of implementing the IADC.

Shortcomings and challenges

The IADC addresses many of the shortcomings identified in the debate on the emerging defense of democracy regime during the 1990s. However, the OAS faces an ongoing challenge in putting the democratic charter into practice in a timely and effective manner. While the Permanent Council and the General Assembly refer to the IADC on a regular basis when issuing statements on democracy, the Chapter IV provisions have not been used in much more than a handful of instances (as will be shown in more detail in Chapter 4 of this book). Apparently, member states find themselves at an impasse in terms of applying the IADC. This is attributable to shortcomings of the IADC as such, to challenges posed to it by the changing nature of the democratic crises it has to address, and to challenges triggered by the transformation of the regional environment.

Main limitations of the IADC

Already very early on, some flaws inherent in the design of the IADC became apparent.[24] These flaws are reducible to three fundamental issues: the legal status of the document; the role of the executive in using it; and its graduated, proportionate approach. It is those areas that the internal OAS review process has repeatedly highlighted as the three main limitations of the IADC.[25]

Regarding the legal status of the document, the IADC is a political accord, not a treaty. It had immediate hemispheric coverage in a political sense, but lacks the precision and rigor of a treaty and is not legally binding. This is certainly a downside of the IADC in comparison to Article 9 of the OAS Charter (the democracy clause created by the

Washington Protocol), even though the former is broader than Article 9's limitation to regime change by force.[26] The democratic charter is the expression of a consensus among the OAS member states to undertake collective action to assist in supporting a democracy in distress and penalize its abolition. Therein resides its strength—and at the same time its weakness, as its invocation is dependent on political will.[27] As a political instrument, it is still plagued by the tensions between new pro-democracy norms and the possibility to protect democracy through collective mechanisms, on the one hand, and more established sovereignty norms, on the other. Thus, other than envisioned by its masterminds, the IADC has not been able to overcome the principle of non-intervention.

The second bone of contention is the central role of the executive in the IADC's application. The decision whether to apply the IADC preventively or in cases of an alteration or interruption of the democratic order depends on the consent of the member state concerned and on the majorities generated among the other member states. The Permanent Council is composed of ambassadors who first and foremost follow instructions from their capitals. This is by no means atypical for decision making at the multilateral level, given that the OAS is an intergovernmental organization and governments took the lead in the creation of the defense of democracy regime.[28] Negotiation, the quest for points of consensus, and the putting together of majority positions forces the 34 active member states to reconcile differences, in such a way that the decisions taken are representative and reflect the collective will.

Yet, the key role of the executives and its consequences for the applicability of the defense of democracy regime is controversial. The requirement of the consent of the affected government even to evaluate a threat to democracy has been characterized by Thomas Legler as "by invitation only" principle.[29] Unless the government of the member state itself is worried that it is being threatened by the situation in a country (when a coup is being attempted or oppositional protests are gaining strength), it will in all likelihood not consent to an outside investigation. If the conduct of the government itself constitutes the danger to democracy, the OAS is doomed to inaction, since that government is unlikely to invoke Article 17 or consent to the invocation of Article 18.[30]

To invoke the reactive mechanisms of Articles 20 and 21, the appraisal of the seriousness of a given situation depends upon the judgment by the other member states. This limits the possibility for intervention, as diplomats are reluctant to point fingers. Even if the SG, backed by the expertise of his staff, pushes for an OAS response in a looming situation of crisis, the consent of the other government representatives either in the Permanent Council or in the General Assembly is not necessarily forthcoming. In a scenario of incomplete or imperfect democracies, and, on occasion, of weak governments, the possibility of setting an adverse precedent that may at some future time be invoked against their own wrongdoings is a specter that haunts a good number of governments. It may be powerful enough to undermine the political will necessary to embark upon collective action under the IADC.

The original rationale to create defense of democracy provisions was the protection of sitting executives to ensure their political survival in the face of antidemocratic threats.[31] In a situation of misbehavior of an elected president, the other member states would not go to the extreme of pressing incumbents to cease being incumbents. Critics thus go as far as to suggest that rather than the defense of democracy, the ultimate aim of the defense of democracy regime is the defense of stability, irrespective of democratic quality. Furthermore, the fact that the process of judging whether there is a threat to democracy is controlled by the governments brings about problems of access for other actors seeking to avail themselves of the IADC's mechanisms, such as parties in opposition and citizen and civil society groups.[32]

The third limitation concerns the lack of a clear threshold determining precisely at what point the OAS should intervene according to the main action clauses in Articles 17–21. While the problem of executive sovereignty predates the adoption of the democratic charter, the possibility of gradual, proportionate diplomatic responses to different types of challenges to democracy was one of the major procedural innovations of the IADC (see Table 3.1). Chapter IV of the charter is an attempt to fine-tune the precision of the different scenarios for the alteration of the democratic constitutional order and of the measures and procedures that may be applied in each case. Upon an impending democratic breakdown or deterioration, the SG and/or the Permanent Council can decide to look into the matter (see Table 3.2). In that sense, the IADC is an advancement compared to Resolution 1080.

Yet, critics point to the uncertain meaning of key terms and the lack of precision in the criteria for defining when and to what extent a country's democratic institutions have been altered, when the OAS is confronted with a situation of unconstitutional alteration or interruption of the democratic order, and when there is a crisis.[33] Except for the cases of a total and utter collapse of democratic institutions (Art. 21) and of a government's request for assistance (Art. 17), it is difficult to delimit each Chapter IV scenario in a precise manner.[34] A lot of discussion concerning the applicability of the IADC hence revolves around the question of which antidemocratic state behavior is serious enough to warrant OAS action. On the one hand, the OAS cannot respond to any minor infraction of the IADC, but only to the most immediate and tangible threats. On the other hand, a series of minor transgressions runs the risk of amounting to an incremental erosion of democracy. At the same time, less clear-cut manifestations of democratic encroachments are not easily identifiable. There is often a shortage of reliable information to assess the magnitude of a situation. Different observers may draw contradictory conclusions from the evidence. The OAS lacks a peer review mechanism to monitor IADC compliance as well as an early warning system that would help to determine unconstitutional alterations.[35]

Complementary to the imprecise definitions of the situations, the measures designed to respond to democratic crises are considered weak. This applies particularly to the preventive measures that are dependent on prior consent of the government concerned. Yet, even the reactive measures leave a lot of leeway for those entitled to initiate a response. The soft language of both Articles 18 and 20 which say that action "may" be taken in response to democratic crises, stands in stark contrast to the definite language of Resolution 1080, according to which the SG was "instructed" to call for an emergency meeting of the Permanent Council in reaction to an unconstitutional interruption of the democratic order.[36] Thus, flexibility—the expansion and potential application of democracy protection to more types of situations—was introduced at the expense of automaticity.

These criticisms of the IADC's design flaws were the spark for a reform initiative to strengthen it, presented at the June 2005 OAS General Assembly in Fort Lauderdale, in the United States. A proposal by the Friends of the Democratic Charter (a network of former heads of state and high-ranking public officials advised by a group of senior academics)[37] envisaged a clearer definition of unconstitutional alteration, as well as a mechanism for greater civil society involvement in monitoring IADC compliance among member states. During the General Assembly, the US government came forward with a draft declaration that called on the Permanent Council to assess routinely any situation that might affect a state's democratic process and to develop mechanisms to ensure that civil society organizations can present their views on issues pertinent to the IADC to the OAS on a systematic and regular basis.[38] This met with broad rejection from the Latin American member states, which feared that their sovereignty would be undermined if the OAS was granted such means of intervention.[39]

Challenges to democracy under the IADC

While enormous progress has been made in the course of the past quarter century in terms of establishing democracy as "the only game in town," the weaknesses and deficiencies of polyarchic rule in Latin America are only too apparent. Without the Cold War umbrella to protect and justify them, pulling off traditional military coups has become more difficult. This does not mean that democratic institutions are not facing other dangers. The nature of threats to democracy in the region has gradually changed, and the sparse use of the IADC may also be attributable to the confusing and fluid situation on the ground in countries facing a democratic crisis.

At the time when Resolution 1080 of 1991 and the Washington Protocol of 1992 were drafted, what their creators had in mind was the sanctioning of coups and coup attempts. Ten years later, the democratic charter of 2001 emerged as a reaction to a different type of threat, the so-called self-coups and other instances of authoritarian backsliding of the 1990s. To address those challenges, the apparently subtle, but nonetheless crucial distinction between unconstitutional "interruptions" and "alterations" was introduced. The former include the classic military coup, as well as its variant, the self-coup. The latter, in turn, refer to more insidious and less easily detectable attempts to betray the will of the people—by stealing elections, usurping the powers of one or more government branches, silencing the media, or otherwise repeatedly and systematically infringing upon freedom of expression.

Yet, where presidents were identified during the 1990s as the principal culprits in undemocratic efforts to circumvent elected legislatures à la delegative democracy, new challenges have emerged since the democratic charter was adopted in 2001. One has been executive-legislative gridlock. Empowered by situations of divided government, legislative alliances have in several countries sought to weaken or impeach presidents for questionable ends. Another recent threat to democracy has been the advent of the "civil society coup" or "impeachment coup," a situation where incumbent elected presidents step back in the face of pressure from mass protests demanding their resignation.[40] All of those scenarios have made it very challenging for the OAS to come to the immediate defense of representative democracy. New challenges that arise cannot always be adequately addressed by the responses tailored to counter previous challenges. As indicated in Table 3.3, the development of institutionalized mechanisms for the defense of democracy by the OAS has lagged behind the evolution of threats to democracy over time. When the IADC—which had been created in response to the executive misbehavior of the 1990s—became operational, the nature of threats had already become more diversified and ambiguous (see Chapter 4 of this book).

In broadening the working definition of threats to democracy, and adding the notion of unconstitutional alteration of the democratic regime to them, the IADC took a significant step forward. The drafters of the democratic charter were reluctant to get into details in terms of what these "alterations" mean. The more precise any such definitions, the greater opposition they were bound to encounter, and the more difficult it would have been to get the document's approval. That said, much of the discussion around the IADC has turned on the need to pin down specific instances of such more ambiguous threats.

For OAS SG Insulza, an atmosphere propitious to such threats— through trends that weaken democratic institutions—is created by developments in three spheres: the rules of the system, by frequent changes in the rules of the democratic game; the judiciary, by weakening its independence; and the media and freedom of expression more generally, by threats to the latter, by attempts to over-regulate the former, excessive concentration of media ownership and attacks on reporters by organized crime. Such trends may lead to the sort of situations that should trigger the enactment of the IADC's provisions.[41] Needless to say, they cannot be any type of rule violation. For the SG, they would include the following:

1 Massive electoral fraud;
2 Widespread human rights violations;
3 Indiscriminate or discriminatory closing of most of the media; and
4 Illegitimate dissolution of and outright interference in a branch of government.[42]

These would all be instances of such gravity that they would justify the invocation of Chapter IV of the IADC. Though quite specific, these categories would still be too general for some observers, who have narrowed them down even further. In a volume commissioned by the Andean Commission of Jurists, Ayala and Bellshaw-Hógg suggested using the essential elements and fundamental components listed in Articles 3 and 4 of the IADC as guidelines to identify when a subversion of the democratic order has taken place and its degree of seriousness.[43] The Friends of the Democratic Charter have come up with a comprehensive list of nine categories of activities that would constitute violations of the IADC and should be considered "democratic crises" in one way or another:

Table 3.3 Main threats to democracy in Latin America and OAS responses

Period	Process	Alternative regime	Collective response tool
1980s	Coups	Military dictatorship	None
1990s	Authoritarian backsliding	Delegative democracy	Resolution 1080, Washington Protocol
2000s	Authoritarian backsliding	Illiberal democracy	IADC

Source: Authors' elaboration.

1 Violation of the integrity of central institutions, including constitutional checks and balances providing for the separation of powers;
2 Holding of elections that do not meet minimal international standards;
3 Failure to hold periodic elections or to respect electoral outcomes;
4 Systematic violation of basic freedoms, including freedom of expression, freedom of association, or respect for minority rights;
5 Unconstitutional termination of the tenure in office of any legally elected official by any other elected or non-elected actor;
6 Arbitrary or illegal removal or interference in the appointment or deliberations of members of the judiciary or electoral bodies;
7 Interference by non-elected officials, such as military officers, in the jurisdiction of elected officials;
8 Systematic use of public office to silence, harass, or disrupt the normal and legal activities of members of the political opposition, the press, or civil society; and
9 Unjustified and repeated use of states of emergency.[44]

It is always possible to add further categories to this already quite extensive list. Ultimately, the determination as to whether a violation impairs the democratic order requires political judgment and cannot be resolved by establishing some predetermined criteria. However, political judgments can be improved by access to the best available empirical evidence, and specifications like the above provide decision makers with exactly the sort of more precise approximation to democratic crises that is needed to ascertain when the IADC should be called into action.

Geopolitical context of the IADC

The unpropitious historical and geopolitical context of its adoption posed another challenge that interfered with the implementation of the IADC. When the democratic charter was signed on 11 September 2001, a number of more pressing issues were about to make it to the top of the inter-American political agenda.[45] The terrorist attacks of 9/11 led to a shift in priorities and distracted US attention from the Western hemisphere towards other parts of the world. As George W. Bush's "War on Terror" gained ground, the United States lost interest in regional cooperation, but at the same time renewed its military presence in Latin America in order to address selected security issues such as illegal migration, drug trafficking, organized crime and, last but not least, terrorist threats. These issues dominated the debate in the inter-American institutions throughout most of the 2000s. In contrast, democracy promotion began to be perceived as an issue of the past that had been tied to a certain moment in time, namely the wave of democratization in the region and the end of the Cold War.[46]

In addition, the IADC turned into a new battleground in the age-old quarrel between the US vision of the OAS as an instrument for advancing its interests in the region and a Latin American vision perceiving the OAS as a body to engage the United States multilaterally while containing its imperial ambitions.[47] Yet, in contrast to earlier time periods when the United States mostly maintained its hegemonic influence in the OAS and the inter-American system, a regional power shift is currently underway with far-reaching consequences. The reassertion of US unilateral projects (like the "War on Terror") and the concomitant emergence of regional powers in South America led to an increasing South American disaffection with hemispheric institutions and a shift from hemispheric to sub-regional cooperation. New multilateral organizations arose that exclude the United States and emerge as potential rivals to the OAS in regional governance, including regional democracy promotion.

The IADC also brought to the fore the increasing ideological divides across the hemisphere. While the adherence to free markets and representative democracy had been largely consensual in the 1990s, these values were questioned by the powerful wave of leftist, nationalist and, in some cases, anti-US, governments which has swept the region since the late 1990s. First indications of an end of consensus on representative democracy became apparent in the preparatory phase of the IADC. In the Declaration of Quebec City of April 2001, Venezuela reserved its position with regard to those passages in the document where the strengthening and active defense of representative democracy was mentioned.[48] Since then, the government of Hugo Chávez and countries aligned with it have expressed repeatedly their skepticism about representative democracy and advanced their rival vision of participatory democracy.

Conclusion

The IADC filled many of the gaps in the preexisting defense of democracy regime. The action clauses of Chapter IV widen the range of possible applications by moving from a mere anti-coup norm towards an anti-authoritarian backsliding norm. They contain provisions not only for reacting to, but also for preventing democratic crises. Article 1 formally establishes democracy as a right that member states have an obligation to promote and defend. Articles 3 and 4 provide a detailed definition of, or set of criteria for, representative democracy, which help clarify what exactly member states and OAS entities like DECO are defending and promoting.

However, soon after its adoption it became clear that the IADC suffers from a number of constraints. Collective actions in support of democracy continue to run up against the existing regional norm of sovereignty and non-intervention. The still tenuous nature of new intervention norms of defending democracy is further captured in the fact that the IADC lacks the status of an international treaty. The difficulties for implementing the IADC from a preventive perspective originate in the need for a modicum of acceptance on the part of the affected government. In some cases, this consent is expressly required (Art. 17 and 18), while other mechanisms implicitly entail some degree of agreement on the part of the affected government, without which any diplomatic initiative that may be undertaken by the OAS (Art. 20) would be condemned to failure. Using the punitive approach is difficult as well, due to the need to determine a critical threshold of seriousness of the violations which has to be passed. There is a certain degree of imprecision in the concepts of alteration and interruption of the democratic order, with consequent drawbacks brought on by the wide margins for political interpretations that this vagueness entails. However, this is an inevitable result of the flexibility that was desired for the collective action mechanisms intended to safeguard democracy in the hemisphere.

The design flaws of the IADC are reinforced by the changing nature of the regional democratic problematique and the geopolitical impasse triggered by the downturn in US–Latin American relations, ideological divergence due to the surge of leftist governments in Latin America since the late 1990s, and the emergence of counter-hegemonic regional projects. The following chapters will review the IADC in action and examine to what extent its advances and shortcomings impact on its performance in times of crisis.

Notes

1 For a discussion on the broader significance of this trend, see Robert A. Pastor, "Collectively Defending Democracy: The Inter-American Model," *Brown Journal of World Affairs* 11, no. 1 (2004): 90–97.

2 Guillermo O'Donnell, "Delegative Democracy," *Journal of Democracy* 5, no. 1 (1994): 55–69.

3 See Catherine M. Conghan, *Fujimori's Peru: Deception in the Public Sphere* (Pittsburgh, Penn.: University of Pittsburgh Press, 2005); Julio Carrión, ed., *The Fujimori Legacy: The Rise of Electoral Authoritarianism in Peru* (Philadelphia, Penn.: Penn State University Press, 2006); Cynthia McClintock and Fabian Vallas, *The United States and Peru: Cooperation—at a Cost* (New York: Routledge, 2003).

4 "Mission of the President of the General Assembly and the OAS Secretary General to Peru," OAS General Assembly Resolution 1753 (XXX-O/00), 5 June 2000.

5 See Andrew Cooper and Thomas Legler, *Intervention without Intervening? The OAS Defense and Promotion of Democracy in the Americas* (New York: Palgrave Macmillan, 2006), 62–83. See also Cynthia McClintock, "The OAS in Peru: Room for Improvement," *Journal of Democracy* 12, no. 4 (2001): 137–40.

6 In personal communication about the drafting process, Luigi Einaudi emphasized that the managerial credit of pulling together the democratic charter goes to the Colombian ambassador to the OAS, Humberto de la Calle, as well as to SG César Gaviria, also a Colombian. Personal interview with Luigi Einaudi, Washington, DC, 23 May 2013. In the aftermath of the process, de la Calle edited a compilation of key documents, speeches, and member states' statements on the IADC. See Humberto de la Calle, ed., *Carta Democrática Interamericana: Documentos e Interpretaciones* (Washington, DC: Organization of American States, 2003), www.oas.org/oaspage/esp/Publicaciones/CartaDemocratica_spa.pdf.

7 "Declaration of Quebec City," Third Summit of the Americas, 22 April 2001, www.iin.oea.org/tercera_cumbre_ingles.htm; also see Enrique Lagos and Timothy D. Rudy, "The Third Summit of the Americas and the Thirty-First Session of the OAS General Assembly," *American Journal of International Law* 96, no. 1 (2002): 173–81.

8 "Resolution of San José, Costa Rica: Inter-American Democratic Charter," OAS General Assembly Resolution 1838 (XXXI-O/01), 5 June 2001; also see Lagos and Rudy, "The Third Summit of the Americas and the Thirty-First Session of the OAS General Assembly."

9 An early assessment of the Charter is found in a 2003 special issue of *Canadian Foreign Policy* 10, no. 3, ed. Maxwell Cameron. For a more recent treatment, see a 2012 special issue of *Latin American Policy* 3, no. 1, ed. Thomas Legler, Riyad Insanally, Santiago Mariani, and Timothy M. Shaw.

10 Thomas M. Franck, "The Emerging Right to Democratic Governance," *American Journal of International Law* 86, no. 1 (1992): 46–91. We are indebted to Heraldo Muñoz for this insight.

11 The Spanish version of the IADC refers to "*elementos esenciales*" in Article 3 and "*componentes fundamentales*" in Article 4. On this distinction and its implications, see Carlos Ayala Corao and Pedro Nikken Bellshaw-Hógg,

Collective Defense of Democracy: Concepts and Procedures (Lima, Peru: Andean Commission of Jurists, 2006).

12 Ayala Corao and Bellshaw-Hógg, *Collective Defense of Democracy*; Enrique Lagos and Timothy D. Rudy, "In Defense of Democracy," *University of Miami Inter-American Law Review* 35, no. 2 (2004): 283–309.

13 See Thomas Legler, "Learning the Hard Way. Defending Democracy in Honduras," *International Journal* 65, no. 3 (2010): 601–18.

14 This is exactly what happened in the case of preventive intervention in Honduras in 2009, and also in the case of Ecuador in 1997, prior to the adoption of the IADC. Faced with a domestic political crisis, Ecuadorian President Abdalá Bucaram called on the OAS for help. However, upon his arrival in the country, SG César Gaviria found that he was not welcomed by the president's opponents, and had to leave. Shortly thereafter, Bucaram was removed from office. See Rubén M. Perina, "The Inter-American Democratic Charter: An Assessment and Ways to Strengthen It," in *The Road to Hemispheric Cooperation: Beyond the Cartagena Summit of the Americas*, ed. The Brookings Institution (Washington, DC: The Brookings Institution, Latin America Initiative, 2012), 77–87.

15 Carlos Ayala Corao, "International Mechanisms for the Collective Protection of Democracy in the Inter-American Democratic Charter," in *Collective Defense of Democracy: Concepts and Procedures*, Carlos Ayala Corao and Pedro Nikken Bellshaw-Hógg (Lima, Peru: Andean Commission of Jurists, 2006), 87–121.

16 See José Miguel Insulza, "Message from the Organization of American States Secretary General," *Latin American Policy* 3, no. 1 (2012): 13–17; César Gaviria Trujillo, "The Inter-American Democratic Charter at Ten: A Commitment by the Americas to the Defense and Promotion of Democracy," *Latin American Policy* 3, no. 1 (2012): 18–25.

17 Ayala Corao and Bellshaw-Hógg suggest that the interruption of the democratic order according to Article 21 is not restricted to a scenario in which the legitimate government is overthrown. This marks an important difference between the IADC and the Washington Protocol. According to them the "unconstitutional interruptions" provision must be understood with a certain breadth and in connection with Article 3 of the IADC— meaning that any case where "essential elements of representative democracy" are infringed could amount to an unconstitutional interruption. Ayala Corao and Bellshaw-Hógg, *Collective Defense of Democracy*.

18 "Ousted ex-President Zelaya Returns to Honduras", CNN.com, 30 May 2011, edition.cnn.com/2011/WORLD/americas/05/28/honduras.zelaya/.

19 Jennifer L. McCoy, "Challenges for the Collective Defense of Democracy on the Tenth Anniversary of the Inter-American Democratic Charter," *Latin American Policy* 3, no. 1 (2012): 33–57.

20 John W. Graham, *A Magna Carta for the Americas: The Inter-American Democratic Charter: Genesis, Challenges and Canadian Connections*, FOCAL Policy Paper FPP-02-09 (Ottawa: Canadian Foundation for the Americas, 2002).

21 Personal interview with José Miguel Insulza, Washington, DC, 19 June 2013. Also see *Update of the Secretary General of the OAS Reports on the Inter-American Democratic Charter Submitted to the Permanent Council in April 2007 and May 2010* (Permanent Council document OEA/Ser.G., CP/ INF. 6222/11 corr. 1), 12 April 2011, which states that the IADC "like any

political program ... is an objective we desire to achieve, but one which probably will never be fully achieved. But the Charter does allow us, whose duty it is to monitor compliance, to use it as a paradigm to see what progress our countries have made in that direction."

22 Personal interview with Peter Hakim, Senior Fellow, Inter-American Dialogue, Washington, DC, 28 May 2013.

23 On the issue of democratic norms, see Dexter S. Boniface, "Is there a Democratic Norm in the Americas? An Analysis of the Organization of American States," *Global Governance* 8, no. 3 (2002): 365–81.

24 Early critical examinations of the IADC are offered by Maxwell A. Cameron, "Strengthening Checks and Balances: Democracy Defence and Promotion in the Americas," *Canadian Foreign Policy* 10, no. 3 (2003): 101–16; Robert A. Pastor, "'A Community of Democracies in the Americas'—Instilling Substance into a Wondrous Phrase," *Canadian Foreign Policy* 10, no. 3 (2003): 15–29; Pastor, "Collectively Defending Democracy"; Thomas Legler, "The Inter-American Democratic Charter: Rhetoric or Reality?" in *Governing the Americas. Assessing Multilateral Institutions*, ed. Gordon Mace, Jean-Philippe Thérien and Paul Haslam (Boulder, Colo.: Lynne Rienner, 2007), 113–30.

25 *The Inter-American Democratic Charter—Report of the Secretary General pursuant to resolutions AG/RES. 2154 (XXXV-O/05) and AG/RES. 2251 (XXXVI-O/06)* (Permanent Council document OEA/Ser.G., CP doc. 4184/07), 4 April 2007; José Miguel Insulza, "Palabras de inauguración del XXXIV Curso de Derecho Internacional," XXXIV Course on International Law of the Inter-American Juridical Committee, Rio de Janeiro, Brazil, 3 August 2007; Jean-Paul Hubert, *Follow-up on the Application of the Inter-American Democratic Charter* (Inter-American Juridical Committee document 317/09, corr. 1), 19 March 2009.

26 It is surprising that Article 9 OAS Charter was not even utilized in reaction to the Honduras coup in 2009, although it clearly would have been applicable.

27 Timothy D. Rudy, "A Quick Look at the Inter-American Democratic Charter of the OAS: What is it and is it 'Legal'?" *Syracuse Journal of International Law and Commerce* 33, no. 1 (2005): 237–48.

28 Personal interview with Carlos Portales, former Permanent Representative of Chile to the OAS, Washington, DC, 24 May 2013.

29 Legler, "The Inter-American Democratic Charter"; Thomas Legler, "The Shifting Sands of Regional Governance: The Case of Inter-American Democracy Promotion," *Politics & Policy* 40, no. 5 (2012): 848–70.

30 Lisa M. Sundstrom, "Carrots and Sticks for Democracy in the OAS: Comparison with the East European Experience," *Canadian Foreign Policy* 10, no. 3 (2003): 45–60.

31 Personal interview with Theodore Piccone, Senior Fellow, Brookings Institution, Washington, DC, 24 May 2013; Legler, "The Inter-American Democratic Charter."

32 Sundstrom, "Carrots and Sticks for Democracy in the OAS"; Hubert, *Follow-up on the Application of the Inter-American Democratic Charter*.

33 Ibid.; also see Mikulas Fabry, "The Inter-American Democratic Charter and Governmental Legitimacy in the International Relations of the Western Hemisphere," *Diplomacy & Statecraft* 20, no. 1 (2009): 107–35.

34 Once again, this difficulty is fertile ground for the political interests of the member states charged with reaching a judgment to prevail in the analysis

of a political crisis in another member state, a crisis which would require triggering the collective action mechanisms set forth in the IADC.

35 Cameron, "Strengthening Checks and Balances."

36 Personal interview with Luigi Einaudi.

37 The group is coordinated by the US-based Carter Center, which has a widely recognized and distinguished record in electoral observation in the region.

38 "Draft Declaration of Florida: Delivering the Benefits of Democracy," OAS General Assembly document AG/doc.4476/05, 1 June 2005. Also see Darren Hawkins and Carolyn M. Shaw, "Legalising Norms of Democracy in the Americas," *Review of International Studies* 34, no. 3 (2008): 459–80.

39 The final declaration watered down the original proposal by authorizing the SG to consult with the Permanent Council and then devise proposals for "gradual initiatives for cooperation, as appropriate" and by barely mentioning civil society's input. These halting measures were further weakened by a phrase calling for respect for the principle of non-intervention and the right of self-determination, two concepts that were not mentioned in the operative part of the draft resolution. See "Declaration of Florida: Delivering the Benefits of Democracy," OAS General Assembly Declaration 41 (XXXV-O/05), 7 June 2005.

40 Legler, "The Inter-American Democratic Charter"; Dexter S. Boniface, "Dealing with Threats to Democracy," in *Which Way Latin America? Hemispheric Politics Meets Globalization*, ed. Andrew F. Cooper and Jorge Heine (Tokyo: United Nations University Press, 2009), 182–201.

41 Remarks by the OAS Secretary General, José Miguel Insulza, at the "Hemispheric Commemoration of the 10th Anniversary of the Interamerican Democratic Charter and Renewal of the Commitment of the Americas to Democracy," Valparaíso, Chile, 3–4 September 2011.

42 Ibid.

43 Ayala Corao and Bellshaw-Hógg, *Collective Defense of Democracy*.

44 See McCoy, "Challenges for the Collective Defense of Democracy on the Tenth Anniversary of the Inter-American Democratic Charter." With the exception of the ninth point, the use of states of emergency, these categories had already been presented in a keynote speech delivered by former US President Jimmy Carter on 25 January 2005 as part of the "Lecture Series of the Americas" at the OAS Headquarters in Washington, DC; see Jimmy Carter, "The Promise and Peril of Democracy," *International Journal of Not-for-Profit Law* 7, no. 2 (2005): 4–9. Five of those criteria had also been listed by Maxwell Cameron in an early attempt to interpret Chapter IV of the IADC; see Cameron, "Strengthening Checks and Balances."

45 Personal interview with Peter Hakim.

46 Personal interview with Theodore Piccone; personal interview with Carlos Portales.

47 Gordon Mace and Louis Bélanger, ed., *The Americas in Transition: The Contours of Regionalism* (Boulder, Colo.: Lynne Rienner, 1999).

48 "Declaration of Quebec City," Third Summit of the Americas, 22 April 2001, www.iin.oea.org/tercera_cumbre_ingles.htm.

4   The OAS democratic paradigm in action

Democratic crises of the twenty-first century

- **Democratic crises in Latin America**
- **OAS responses to democratic crises**
- **Evaluating the IADC record**
- **Conclusion**

Although Latin America has made impressive democratic gains over the last several decades, democratic stability remains elusive. What in some cases could be viewed as democratic stability might be described in other cases as democratic stagnation. In some other countries, there are in fact distinctly regressive tendencies. In a recent survey of threats to democracy in the region, Jennifer McCoy identified more than 60 different episodes of democratic crisis in Latin America for the period 1990–2011.[1] Since 1985, more than a dozen elected presidents in the region were forced to leave office before the end of their regular term.[2] While the quality of democracy has remained on average nearly the same since 2001—as positive and negative developments tend to cancel each other out—expert assessments reveal significant deficiencies in a number of countries along different dimensions of democracy (as depicted in Table I.1).

Crises of democracy, the subject of this chapter, result from factors very similar to those identified as determinants of democratic breakdown in the past, namely regime performance and institutional design. While the deep, underlying causes of Latin American democratic fragility are social and economic, and can be traced back to the origins of profoundly unequal societies where the legacies of the *hacienda* and the *encomienda* still linger, their inability to modernize their political systems also plays a part. The ability of many Latin American democratic regimes to solve basic social problems is still insufficient. As a number of studies have shown, Latin America's condition as the most unequal region in the world in terms of income distribution cannot but affect the functioning of its political system, particularly as in most countries the financing of political parties and political campaigns is quite unregulated. Much the same can be said about the impact on citizens who find themselves under the poverty line, thus experiencing severe limitations to the exercise of their economic and social rights. For much of the 1990s, programs of neoliberal reform, by dismantling sizeable portions of the state apparatus, further weakened state capacity to deal with these inequalities. Other problems include weaknesses in the rule of law, corruption, and high levels of criminal violence.[3]

Concerning institutional design, it has long been argued that presidentialism, particularly when combined with proportional electoral systems that generate multiparty systems and minority governments, promotes intractable congressional-executive conflicts. There is a huge gap between the high expectations Latin American citizens have of their presidents and the actual capacity of executives in the face of political fragmentation and weak party discipline in the legislature.[4] Dysfunctional political arrangements with few controls on the role of money in politics, with hyper-centralized polities that leave little room for decentralization and regional autonomy and with mass media monopolies controlled by big business, all contribute to an imperfect public space in which to conduct the sort of deliberations that are so critical in a democracy is not made easy. Hence, the condition of Latin American democracies remains precarious.

Yet, as discussed in Chapter 3, the nature of challenges to democracy in the region changed over time. In the past, threats to democracy emanated from unelected actors such as the military which toppled elected governments in *coups d'état*. Mainwaring and Pérez-Liñán document a sea change in Latin American politics around the year 1978, stating that afterwards those regime breakdowns "virtually ceased to occur."[5] While there were few military regimes by 1990, the armed forces remained influential, and coups, coup attempts and coup threats still were prime concerns. Since then, however, a new pattern of instability caused by civilian actors has emerged. Authoritarian-minded incumbents initiated self-coups and backsliding that threatened to undermine the democratic constitutional order. In these democratic crises of the 1990s, incumbent presidents overreached in their efforts to accumulate political power at the expense of democratic accountability and the rule of law, were personally involved in corruption scandals, or responded to mass protests with repressive force. In the new millennium, more ambiguous crises involving challenges to the executive by legislators or civilian protesters arose.

The purpose of this chapter is to explore international reactions to those developments. Specifically, the chapter examines OAS reactions to situations of democratic crisis and democratic decline in Latin America after the adoption of the IADC. The first section presents our concept and typology of democratic crisis and delimits it from the concept of democratic decline. It also gives an overview of democratic crises and decline in Latin America from 1990 to 2012. The second section outlines possible regional reactions to democratic crises, including the instruments that the IADC offers, and examines the regional reaction to those democratic crises that occurred after the approval of the IADC in 2001. The third section summarizes case study evidence and discusses whether there are any identifiable patterns as to which types of situations are likely to be countered with which type of measures.

Democratic crises in Latin America

Defining democratic crisis

So far, the concept of democratic crisis is rather vague and diffuse.[6] In general, two uses of the term "crisis" can be found: acute crisis and latent crisis. In our understanding, democratic crises are acute crises. They are clearly discernible events that unfold over a limited time span and directly threaten the democratic political institutional order. The criterion of acuteness distinguishes our definition from latent crises of democracy—of the kind with which mature democracies of the Organisation for Economic Co-operation and Development (OECD) world have been diagnosed since the 1970s by authors as diverse as Habermas, Huntington, and Crouch.[7] Latent crises drag on, and while formal institutions remain in place, democracy slowly hollows out from within. Our concept of crisis is also distinct from more recent diagnoses of democratic rollback, democratic regression, authoritarian backsliding, or loss in democratic quality affecting those countries that have made transitions to democracy in the course of the "third wave" of democratization since 1974.[8] Acute democratic crises and democratic decline do not necessarily coincide. A crisis might be the starting point or culmination of democratic decline, but might as well be a sign of unfinished democratic consolidation.

Furthermore, our concept of crisis is connected with challenges to the political system of such a kind and degree that the persistence of the system is threatened. The system is facing a potential breakdown, or structural changes of a fundamental character.[9] Such challenges could occur rather unexpectedly, but could also be the consequence of an incremental dangerous development. The criterion of being a direct threat to the political institutional order distinguishes democratic crises from indirect threats to the proper functioning of political institutions. Structural problems, such as high levels of criminal violence, contestations over the monopoly on the use of force, ongoing internal conflict, or transitions from civil war to peace occurring under a formally democratic regime may potentially undermine the democratic fabric. In any case, these are longer-term processes that may or may not affect the integrity of democratic institutions.

In line with Boniface, we argue that the nature of democratic crises varies according to the strategies actors employ and the agents of change.[10] The first dimension looks to the incidents that spark the crisis. Democratic crises can be unambiguous or ambiguous. To be considered unambiguous crises, the event must be in violation of existing laws. In this case, strategies of change, such as the use or credible threat of force against an elected government, are patently illegal. In turn, crises are ambiguous when strategies of change are legal or quasi-legal. In such cases, the procedures channeling the crisis are either formally contained within the existing legal framework, but widely perceived as of a dubious character, or on the borderline of what is allowed by existing laws. An example of an ambiguous crisis is when violent pressure to remove an elected president is combined with nominal respect for the constitution and the rule of law.[11]

A second dimension capturing variation in democratic crises is to look not so much to the *how* as to *who* precipitates such crises. McCoy singles out five distinct sources or origins of democratic crises: traditional military force, incumbent elected leaders, conflict between different branches of government, armed non-state actors, and unarmed non-state actors.[12] Boniface draws a more general distinction between endogenous and exogenous agents of change.[13] We combine Boniface's and McCoy's approaches. In the case of endogenous agents of change, the threat to democracy is internal to the regime, meaning that it results from the undemocratic behavior of constitutionally elected officials (generally, in an attempt to subvert the democratic process). This category of agents hence includes McCoy's incumbent leaders and intra-governmental conflict. In turn, in the case of exogenous agents of change, the challenge emanates from outside the regime—that is, from unelected persons or institutions, generally those whose interests are challenged by the incumbent government's policies. This covers McCoy's traditional military force and non-state actors.

Using these categories enables us to map a fourfold typology of democratic crises, as illustrated by Table 4.1. Unambiguous endogenous crises typically arise when incumbent presidents wish to accumulate political power at the expense of democratic accountability and the

Table 4.1 Taxonomy of democratic crises

		Origin	
		Endogenous	*Exogenous*
Strategy	*Unambiguous*	Self-coup (*autogolpe*) Electoral fraud	Coup Coup attempt Coup threat
	Ambiguous	Electoral irregularity Inter-branch conflict Constitutional change	Forced resignation

Source: Authors' elaboration based on Dexter S. Boniface, "Dealing with Threats to Democracy," in *Which Way Latin America? Hemispheric Politics Meets Globalization*, ed. Andrew F. Cooper and Jorge Heine (Tokyo: United Nations University Press, 2009), 182–201.

rule of law. They are indisputable disruptions of democracy, such as widespread and proven fraud in an election, the unconstitutional closing down of a branch of state power, massive human rights violations, or the shutting down of media outlets. The most extreme form is the self-coup (*autogolpe*), where a democratically elected president sets out to transform his government into dictatorial rule by suspending the constitution and closing parliament and the constitutional court. In that context, presidents deny freedoms, inhibit political mobilization, and apply other forms of political repression, thus undermining political rights and civil liberties.

Ambiguous endogenous crises may involve the same agents as their unambiguous endogenous counterparts, but are characterized by the use of quasi-legal or legal strategies. Yet, these situations may substantially curtail the exercise of democracy. Examples include dubious, but not outright illegal constitutional changes, stalemate resulting from power struggles and divisions within the government coalition or within the presidential party, and action by the congress or the judiciary to disempower the elected president.

Unambiguous exogenous crises result from the illegal actions of unelected agents, such as the security forces. Latin America's armed forces have historically been the most crucial unelected actors challenging constitutionally elected governments. Thus, typical forms of unambiguous exogenous crisis are military *coups d'état*, coup attempts, or threats and allegations of a coup. While clear-cut military coups have receded in recent years, Boniface argues that military officials and other unelected actors have learnt to adapt their strategies in the face of international norms supportive of democracy and tend to use more discreet ways to threaten democracy. In what has been termed a "coup under the table," they pressure and intimidate elected presidents while publicly demonstrating respect for the constitution.[14]

Exogenous threats to democracy are not limited to the military but might come from a variety of unelected actors, including civil society organizations and ordinary citizens. Most frequently, these crises take the form of massive social mobilization and protest. This type of crisis is ambiguous for two reasons. First, mass mobilization as such is not illegal, as it is protected by the freedom of assembly and the right to demonstrate. Social protest might even enhance the quality of democracy when it articulates the demand from marginalized sectors of the population to play a more central role in politics and opens new channels of political participation. However, those legitimate motives have to be weighed against the danger that violent protest is instrumentalized as an illegal substitute for formal impeachment proceedings. Second, the category of ambiguous exogenous crisis is difficult to disentangle from other developments that threaten democracy, as challenges to the government by mass mobilization frequently coincide with intra-governmental rifts or are reinforced by coup allegations.

Democratic crisis and decline in Latin America

Table 4.2 identifies the democratic crises that have occurred in Latin America since the end of the Cold War (1990–2012), a time period

Table 4.2 Democratic crises in Latin America, 1990–2012

	Endogenous	*Exogenous*
Unambiguous	Peru 1992 Guatemala 1993 Dominican Republic 1994 Peru 2000 Haiti 2000	Haiti 1991 Venezuela 1992 Paraguay 1996 Paraguay 1999–2000 Ecuador 2000 Venezuela 2002 Haiti 2004 Honduras 2009 Ecuador 2010
Ambiguous	Ecuador 1997 Ecuador 2005 Nicaragua 2005 Bolivia 2008 Paraguay 2012	Argentina 2001 Bolivia 2003 Bolivia 2005

Source: Authors' elaboration.

deliberately chosen to highlight the new regional context marked by a growing normative commitment to democracy in the Western hemisphere and in the OAS. The table shows that democratic crises in Latin America have run the gamut, with a considerable variety of types. What the table also illustrates is that these crises have been concentrated in a number of countries—Haiti, Bolivia, Ecuador and Paraguay stand out among them, while others, like Nicaragua, Guatemala, Peru, Venezuela and Honduras, appear more intermittently. Since the days of the coup attempts and self-coups of the 1990s, crisis situations in Latin America have become more ambiguous. It seems as if unambiguous crises happened to a disproportionate extent in the early stages of democratization, whilst the functioning of democratic institutions was still heavily constrained by the legacies of authoritarian rule or civil war. As long as a country lingers in a state of emergency-like situation, rulers seem to act on the assumption that the population might be more inclined to tolerate a violation of democratic norms.

Unambiguous abuses by the president himself appear to be a phenomenon of the 1990s. With the onset of the new millennium, new types of threats have surfaced. The nature of the presidential system implies that the president might face challenges both when he is too weak and when he is too strong. Presidents have increasingly been challenged by mass demonstrations putting them under pressure to resign. Pérez-Liñán has argued that popular protest has replaced military interference as the extra-institutional source of democratic crisis.[15] In Argentina (2001), Bolivia (2003, 2005), Ecuador (2000, 2005) and Venezuela (2002) the ousting of incumbent elected presidents occurred in the midst of popular mobilization. Another recent cause of democratic crises that played a role in Ecuador (2005), Nicaragua (2005), Honduras (2009) and Paraguay (2012) is executive-legislative gridlock resulting from the executive's lack of a power base in the legislature or shifting legislative coalitions.

The types of crises overlap to a certain extent, and in a number of cases, the placement in one particular cell is a simplification, given a combination of several factors at work. For example, the ability of the legislature to remove the president from office ultimately hinges on the degree of popular mobilization against the government.[16] Inter-branch conflicts in Ecuador that resulted in presidential breakdown (1997, 2005) as well as the conflict between the executive and the prefects about autonomy status in Bolivia (2008) were also accompanied by mass mobilization. Even when the military pulled the strings in ousting a democratically elected president, as in Ecuador (2000), Venezuela (2002) and Honduras (2009), mass outpourings of popular discontent backed military action. When a broad social coalition takes to the streets to demand presidential resignation, the fall of the administration is usually in sight. Most presidential breakdowns were a result of a combination of institutional factors, the machinations of a counter-elite (in some cases, with support of the military) and social protest. While Table 4.2 lists acute democratic crises, Table 4.3 draws on annual expert ratings of the level of democracy to identify episodes of democratic decline. The measurements focus on different aspects of the democratic political order: Polity IV captures political participation as well as executive recruitment and executive constraints, whereas Freedom House assesses political rights and civil liberties.[17] Both projects

Table 4.3 Democratic decline in Latin America, 1990–2012

	Polity IV	*Freedom House*
Decline within democracy	Bolivia (2003–12) Colombia (1995–2012) Ecuador (1997, 2000–05) Paraguay (1998) Venezuela (1992–2005)	Argentina (1992–99) Bolivia (2002) Ecuador (1991–95) Mexico (2006–09)
Decline from democracy to semi-democracy	Dominican Republic (1994–95) Ecuador (2007–12) Haiti (1999) Peru (1992–2000) Venezuela (2006–08)	Argentina (2001–02) Bolivia (1995, 2003–12) Brazil (1993–2001) Dominican Republic (1993) Ecuador (1996–97, 2000–12) Honduras (1993–96, 1999–2008) Mexico (2010–12) Venezuela (1992–95, 1999–2004)
Decline within semi-democracy	Haiti (2000–03, 2010–12) Venezuela (2009–12)	Brazil (1997–99) Colombia (1994–97, 1999–2004, 2008–12) Dominican Republic (1994–95) Guatemala (1991–95, 2002–05, 2009–10) Haiti (1998–99) Honduras (2009–12) Nicaragua (1992–95, 1999–2012) Paraguay (1994–2002) Peru (1991–99) Venezuela (2005–12)
Breakdown from democracy to autocracy	Haiti (1991–93)	Haiti (1991–93, 2000–05)

Source: Authors' elaboration based on Polity IV, www.systemicpeace.org/ polity/polity4.htm; and Freedom House, www.freedomhouse.org.

also group the countries into three regime categories roughly corresponding to democracy, semi-democracy and autocracy, and register transitions from one category to the other.[18] Table 4.3 illustrates that acute democratic crises in Latin America were frequently embedded in more subtle, latent, stepwise processes of democratic decline. In turn, drastic deteriorations in long-term processes of democratic decline did not necessarily coincide with a democratic crisis. Numerous episodes of democratic decline happened incrementally without registering an acute crisis event.

It would certainly be easier to tailor OAS reactions to democratic challenges if the distinction between crisis and decline coincided with the categories stipulated by the IADC: "unconstitutional interruption of the democratic order" and "unconstitutional alteration of the constitutional regime that seriously impairs the democratic order." However, democratic crises do not always amount to an interruption of the democratic order, and in some cases, when crises are short lived and quickly reversed (as in the case of the attempted *autogolpe* in Guatemala in 1993), it is not even clear whether they fulfill the IADC definition of alteration. Yet, in general terms, the concept of unconstitutional alteration put forth by the IADC suggests that the OAS should take a broad view and consider both democratic crises and decline. We will hence also briefly consider how the OAS has accounted for more long-term democratic decline in the countries affected. The subsequent analysis focuses on OAS responses to democratic crises after the adoption of the IADC in 2001.

OAS responses to democratic crises

The OAS has sometimes played a role in reversing or containing democratic crises over the past 20 years, though the record is uneven.[19] Responses to democratic crises by regional organizations are in essence external interventions. In its broadest definition, intervention refers to actions that influence the domestic affairs of a sovereign state. The spectrum of influences ranges from low coercion to high coercion.[20] The highest amount of coercion, forcible interference by military invasion, is seldom applied for the sake of defending democracy. At the low end of the scale, intervention may be simply a declaration of support for a challenged incumbent, a declaration of concern or a condemnation of illegal acts. A little further along the spectrum of coercion is what we termed facilitation in Chapter 1—the use of diplomatic measures ranging from the deployment of observers or fact-finding missions to good offices and mediation. Toward the coercive end of the spectrum are the threat and the actual enactment of sanctions, such as an

Table 4.4 OAS responses to democratic crises, 2001–12

Democratic crises		OAS responses		
		Declarations	Facilitation	Sanctions
Unambiguous	Venezuela 2002	Yes	Art. 20	No
exogenous	Haiti 2004	Yes	Ad hoc	No
	Honduras 2009	No	Art. 17	
			Art. 20	Art. 21
	Ecuador 2010	Yes	Ad hoc	No
Ambiguous	Argentina 2001	No	No	No
exogenous	Bolivia 2003	Yes	No	No
	Bolivia 2005	Yes	No	No
Ambiguous	Ecuador 2005	No	Art. 18	No
endogenous	Nicaragua 2005	No	Art. 18	No
	Bolivia 2008	No	Ad hoc	No
	Paraguay 2012	No	Ad hoc	No

Source: Authors' elaboration.

economic blockade or membership suspension. Apart from coerciveness, the format of measures is of particular interest when examining the IADC's record in defending democracy. The primary question here is whether responses to democratic crises happen pursuant to formal provisions, i.e. by invoking the IADC, or ad hoc. Secondary questions include whether the measure is preventive or reactive, and whether it is initiated by the state concerned or by the organization. These differentiations are tacitly guiding the brief case studies that follow (see Table 4.4).

Unambiguous exogenous crises: coups, coup attempts and coup threats

Military interference in domestic politics is on the wane, but while the replacement of a civilian government by military rule does not seem a realistic perspective any longer in the region, a number of post-2001 crises have involved the security forces or armed non-state actors. In most instances, though, this went hand in hand with mass mobilization and/or clashes between an elected president and his opponents, and especially in the cases of Haiti and Honduras, one might well argue that the illegal ouster of the president was provoked in part by the incumbent's questionable behavior.

Venezuela, 2002

The first time the OAS acted in defense of democracy under the IADC framework was in response to the interruption of the democratic order in Venezuela in April 2002. The implementation of several substantive reforms by the government of President Hugo Chávez Frías created a highly polarized situation. Despite months of heightening tensions prior to the April 2002 coup, neither Chávez nor the OAS resorted to the preventive mechanisms contained in Articles 17 and 18 of the IADC. On 12 April 2002, the clash turned violent. That same day, General Lucas Rincón, the minister of defense, announced that President Chávez had been dismissed and that Pedro Carmona Estanga, president of Venezuela's Federation of Chambers of Commerce and Manufacturers' Associations (Fedecámaras) was appointed to head a "Democratic Transition and National Unity Government." The de facto president abolished the constitution and dissolved the branches of government, including the National Assembly and the Supreme Court. Those decisions exacerbated citizens' rejection of the interruption of the constitutional order and led a majority faction of the armed forces to support a restoration of the democratically elected government. On 14 April, Chávez was reinstated as constitutional president of Venezuela.

In reaction to the coup, the OAS Permanent Council met on 13 April 2002 and, for the first time, used the mechanisms provided by Chapter IV of the IADC (specifically, Art. 20). Resolution 811 condemned the alteration of constitutional order and the acts of violence that had led to the loss of human life. It authorized a special mission of the SG to Caracas "with the aim of carrying out a fact-finding mission and undertaking the necessary diplomatic initiatives, including good offices, to promote as quickly as possible the normalization of the democratic institutional framework."[21] In accordance with Article 20, the Permanent Council also convoked a special session of the General Assembly to consider the crisis in Venezuela. The preference for Article 20 was controversial. At the height of the crisis, Venezuelan ambassador Jorge Valero demanded that the Permanent Council invoke Article 21 to suspend Venezuela from the OAS in response to the *coup d'état*.[22] In contrast, the George W. Bush Administration failed to condemn the coup against Chávez, a leader it disliked.

When the special session of the General Assembly convened on 18 April, Chávez had already returned to power. The General Assembly expressed satisfaction with the restoration of the constitutional order and the democratically elected government and supported the government's initiative to convoke a national dialogue in the interest of reconciliation.[23] During its regular session on 4 June 2002, the General Assembly reiterated its support for the dialogue process in the "Declaration on Democracy in Venezuela."[24] On this basis, the OAS, together with UNDP and the Carter Center, facilitated a dialogue between the Venezuelan government and the opposition, grouped together under the name Coordinadora Democrática de Venezuela (Democratic Focal Point of Venezuela).[25] Based on an initial "Declaration of Principles for Peace and Democracy," signed on 15 October, a negotiation and dialogue roundtable was established in Venezuela on 8 November. The OAS SG was appointed international facilitator with the technical support of the three organizations already involved.[26] During the mediation period, which lasted approximately seven months (from 8 November 2002 to 23 May 2003), two further agreements were adopted. The "Declaration against Violence and for Peace and Democracy" was signed on 18 February 2003, followed, on 23 May, by the signing of an agreement between the government of Venezuela and Coordinadora Democrática and the organizations supporting it. The latter agreement proposed an electoral way out of the crisis.[27]

Apart from electoral observation missions, the OAS has not interfered with the trajectory of democracy in Venezuela in the years following the short-lived coup, despite ample grounds for doing so. The country subsequently experienced democratic decline under the Chávez government, as registered both by Polity IV and Freedom House between 1999 and 2012, including a deterioration in the quality of elections, the erosion of the separation of powers, a judicial reform that stacked the judiciary with the president's appointees, and a decline in civil liberties and civilian power (see Table 4.3).

Haiti, 2004

Since the fall of the infamous Duvalier dictatorship, the OAS played a central role in Haiti's slow and turbulent journey towards democracy. The organization reacted forcefully, by invoking its Resolution 1080 for the first time, when in September 1991 President Jean-Bertrand Aristide was deposed by the military several months after his election. It helped negotiate the Haitian army's withdrawal and Aristide's return to the country in 1994.[28] Yet, Aristide's democratic credentials, along with his popular support, were mostly gone by the time the IADC was adopted. The democratic crisis of 2004 is the culmination of a longer phase of democratic decline that took its course four years earlier, when Aristide's supporters engaged in widespread electoral fraud in the legislative and municipal elections of May 2000. As a reaction, the opposition boycotted the presidential elections of 26 November 2000, resulting in a landslide victory for Aristide. In the following years, an increasingly unified opposition distrustful of Aristide mounted. He was accused of being corrupt and exerting ever more dictatorial control over the country.

The OAS continuously tried to stabilize democracy in the country. It monitored the flawed elections in 2000, and over the course of the following three years it sought to broker a solution to the ensuing political stalemate between the government and the opposition. The organization also investigated an armed attack on the presidential palace on 17 December 2001. In March 2002, the OAS established a "Special Mission to Strengthen Democracy," in order to help move the country towards new elections.[29] Another regional actor involved was the Caribbean Community (CARICOM), which along with the OAS devised a power-sharing plan that would have required the president to appoint a new prime minister who would be neutral and independent, and to establish a multiparty governing council. However, because nothing less than Aristide's resignation was acceptable to his intransigent opponents, all mediation efforts were inevitably doomed.[30] The United States did little to discourage Aristide's opposition, made up at least in part of criminals and thugs with connections to Haiti's last dictatorship, from thinking that it could oust President Aristide by force.

Political instability reached its apex in early 2004. During January, the Aristide government was shaken by the announcement of a general strike, almost daily mass protests in which demonstrators demanded Aristide's resignation, and an armed uprising led by former military and paramilitary soldiers. After taking over more than half of the country, they threatened to march on the capital, Port-au-Prince, and to execute the president and his supporters. On 29 February 2004 Aristide abruptly resigned and fled from Haiti. As was required by the constitution, Boniface Alexandre, the chief justice of the Supreme Court, was sworn in as interim president.

In the moment of crisis, OAS reactions were low-key. In spite of the organization's continuous engagement in the country, it did not occur to Aristide to invoke the self-help clause contained in Article 17 IADC following the armed attack on the presidential palace in 2001, nor did he use it in the weeks leading up to his ouster. The OAS on its part also did not invoke Article 20 in response to the use of force to overthrow the president. Before Aristide's departure, the OAS had condemned the violence and expressed its support for the constitutional government.[31] However, Resolution 862, which was passed by the Permanent Council just days before Aristide's forced resignation and called upon the UN Security Council to resolve the crisis, did not contain a single reference to the IADC.[32] It was only in its regular session in June that the General Assembly referred to Article 20 IADC and acknowledged that there had been an "alteration of the constitutional regime which began prior to February 29, 2004, and which has damaged the democratic order in Haiti."[33] The OAS foreign ministers committed to undertaking all the diplomatic initiatives necessary to restore democracy and urged the Haitian transitional government to hold new elections as soon as possible. After Aristide's fall, the UN on 30 April 2004 established the UN Stabilization Mission in Haiti (MINUSTAH) to "secure and stabilize" the country, facilitate humanitarian aid, and establish law and order for an initial six-month period which has since then repeatedly been extended.[34]

Honduras, 2009

During the first half of 2009, controversial actions by the elected President José Manuel Zelaya of Honduras led to increasing opposition to the president from other branches of government, including factions of his own party in congress, and to heightened political polarization. The main bone of contention was Zelaya's proposal to hold a referendum on the convocation of a national constitutional assembly. The proposal was deemed illegal by Honduran courts, due to its alleged intention to eliminate the presidential term limit. Things became so bad that the Honduran military ousted President Zelaya on 28 June 2009. Subsequently, the parliament appointed the head of that legislative body, Roberto Micheletti, as interim president for the remainder of Zelaya's term in office.

The causes and the progression of the Honduran crisis will be portrayed in more detail in Chapter 5, as it was in many ways a crucial case. One of the reasons for this is that almost the full range of instruments of Chapter IV IADC was applied, starting with the invocation of Article 17 by the Honduran government two days before the *coup d'état*.[35] On the day of the coup, the Permanent Council condemned political events in Honduras and the arbitrary detention and expulsion from the country of the constitutional president, and invoked Article 20, calling for a special session of the General Assembly.[36] When the de facto government rejected the demand to return President Zelaya to his constitutional functions within 72 hours, the OAS General Assembly on 4 July 2009 invoked Article 21 and suspended Honduras from the exercise of its right to participate in the OAS.[37] The organization was also involved in the ensuing mediation process between Zelaya and interim President Micheletti.

Ecuador, 2010

Despite several presidential breakdowns in 1997, 2000 and 2005 (see Table 4.2), and a process of steady democratic decline from democracy to semi-democracy (see Table 4.3), the country was surprisingly stable since Rafael Correa became its president in 2007. On 30 September 2010, however, that relative calm was shattered, as police and soldiers staged a mutiny over some aspects of a new law that their leaders said would reduce benefits for the security forces. The rebels seized the main airport and stormed congress. Ecuador's government declared a state of emergency, and army chief Ernesto González called on rebels to end the uprising. President Correa tried to resolve the conflict directly by visiting one police installation in an attempt to negotiate. After a tear gas canister exploded near the president, he was transferred to the Police Hospital in Quito, where he was held hostage by the dissident police units that controlled the building. Elite forces from the police and the military rescued Correa. Although it is still not clear whether the original intention of the police was to overthrow Correa, he and his government called the protests a coup attempt, citing evidence that the destabilization efforts had been planned during the weeks preceding the uprising. Others beg to differ, pointing out that the military high command did not break with Correa and that Correa at no time lost control of the government, nor did anyone try to succeed him.

Faced with the imminent risk of an alteration of the constitutional order, the OAS Permanent Council held an emergency meeting at the request of the Permanent Representative of Ecuador to the OAS. SG José Miguel Insulza made a call to governments and multilateral institutions in the region to "stop the coup d'état from becoming a reality."[38] After analyzing the crisis in the country, the Permanent Council adopted a resolution by acclamation on the same day as the police uprising. They repudiated what had happened, expressed firm support for the constitutional government, and made a strong appeal to Ecuador's law enforcement personnel, as well as to the political and social sectors, to avoid all acts of violence that could further exacerbate the situation of political instability.[39] In the same vein, the United States and nearly every government in Latin America, right or left, condemned the uprising and declared unconditional support for Correa and Ecuador's constitutional order. Peruvian President Alán García also called a meeting of regional leaders under the umbrella of UNASUR.[40] Pursuant to the mandate in the Permanent Council resolution, the SG traveled to Ecuador on 1 October to express his support for and solidarity with President Correa. The immediate regional response helped contain the crisis and dissuade the destabilizing sectors from further action. Other determining factors were the backing of the citizenry and the support of the armed forces for the constitutional government of Ecuador.

Ambiguous exogenous crises: mass protest and forced resignation

As has been pointed out above, in several instances popular protest has replaced military intervention as the extra-institutional (exogenous) instrument generating or marking the end of a presidential crisis.

Argentina, 2001

In late 2001, only a few months after the adoption of the IADC, the first case of massive social mobilization of ordinary citizens that ultimately led to the ouster of a democratically elected president took place in Argentina. The government of Fernando de la Rúa, elected in 1999, was unable to contain an economic depression that caused widespread unemployment, the end of the peso's fixed exchange rate to the US dollar, and ultimately, a default on the country's foreign debt. Throughout 2001, capital flight had reached new heights, and public discontent was widespread. On 2 December 2001 the government enacted measures that effectively froze all bank accounts, which triggered a period of civil unrest and rioting, with the most violent incidents taking place on 19 and 20 December in Buenos Aires and other large cities around the country. However, in spite of violent protests in the streets, the Argentine crisis ultimately was resolved through legal-constitutional means.[41] Hence, there was no need for regional actors to intervene in defense of democracy, and the only OAS response was a statement by SG César Gaviria on 20 December, the day of de la Rúa's resignation, in which he regretted the climate of violence in Argentina and called for a constitutional succession process.[42]

Bolivia, 2003

In 2003, Bolivia experienced civil disorder that culminated in a presidential resignation. President Gonzalo Sánchez de Lozada had been elected in 2002 with the support of only 22.5 percent of the popular vote.[43] Only a few months after he took office, social protest erupted against several governmental measures.[44] Bolivia's poor indigenous majority had grown increasingly disenchanted with free market reforms and US-backed policies to eradicate coca, the plant that is the raw material for cocaine. However, coca is also chewed to stave off hunger and as a natural stimulant in the Andean mountain nation, and eradication policies deprived thousands of poor indigenous farmers of their livelihood. An agreement between the Lozada government and the US Administration to continue eradication policies and the lack of an alternative plan for rural development triggered a violent confrontation between coca growers and government forces in December 2002. Twelve people were killed, many more wounded. On 12 and 13 February 2003, a demonstration against a proposed reform of the national police force turned into a general protest against the government, with students and other civilians joining. The ensuing armed confrontation between police and military forces left 17 dead and hundreds wounded.

The wave of protest that ultimately led to the president's resignation started in September 2003. By that time, the protest movement had grown into a heterogeneous group composed of the landless movement, peasant workers, coca growers, indigenous movements, pensioners, and neighborhood associations. The common ground in protesters' demands was the plea for President Sánchez de Lozada to resign. The popular outrage against the president was sparked by a controversial proposal to export gas to the United States and Mexico, which was considered a privatization of resources whose revenues should rather go to the people of Bolivia.[45] The protests paralyzed the capital, La Paz, and the nearby city of El Alto. Calls for presidential resignation intensified when the violent repression of the protests resulted in dozens of civilian deaths. Vice-President Carlos Mesa as well as the head of the center-right New Republican Force party, a partner in his ruling coalition, withdrew their support for Sánchez de Lozada. On 17 October 2003, as tens of thousands of miners, farmers and *indígenas* marched to the center of La Paz demanding the president's departure, Sánchez de Lozada had to resign, and Carlos Mesa was installed as successor.

The OAS followed the events closely and issued several resolutions, but did not resort to the IADC. The organization's actions were inconsistent. Until a few days before the president's demise, the OAS rejected the use of violence and any action to disrupt the democratic system in Bolivia, supported the president, and underlined the OAS's "firm resolve" to apply and enforce the mechanisms set out in the IADC.[46] Despite this rhetoric, the preventive clauses were not invoked in the midst of massive popular protests demanding the president's resignation, nor were any reactive measures considered. Following the forced resignation, the OAS immediately expressed its support for the succession of power to the vice-president.[47] No further action supporting democracy in Bolivia was taken, although the re-occurrence of democratic crises in 2005 and 2008 as well as slow democratic decline from 2003 onwards, particularly pronounced in the area of political rights and civil liberties (see Table 4.3), indicate that there might have been good reasons for the OAS to monitor the situation in the country.

Bolivia, 2005

Barely two years later Bolivia faced déjà-vu, when President Carlos Mesa submitted his resignation in June 2005 in the context of political and social upheaval. Renewed anti-government protests began in late 2004 when the government announced the end of fuel subsidies. From March 2005 onwards, contestation arose around the question of whether congress should increase taxes on foreign oil companies that had flocked to the country to extract Bolivian oil and gas. Protesters demanded the nationalization of the oil industry and a constitutional assembly to write a new constitution giving stronger representation to the indigenous population. The crisis pitted indigenous and labor groups from the poorer eastern highlands, including La Paz and its poor satellite city of El Alto, against ruling blocks from Santa Cruz in the east and Tarija in the south (the center of gas and petrol reserves) that are pursuing greater autonomy. La Paz was paralyzed by weeks of street blockades, food shortages and a public transport strike. The turmoil prompted Mesa on 6 June to render his resignation to congress, which on 9 June voted unanimously to accept it. After two congressional leaders had renounced their rights to succeed, Bolivia's head of the Supreme Court, Eduardo Rodríguez Veltzé, was sworn in as interim president on that same day, clearing the way for early elections. Presidential elections in December 2005 were won by Evo Morales of the Movement Towards Socialism (MAS) party, one of the leaders of the demonstrations and the first indigenous person to be elected head of state.

In view of the uncertainties surrounding his resignation, President Carlos Mesa omitted the OAS, which would normally have been the first port of call, and rather asked the governments of Argentina and Brazil and the UN to send observers.[48] Thus, in spite of following closely the developments in Bolivia,[49] the OAS had no possibility to operate on the basis of the IADC. Yet, after Mesa resigned, which happened to take place during the regular session of the General Assembly, the OAS offered its cooperation.[50] A few weeks later, the Permanent Council declared its support for the preservation of democratic institutions and the electoral process.[51] An agreement between the government of Bolivia and the OAS also paved the way for the hemispheric body to provide assistance to Bolivian authorities for the country's constituent assembly process.

Ambiguous endogenous crises: inter-branch conflicts

While in the 1990s executives were the main agents of change in undemocratic efforts to control and bypass other branches of power, in more recent situations it has been powerful legislative alliances that intentionally sought to weaken presidents—albeit sometimes in reaction to executive misbehavior.

Ecuador, 2005

In Ecuador, President Lucio Gutiérrez, elected in 2002, faced growing protests over maneuvers supposedly aimed at cementing his control over all branches of power. The court crisis was set in motion in November 2004 when the Supreme Court judges sided with opposition politicians in a failed effort to impeach Gutiérrez on allegations of corruption. Gutiérrez removed the judges in December 2004. In April 2005, after new judges had been installed, they decided to annul corruption charges leveled against former President Abdalá Bucaram, thereby making it possible for him to return to the country. Gutiérrez's opponents accused him of cutting a deal with Bucaram to stack the Supreme Court in his favor as payback for key votes that Bucaram's political party had provided to block the impeachment drive in congress. The decision also roused the population of Quito. In an attempt to contain the mobilization of the population and stem the discontent, the president again dismissed the court and decreed a state of emergency. That last decision incensed the ire of the people even more and increased protest against Gutiérrez's government. Under those circumstances, congress removed Gutiérrez from office on 20 April 2005 and replaced him with Vice-President Alfredo Palacio. Hence, Gutiérrez was forced from power by a combination of angry crowds of demonstrators, a signal of no confidence from the military and a hasty vote by the Ecuadorean congress. Due to the preceding inter-branch tensions, that last act provided merely a veneer of constitutionality to the curtailment of an elected president's term.[52]

The OAS was at the time of the crisis paralyzed over the choice of a new SG. Yet, on 22 April 2005, the Permanent Council, in keeping with an invitation issued by the delegation of Ecuador at the Permanent Council meeting, invoked Article 18 IADC, which made its debut as the grounding for a high-level mission to Ecuador led by Acting SG Luigi Einaudi.[53] When the report submitted by the high-level mission raised questions regarding the legality of constitutional succession, a special mission to observe the selection of members of the Supreme Court of Justice was appointed from June to November 2005.[54] It is worth noting, though, that in spite of its preventive intention, Article 18 made its appearance only after Gutiérrez had left office. Neither Article 18 nor any other IADC measures were invoked in December 2004 when the president unconstitutionally undermined the separation of powers between the executive and the judiciary, nor in the weeks prior to his demise.

Nicaragua, 2005

An institutional-political crisis was unleashed in Nicaragua in 2005 when internal factions aligned in an attempt to implement constitutional changes that tilted the balance of power in favor of the legislative branch, to the detriment of the executive. President Enrique Bolaños refused to publish the partial reform of the constitution, which prevented it from entering into force. That decision triggered a clash between the executive and legislative branches of government. The Supreme Court of Justice became involved in the dispute when it ratified the constitutional amendments introduced by the National Assembly.

The turn events were taking and the impasse created between the branches of government led the government of Nicaragua to request the deployment of a mission of the OAS in line with Article 18 IADC. To that end, on 7 June 2005 the annual OAS General Assembly made reference to Article 18 IADC as the basis of authorization for sending a mission headed by newly elected SG Insulza to Nicaragua for the purpose of facilitating a dialogue between the government and the major political parties.[55] The high-level mission was succeeded by a special mission which spent five months in Nicaragua, from June to October 2005. The OAS work of facilitating an end to the crisis culminated with the deployment of an electoral observation mission, which was present during regional elections in March 2006, as well as during the presidential and legislative elections held in November of that year.

The response to the democratic crisis in Nicaragua marked the first use of Article 18 as it was meant to be used: as a preventive diplomatic tool. In contrast to the previous reluctance of threatened governments in the region to consent to Article 18, the impulse in Nicaragua came largely from the Bolaños government itself. It found itself compelled to turn abroad for assistance in a political battle in which it was facing an

alliance of powerful enemies like former Liberal Constitutionalist President Arnoldo Alemán and former Sandinista President Daniel
Ortega.[56] However, despite the agitated political situation and Freedom House surveys revealing that Nicaragua was in the midst of an
extended phase of democratic decline (see Table 4.3), no follow-up
action in support of democracy in the country was taken.

Bolivia, 2008

Forming the backdrop of Bolivian crisis of 2008 were clashes regarding
a referendum for approving a new constitution. The central government was faced with opposition from certain sectors, especially the
prefects and civic committees of the departments in the so-called "half-
moon," which were demanding greater autonomy. The conflict was
accompanied by mass protests on both sides and some violence, and
hence has features of both an endogenous and an exogenous crisis.

The actions undertaken by the OAS stemmed from a request by
the government of President Evo Morales. The Bolivian minister of
foreign affairs, David Choquehuanca, addressed the Permanent Council
on several occasions to request OAS assistance in the troubling
events. In retrospect, some interpreted this request as recourse to
Article 17 IADC. On 3 May 2008, the Permanent Council affirmed the
readiness of the OAS to provide assistance to the government of
Bolivia in implementing a process of dialogue with the opposition
and strengthening democracy.[57] In order to comply with the mandate
arising from the resolution, the OAS monitored the political situation in Bolivia and special representatives visited Bolivia repeatedly
to open channels of communication between political and social
players who were not talking to each other directly. The organization also acted as guarantor of the transparency of the recall referendum
for the office of president and of eight of the nine prefects, which took
place on 10 August. In October, it participated in the dialogue between
the central government and the prefects. Finally, the OAS was present, along with other international organizations, in the negotiations at the roundtable installed in the national congress, leading to
a political agreement among the different political parties to hold the
postponed constitutional referendum on 25 January 2009.[58]

Paraguay, 2012

Another severe conflict between the executive and the legislative branches in government occurred in Paraguay in 2012. In 2008, Fernando

Lugo, a left-wing former bishop, became the first freely elected leftist president of Paraguay, bringing an end to 61 years of rule by the right-wing Colorado Party. However, the coalition backing him did not have a majority in any of the two legislative chambers, and in order to pass new bills, he was forced to form ad hoc alliances with opposition parties which on other occasions were blocking his proposals. Lugo's administration soon ran afoul of conservative elites who were afraid of the political space he was opening up for reform and saw his anti-poverty initiatives as an existential threat to their grip on power. Since Lugo was elected, many political actors had been waiting for him to make a mistake that could generate sufficient political support for his impeachment.[59]

Lugo's political enemies saw their chance to move against him on 15 June 2012, when a clash between police and landless squatters near the eastern town of Curuguaty resulted in the deaths of 11 farmers and six officers. The Chamber of Deputies cited this event as well as insecurity, nepotism and a controversial land purchase to vote 76 to 1 to impeach Lugo on 21 June 2012 for "poor performance of his duties." The next day the shaken president was given just two hours to defend himself before the Senate, which upheld the charge by 39 votes for Lugo's removal and four for his continuity. This ended his mandate and turned Vice-President Federico Franco into the new president of Paraguay. While the impeachment process strictly followed the provisions laid out in the constitution, the speed with which it was conducted created an aura of illegitimacy. The legal formality obscures the fact that Lugo's ouster, long desired by those who opposed his democratic reforms, was politically motivated. Lugo and his supporters denounced the impeachment as a "parliamentary *coup d'état*." The presidents of Paraguay's neighbor states shared this interpretation. Brazilian President Dilma Rousseff proposed suspending Paraguay's membership in MERCOSUR and UNASUR.[60] Other governments in the region likewise condemned the proceedings and announced that they would not recognize Franco as president.[61]

In turn, the OAS was more hesitant in its response. While there were several special meetings of the Permanent Council to follow the impeachment proceedings and its consequences, the body did not issue an official declaration, nor did it make use of the mechanisms provided for in the IADC. Although critical of the haste that marked the impeachment process, the OAS ultimately decided to take a cautious approach and refrained from second-guessing the interpretation of a member state's constitution.[62] However, SG Insulza followed the situation closely and voiced concerns on the violation of the principles of due process and the legitimate right of every accused person to defend themselves.[63] From 1 to 3 July, he travelled to Paraguay for an informative visit during which he held a series of meetings with former President Lugo and with other political actors. Upon his return, he presented a report to the Permanent Council in which he advised against a suspension of Paraguay from the OAS, as this would have serious economic consequences for the country and could exacerbate the divisions within Paraguayan society.[64] However, the OAS remained involved and sent several observer missions over the following months to foster political dialogue and to help the country prepare for the 2013 elections.

Evaluating the IADC record

So far, the number of cases in which the mechanisms stipulated by Chapter IV of the IADC were explicitly invoked is minuscule, even more so when looking at the frequency of democratic crises and instances of democratic decline illustrated by Table 4.2 and Table 4.3. The picture becomes a bit different, however, when ad hoc reactions are accounted for. The attempt to match the type of democratic crisis with the coerciveness of OAS responses reveals a clear pattern (see Table 4.4). While ambiguous exogenous crises have been countered with declarations, at best, all ambiguous endogenous crises have been dealt with by means of facilitation. Unambiguous exogenous crises led to the most coercive responses, involving both facilitation and sanctions. Looking more specifically at the application of the IADC, all uses of the reactive clauses (Art. 20 and 21) have happened in response to unambiguous crises, such as Venezuela in 2002 and Honduras in 2009. In Haiti in 2004, Article 20, while not formally invoked, was referred to at least in retrospect. In turn, the preventive clauses (Art. 17 and 18) have been used mainly in response to ambiguous crises originating from endogenous actors, such as Ecuador and Nicaragua in 2005, and, one may add, Honduras in 2009 before the military staged the *coup d'état*. In ambiguous exogenous crises, like in Bolivia in 2003 and 2005, the presidents refrained from invoking the self-help clause of Article 17.

In sum, unambiguous crises are generally more likely to trigger a more coercive response. However, a more diffuse, ambiguous nature of democratic crises makes a clear-cut reaction not only less likely, but also, in many cases, less desirable. Often enough less seems to be more when it comes to crisis mitigation that goes beyond the protection of a sitting executive and thus requires a more balanced approach in order to mediate between the parties involved in the dispute. Additionally, the apparent scarcity of IADC use, especially of its defense of democracy provisions in Chapter IV, should not be taken to mean that it has not performed a valuable function. In some cases, the mere prospect of invoking the IADC might have served as a means to strengthen democracy and facilitate OAS democracy promotion activities.[65]

Future OAS interventions on the basis of the IADC will be complicated by the fact that democratic crises have tended to become more ambiguous in nature. Not only has the number of the ambiguous crises versus the unambiguous crises soared in the new millennium, but the boundaries between the types identified in Table 4.1 have become increasingly blurred. Twenty-first-century democratic crises in Latin America frequently involve both endogenous and exogenous actors using both illegal and semi-legal or legal strategies. This is exemplified by the contestation over what types of situation constitute a "coup." Divergence about the appropriateness of this label reigned especially in the most recent democratic crises of Honduras (2009), Ecuador (2010), and Paraguay (2012). Another consequence of the ambiguous nature of crises is the difficulty for external actors to identify their origin. The OAS has repeatedly been faced with the challenge to decide whether to condemn action that might be unconstitutional, but is itself a reaction to questionable developments (such as the forced resignation of a leader who himself violated the constitution). When making such debatable choices, it is ever more problematic to uphold the claim to be a neutral arbiter.

Acute crises are more likely to trigger international reactions than creeping processes of democratic decline, irrespective of whether their impact on democratic institutions is more severe or not. The concept of unconstitutional alteration stipulated by Articles 19 and 20 IADC suggests that the OAS should take into consideration both democratic crises and decline. However, in a number of instances of democratic decline that common sense would clearly interpret as alterations, no OAS reaction came forward. The majority of acute democratic crises were followed by subsequent years of democratic decline, but OAS intervention usually ended after the nearest election date, at the latest. Venezuela, Ecuador, Bolivia, Nicaragua, and to some extent Honduras are cases in point. The passage on unconstitutional alteration further defines it as an event "that seriously impairs the democratic order." Hence, the practice of IADC application for the defense of democracy so far has paid priority attention to the most immediate and tangible threats. Thus, it is to be expected that processes of decline are unlikely to trigger an international reaction until they reach a certain threshold or culmination point and result in a specific, discernible event or change—in other words, an acute situation which requires immediate action in order to avoid, stop, or even reverse democratic backsliding.

Conclusion

The review of OAS responses to democratic crises reveals that most of the strengths and weaknesses of the IADC highlighted in Chapter 3 are in fact relevant for its real-world application. First, the role of executive sovereignty mitigates the effectiveness of the IADC in the defense and promotion of democracy, as many measures depend on the explicit or passive consent of the government concerned. For the aim of defending democracy, this could be both beneficial and detrimental, depending on the nature of the threat. The tendency that executives increasingly are not the origins, but the targets of democratic challenges might make presidents more willing to turn abroad for assistance and should hence make the recourse to the IADC more likely. Yet, this does not rectify, but might even reinforce the IADC's bias in favor of executives, in the sense that the IADC primarily serves the protection of sitting executives, but is a less suitable tool once other components of the democratic system are undermined.

Second, the flexibility of the IADC's instruments (in contrast to the automaticity of Resolution 1080) likewise exhibits positive and negative consequences. As the short case studies above have shown, the broadened focus of the IADC—which deals with both interruptions and alterations of the constitutional order, and enables reactive as well as preventive action—creates a lot of leeway to find adequate responses to diverse challenges. Applicability is undermined, however, by the increasingly opaque character of democratic crises and the ensuing mismatch between situations stipulated in the IADC and the nature of the situations on the ground. This might entail a "conceptual stretching" of IADC terminology that does anything but help to clarify how to address newly emerging challenges. The "coup inflation" is a case in point. Recently, the term "coup" has been used for cases that some would not consider an unambiguous challenge from an exogenous actor, let alone a classic *coup d'état*. As a consequence, the anti-coup norm is eroding. On the one hand, there is no consensus on what constitutes an illegal coup in contrast to a coerced resignation that might have some legitimacy when impelled by mass protests. On the other hand, events that do meet the classic definitional criteria are sometimes welcomed for ideological reasons by some external powers that would otherwise have the duty, according to the democratic solidarity paradigm, to intervene in response to what would normally be considered an illegal regime change.

This leads to a third problem that has surfaced in some of the cases depicted above and will take center stage in the next chapter: collisions between regionally agreed norms and individual states' interests. The OAS as international organization (and its bureaucracy) stands firm in its commitment to democracy, whereas the stance of the United States and aspiring regional powers like Brazil and Venezuela may diverge from the democratic consensus due to the existence of competing (geo) political priorities.

Notes

1 Jennifer L. McCoy, "Challenges for the Collective Defense of Democracy on the Tenth Anniversary of the Inter-American Democratic Charter," *Latin American Policy* 3, no. 1 (2012): 33–57.

2 See Latinobarómetro, "Informe Flash Paraguay 1995–2012," 27 June 2012, www.latinobarometro.org/latino/latinobarometro.jsp.

3 Dexter S. Boniface, "Dealing with Threats to Democracy," in *Which Way Latin America? Hemispheric Politics Meets Globalization*, ed. Andrew F. Cooper and Jorge Heine (Tokyo: United Nations University Press, 2009), 182–201; John A. Peeler, *Building Democracy in Latin America* (Boulder, Colo.: Lynne Rienner, 2009).

4 Arturo Valenzuela, "Latin American Presidencies Interrupted," *Journal of Democracy* 15, no. 4 (2004): 5–19.

5 Scott Mainwaring and Aníbal Pérez-Liñán, "Latin American Democratization since 1978: Democratic Transitions, Breakdowns, and Erosions," in *The Third Wave of Democratization in Latin America: Advances and Setbacks*, ed. Frances Hagopian and Scott Mainwaring (Cambridge: Cambridge University Press, 2005), 14–59 (20).

6 While the concept of democratic crisis as such has only received scant attention, some subsets of democratic crises have been studied more extensively, most notably *coups d'état* and the phenomenon of failed presidencies. The literature on military intervention in politics is almost unmanageable and has for the Latin American context emphasized the armed forces' propensity to act as guardians and protect "national security" against external as well as internal enemies. Classics on coups and the military in politics include Samuel P. Huntington, *The Soldier and the State: The Theory and Politics of Civil-Military Relations* (Cambridge, Mass.: Harvard University Press, 1957); Samuel E. Finer, *The Man on Horseback: The Role of the Military in Politics* (London: Pall Mall, 1962); Stanislav Andreski, *Military Organization and Society* (Berkeley and Los Angeles: University of California Press, 1968); Eric A. Nordlinger, *Soldiers in Politics: Military Coups and Governments* (Englewood Cliffs, N.J.: Prentice Hall, 1977); and for Latin America Alfred Stepan, *The Military in Politics: Changing Patterns in Brazil* (Princeton, N.J.: Princeton University Press, 1971); Guillermo O'Donnell, *Modernization and Bureaucratic-Authoritarianism:*

Studies in South American Politics (Berkeley: Institute of International Studies, University of California, 1973); Alain Rouquié, *The Military and the State in Latin America* (Berkeley: University of California Press, 1989). Given the centrality of the executive in Latin American political systems, and the frequency of failed presidencies even after democratization, much work has recently been devoted to the perils of presidentialism and the causes and consequences of executive instability. See Valenzuela, "Latin American Presidencies Interrupted"; Kathryn Hochstetler, "Rethinking Presidentialism: Challenges and Presidential Falls in South America," *Comparative Politics* 38, no. 4 (2006): 401–18; Kathryn Hochstetler and Margaret E. Edwards, "Failed Presidencies: Identifying and Explaining a South American Anomaly," *Journal of Politics in Latin America* 1, no. 2 (2009): 31–57; Aníbal Pérez-Liñán, *Presidential Impeachment and the New Political Instability in Latin America* (Cambridge: Cambridge University Press 2007); Mariana Llanos and Leiv Marsteintredet, ed., *Presidential Breakdowns in Latin America: Causes and Outcomes of Executive Instability in Developing Democracies* (New York: Palgrave Macmillan, 2010).

7 Michel J. Crozier, Samuel P. Huntington and Joji Watanuki, *The Crisis of Democracy: Report on the Governability of Democracies to the Trilateral Commission* (New York: New York University Press, 1975); Jürgen Habermas, *Legitimation Crisis* (Boston, Mass.: Beacon Press, 1975); Colin Crouch, *Post-democracy* (Cambridge: Polity Press, 2004). We owe the hint to this debate to Wolfgang Merkel.

8 Larry Diamond, "The Democratic Rollback. The Resurgence of the Predatory State," *Foreign Affairs* 87, no. 2 (2008), 36–48; Arch Puddington, "The 2007 Freedom House Survey. Is the Tide Turning?" *Journal of Democracy* 19, no. 2 (2008): 61–73; Steven Levitsky and Lucan A. Way, *Competitive Authoritarianism: Hybrid Regimes after the Cold War* (Cambridge: Cambridge University Press, 2010).

9 For similar reflections on the concept of political crisis see Palle Svensson, "Stability, Crisis and Breakdown: Some Notes on the Concept of Crisis in Political Analysis," *Scandinavian Political Studies* 9, no. 2 (1986): 129–39.

10 Boniface, "Dealing with Threats to Democracy."

11 Ibid.

12 Jennifer L. McCoy, "International Response to Democratic Crisis in the Americas, 1990–2005," *Democratization* 13, no. 5 (2006): 756–75; McCoy, "Challenges for the Collective Defense of Democracy on the Tenth Anniversary of the Inter-American Democratic Charter."

13 Boniface, "Dealing with Threats to Democracy."

14 Ibid., 186.

15 Pérez-Liñán, *Presidential Impeachment and the New Political Instability in Latin America.*

16 Ibid.; Hochstetler, "Rethinking Presidentialism."

17 Polity IV constructs two 10-point scales capturing the democratic and autocratic characteristics of a country which are frequently combined into the 21-point scale Polity score. See the project website for further information: www.systemicpeace.org/polity/polity4.htm. Freedom House rates countries on a seven-point scale for both political rights and civil liberties. Further information is available on the organization's website: www.freedom house.org.

18 The exact terms for the three regime categories in Polity IV are "Democracy," "Anocracy" and "Autocracy"; Freedom House distinguishes between "Free", "Partly Free" and "Not Free."

19 Arturo Valenzuela, "Paraguay: The Coup that Didn't Happen," *Journal of Democracy* 8, no. 1 (1997): 43–55; Andrew F. Cooper and Thomas Legler, *Intervention Without Intervening? The OAS Defense and Promotion of Democracy in the Americas* (New York: Palgrave Macmillan, 2006); Andrew F. Cooper and Thomas Legler, "A Tale of Two Mesas: The OAS Defense of Democracy in Peru and Venezuela," *Global Governance* 11, no. 4 (2005): 425–44; Barry S. Levitt, "A Desultory Defense of Democracy: OAS Resolution 1080 and the Inter-American Democratic Charter," *Latin American Politics and Society* 48, no. 3 (2006): 93–123; Craig Arceneaux and David Pion-Berlin, "Issues, Threats, and Institutions: Explaining OAS Responses to Democratic Dilemmas in Latin America," *Latin American Politics and Society* 49, no. 2 (2007): 1–31.

20 See Joseph S. Nye and David A. Welch, *Understanding Global Conflict and Cooperation: An Introduction to Theory and History* (Boston, Mass.: Longman, 2011), 197–98.

21 "Situation in Venezuela," OAS Permanent Council Resolution 811 (1315/02), 13 April 2002.

22 Thomas Legler, "The Inter-American Democratic Charter: Rhetoric or Reality?" in *Governing the Americas: Assessing Multilateral Institutions,* ed. Gordon Mace, Jean-Philippe Thérien and Paul Haslam (Boulder, Colo.: Lynne Rienner, 2007), 113–30 (120).

23 "Support for Democracy in Venezuela," OAS General Assembly Resolution 1 (XXIX-E/02), 18 April 2002.

24 "Declaration on Democracy in Venezuela," OAS General Assembly Declaration 28 (XXXII-O/02), 4 June 2002.

25 "Support for the Process of Dialogue in Venezuela," OAS Permanent Council Resolution 821 (1329/02), 14 August 2002.

26 "Support for the Democratic Institutional Structure in Venezuela and the Facilitation Efforts of the OAS Secretary General," OAS Permanent Council Resolution 833 (1349/02), 16 December 2002.

27 For a more detailed account of the mediation, see Cooper and Legler, *Intervention Without Intervening?* Cooper and Legler, "A Tale of Two Mesas"; Thomas Legler, "Venezuela 2002–4: The Chávez Challenge," in *Promoting Democracy in the Americas,* ed. Thomas Legler, Sharon F. Lean and Dexter S. Boniface (Baltimore, Md.: Johns Hopkins University Press, 2007), 204–24; Jennifer McCoy and Francisco Diez, *International Mediation in Venezuela* (Washington, DC: United States Institute of Peace Press, 2011); Randall R. Parish Jr, Mark Peceny and Justin Delacour, "Venezuela and the Collective Defence of Democracy Regime in the Americas," *Democratization* 14, no. 2 (2007): 207–31.

28 During the interval of military rule, the OAS, in collaboration with the UN, formed a joint civilian mission (MICIVIH), which monitored the human rights conditions in the country and which, once civilian rule was restored, was transformed into an institution-building effort focusing on judicial and police reform. See Sebastian von Einsiedel and David M. Malone, "Peace and Democracy for Haiti: A UN Mission Impossible?" *International Relations* 20, no. 2 (2006): 153–74.

29 On the establishment and mandate of the mission, see "The Situation in Haiti," OAS Permanent Council Resolution 806 (1303/02), 16 January 2002; "Support for Strengthening Democracy in Haiti," OAS Permanent Council Resolution 822 (1331/02), 4 September 2002.

30 On the Haitian crisis, see Yasmine Shamsie, "Building 'Low-Intensity' Democracy in Haiti: The OAS Contribution," *Third World Quarterly* 25, no. 6 (2004): 1097–115; David M. Goldberg, "Haiti 2004: CARICOM's Democracy Promotion Efforts," in *Promoting Democracy in the Americas*, ed. Thomas Legler, Sharon F. Lean and Dexter S. Boniface (Baltimore, Md.: Johns Hopkins University Press, 2007), 177–203.

31 "Support for Public Order and Strengthening Democracy in Haiti," OAS Permanent Council Resolution 861 (1400/04), 19 February 2004.

32 "Situation in Haiti," OAS Permanent Council Resolution 862 (1401/04), 26 February 2004.

33 "Situation in Haiti: Strengthening of Democracy," OAS General Assembly Resolution 2058 (XXXIV-O/04), 8 June 2004.

34 Jorge Heine and Andrew S. Thompson, ed., *Fixing Haiti: MINUSTAH and Beyond* (Tokyo: United Nations University Press, 2011).

35 "Situation in Honduras," OAS Permanent Council Resolution 952 (1699/09), 26 June 2009.

36 "Current Situation in Honduras," OAS Permanent Council Resolution 953 (1700/09), 28 June 2009. The special session convened between 30 June and 4 July 2009; see "Resolution on the Political Crisis in Honduras", OAS General Assembly Resolution 1 (XXXVII-E/09), 1 July 2009.

37 "Suspension of the Right of Honduras to Participate in the Organization of American States," OAS General Assembly Resolution 2 (XXXVII-E/09), 4 July 2009.

38 "OAS Permanent Council Repudiates Events in Ecuador and Supports the Government of President Correa," OAS press release E-360/10, 30 September 2010.

39 "Situation in the Republic of Ecuador," OAS Permanent Council Resolution 977 (1772/10), 30 September 2010.

40 Brazil called for coordinated action on the part of UNASUR, OAS, and MERCOSUR in order to maintain democratic stability, and external support for the challenged president came from both the OAS and UNASUR. According to some observers, UNASUR played a more visible role than the OAS: the South American presidents convened in Argentina on the very day of the Ecuadorean crisis. See Detlef Nolte and Leslie Wehner, "UNASUR and Regional Security Governance in the Americas," in *Regional Organisations and Security: Conceptions and Practices*, ed. Stephen Aris and Andreas Wenger (London: Routledge, 2014), 183–202.

41 Steven Levitsky and María Victoria Murillo, "Argentina Weathers the Storm," *Journal of Democracy* 14, no. 4 (2003): 152–66; Mariana Llanos, "Presidential Breakdown in Argentina," in *Presidential Breakdowns in Latin America: Causes and Outcomes of Executive Instability in Developing Democracies*, ed. Mariana Llanos and Leiv Marsteintredet (New York: Palgrave Macmillan, 2010), 55–71.

42 "Gaviria Calls for Constitutional Transition in Argentina," OAS press release E-251/01, 20 December 2001.

43 As no candidate for the presidency received over 50 percent of the vote, the national congress was required to elect a president.

44 The sequence of social protests in 2002–03 is described by Miguel A. Buitrago, "Civil Society, Social Protest, and Presidential Breakdowns in Bolivia," in *Presidential Breakdowns in Latin America: Causes and Outcomes of Executive Instability in Developing Democracies*, ed. Mariana Llanos and Leiv Marsteintredet (New York: Palgrave Macmillan, 2010), 91–107.

45 A minor issue that increased the outrage was that the export of gas was supposed to work via a port in Chile, with which Bolivia maintains a longstanding territorial dispute about its access to the Pacific.

46 "Support for the Constitutional Government of the Republic of Bolivia," Permanent Council Resolution 838 (1355/03), 14 February 2003; "Statement of OAS Secretary General César Gaviria on Violence in Bolivia," OAS press release E-198/03, 13 October 2003; "Support for the Constitutional Government of the Republic of Bolivia," Permanent Council Resolution 849 (1384/03), 13 October 2003.

47 "Statement by OAS Secretary General on Events in Bolivia," OAS press release E-202/03, 17 October 2003; "Support for the Constitutional Process in the Republic of Bolivia," Permanent Council Resolution 852 (1387/03), 22 October 2003.

48 One reason was that the new OAS SG came from the ancient rival Chile. See Günther Maihold and Jörg Husar, *Democracy in Crisis in Latin America*, SWP Comments 26 (Berlin: Stiftung Wissenschaft und Politik, 2005), www.swp-berlin.org/fileadmin/contents/products/comments/comment s2005_26_ilm_husar_ks.pdf.

49 In March 2005 Acting SG of the OAS Luigi Einaudi issued two statements on the political crisis in Bolivia, as evidenced by OAS press releases.

50 "Declaration of the General Assembly on the Situation in Bolivia," OAS General Assembly Declaration 42 (XXXV-O/05), 7 June 2005.

51 "Support for Democracy in Bolivia," Permanent Council Resolution 885 (1499/05), 26 July 2005.

52 On the Ecuadorean crises 2004–05, see Barry S. Levitt, "Ecuador 2004–5: Democratic Crisis Redux," in *Promoting Democracy in the Americas*, ed. Thomas Legler, Sharon F. Lean and Dexter S. Boniface (Baltimore, Md.: Johns Hopkins University Press, 2007), 225–45.

53 "Support by the Organization of American States for the Republic of Ecuador," Permanent Council Resolution 880 (1478/05), 22 April 2005.

54 "Report to the Permanent Council on the Situation in Ecuador," Permanent Council Document 4028/05 corr. 1, 20 May 2005; and "Support to the Republic of Ecuador by the Organization of American States," Permanent Council Resolution 883 (1484/05), 20 May 2005, which once again invoked Art. 18 IADC.

55 "Support for Nicaragua," General Assembly Declaration 43 (XXXV-O/05), 7 June 2005; also see "Support for Nicaragua," Permanent Council Resolution 892 (1507/05), 9 September 2005, which was issued in response to the SG's report on the results of the high-level mission to Nicaragua.

56 Legler, "The Inter-American Democratic Charter."

57 "Support for the Process of Dialogue, Peace, and for Democratic Institutions in Bolivia," Permanent Council Resolution 935 (1648/08), 3 May 2008. The resolution does not make reference to Article 17 IADC (which is

why Bolivia is listed as a case of ad hoc facilitation in Table 4.4). Yet, other OAS documents claim that the request from the Bolivian government was made under that provision. See OAS, *Tenth Anniversary of the Inter-American Democratic Charter: A Hemispheric Commitment to Democracy* (Washington, DC: Organization of American States, 2011), 30; *Report of the Secretary General Concerning Compliance with Operative Paragraph 3 of Resolution AG/Res.2480 (XXXIX-O/09) "Promotion and Strengthening of Democracy: Follow-up to the Inter-American Democratic Charter"* (Permanent Council document OEA/Ser.G., CP/doc.4487/10), 4 May 2010. The latter offers a detailed account of OAS actions during the 2008 Bolivian crisis.

58 UNASUR decided to send its own mission to Bolivia to mediate in the conflict. SG Insulza criticized this decision as he would have preferred a joint mission. Some say that in the end, the activities of the UNASUR mission proved more important than those of the OAS in the resolution of the Bolivian crisis. See Nolte and Wehner, "UNASUR and Regional Security Governance in the Americas."

59 "Lugo Impeachment Rumors are Back, but Nothing Concrete or Imminent," WikiLeaks cable 09ASUNCION621, Embassy Asunción (Paraguay), 23 October 2009.

60 In fact, MERCOSUR as well as UNASUR suspended Paraguay in accordance with their democratic clauses.

61 On the evolution and evaluation of the Paraguayan democratic crisis, see Mariana Llanos, Detlef Nolte, and Cordula Tibi Weber, *Paraguay: Staatsstreich oder "Misstrauensvotum"?* GIGA Focus Lateinamerika 8 (Hamburg: German Institute of Global and Area Studies, 2012); Leiv Marsteintredet, Mariana Llanos and Detlef Nolte, "Paraguay and the Politics of Impeachment," *Journal of Democracy* 24, no. 4 (2013): 110–23.

62 Personal interview with Kevin Casas-Zamora, Secretary for Political Affairs, OAS General Secretariat, Washington, DC, 24 May 2013.

63 "OAS Secretary General Raises Doubts about Respect for Legitimate Self-Defense in Impeachment that Ousted the Former President of Paraguay," OAS press release E-229/12, 23 June 2012.

64 "OAS Permanent Council Receives Report of the Secretary General and Delegation to Paraguay," OAS press release E-247/12, 10 July 2012.

65 John W. Graham, *A Magna Carta for the Americas: The Inter-American Democratic Charter: Genesis, Challenges and Canadian Connections,* FOCAL Policy Paper FPP-02-09 (Ottawa: Canadian Foundation for the Americas, 2002).

5   The OAS democratic paradigm in action

The case of Honduras

- **Chronicle of a crisis foretold**
- **The coup that dare not speak its name**
- **The regional reaction**
- **Explaining the Honduras fiasco**
- **Conclusion**

Honduras seems an unlikely setting for a major international crisis. One of the smallest and poorest countries in Latin America, it is mostly known for having originated the expression "banana republic," due to the degree it was dominated by the United Fruit Company in the 1940s and 1950s. Even at the height of the Central American revolutionary upsurge in the 1980s, Honduras managed to stay apart from the maelstrom of violence that engulfed the isthmus at the time. Yet, during the second half of 2009, events in Honduras dominated the inter-American agenda, led to a major change in the dynamics of US–Latin American relations,[1] and became a contentious issue between the Western hemisphere's two leading powers, i.e. the United States and Brazil.[2] Why was Honduras considered to be so critical for the present and future state of democracy in the Americas? Why was it that a country smaller than North Carolina (112,000 square km) of a mere 7.4 million people, the fourth poorest in the Western hemisphere, with a per capita income of US$1,900, half of the regional average,[3] turned into the most critical item on the inter-American agenda for several months?

As was analyzed in Chapter 4, since 2001 there have been a number of cases in which elected heads of state in Latin America have ended their terms prematurely and abruptly.[4] On a number of those occasions democratic crises triggered the various mechanisms set up within the inter-American system to deal with them.[5] Yet, in none of them did we see anything similar to what happened in Honduras: a president taken at gunpoint out of his home in the early hours of the morning of 28

June 2009, put on a plane and flown abroad. Accordingly, there was a strong reaction against the overthrow of an elected president. For the first time since its creation, the OAS voted unanimously to suspend one of its members.[6] The coup was condemned by the United States and Canada as well as by most, if not all, Latin American governments. The US visas of leading Honduras officials were revoked, military cooperation programs were frozen, and (quite exceptionally) funding from international financial institutions like the World Bank and the International Monetary Fund (IMF) came to a standstill.

A frequent conclusion drawn from the Honduran case is that if the international community was unable to restore democracy in Honduras, it would have serious difficulties in doing so anywhere else. Honduras put into question 20 years of relative democratic stability and continuity in Latin America. To allow the precedent of the Honduras coup to stand would have serious consequences. Given that Honduras is one of the poorest and smallest states in the region and that the classification of the forced removal of President José Manuel ("Mel") Zelaya as an unconstitutional military coup was widely consensual, the expectation was that of forceful OAS actions in defense of democracy which would successfully reverse the coup. Yet, in spite of the initial international repudiation of the coup, the heavy involvement of the OAS in efforts to return to democracy, and protracted multiparty negotiations involving many domestic and international actors, Zelaya was not restored to power.[7]

This chapter dissects the reasons for this counterintuitive outcome and discusses whether it can be considered a failure of the common defense of democracy regime. The first section examines the background to the Honduran crisis; the second, the course of events and the nature of the "constitutional interruption" of 28 June 2009; the third, the regional reaction to it, paying special attention to the policy of the Barack Obama Administration; while the fourth section reviews a set of explanations for the Honduran fiasco.

Chronicle of a crisis foretold

What transpired on 28 June 2009 in Honduras was by no means accidental. Neither was it the product of an unfortunate concatenation of events. Rather, it was the result of deep divisions in Honduran society and of an acute polarization in that seemingly most tranquil of Central American nations, a polarization that its political elite was unable to resolve peacefully, and that was further deepened following the ouster of the president. This polarization had its ultimate roots in a deeply unequal society (with a Gini coefficient of 0.55) marked by stagnant social and economic development.[8] It cut across families, communities, neighborhoods and all sorts of associations in a way not seen in Honduras in many decades.[9]

Divisions within the political elite were often more personal than ideological. Zelaya was an unlikely candidate to be cast in the role as a threat to the Honduran establishment. If anything, he was very much part of it. A rancher and businessman (known for going around in a cowboy hat and boots, sporting a broad moustache), he comes from a land-owning family in the logging and cattle-raising business. As a leading member of the PLH, the Partido Liberal de Honduras, one of the two main parties in the country, he had already been the party's standard-bearer in the 2001 elections before winning the presidency in 2005.[10] There was nothing in his background, discourse or trajectory until then that presaged the polarization that would obtain in Honduras mid-way into his presidency.[11]

However, the crisis was also rooted in the feeble and imperfect arrangements of Honduran democracy and its constitutional scaffold-ing.[12] The rigidities, deficiencies, overlaps and glaring loopholes of Honduran political institutions go a long way towards explaining not only the crisis itself, but the passionate debate that followed it, both at home and abroad, on the question as to whether what took place was an old-fashioned military coup or an orderly transfer of power within the parameters of existing constitutional norms.[13]

In addition, transnational politics came into play. The rise in the price of oil was starting to have an inordinate impact on Honduras, its balance of payments and its balance of trade—not surprising in a small country without significant energy sources of its own, and which depends heavily on the export of coffee and bananas. With Venezuela offering discounted oil at favorable conditions to a number of Latin American and Caribbean nations upon joining ALBA, the Zelaya government suddenly saw a way out of its predicament.[14] This was by no means uncontroversial, but in the end, the Honduran parliament, where Zelaya did not have a majority (as it was controlled by another faction of his own party) went along with it, after some protracted and convoluted negotiations and backroom deals. Zelaya visited Venezuela and Cuba. ALBA met in Tegucigalpa, with leaders of the various member states (like Bolivia, Ecuador and Nicaragua) making strong anti-US statements, and Honduras was drawn into the whirlwind of regional politics in a way that had not happened before. Zelaya also implemented a number of progressive policy measures, like a drastic increase in the minimum wage, and a raise in teachers' salaries, which increased his popularity, but did not go down well with the Honduran elite.

Several ALBA members had given themselves new constitutions, in an effort to adapt their political institutions to twenty-first-century realities. At some point, Zelaya concluded that Honduras needed one as well. The anachronistic Honduran constitution was emblematic of the backwardness of Honduran institutions. Polls showed that this issue resonated with the voters, and the government saw in this a winning issue that would allow Zelaya to leave his mark on the country.

A constitution as bad as they come

It is difficult to escape the conclusion that the Honduran constitution itself, the proposed change of which was so much at the center of the dispute, played no small part in the whole imbroglio. In place since 1982, with 378 articles, and 20-plus reforms since its enactment, the constitution is one of the longest and most dysfunctional anywhere. Given the country's long history of military rule and dictatorships, the drafters of the document went overboard to put in place safeguards to guarantee the stability and continuity of democratic institutions. In so doing, however, they overreached, and ended up with constitutional and legal monstrosities that undermine their very goal. Many key constitutional provisions differ quite drastically from established constitutional practices and doctrine in Latin America. In so doing, they do not just open the door for conflicts of various kinds, but actually invite their occurrence. In brief, its key features are the following:

- *Extreme rigidity.* As if wishing to leave the constitution in place in perpetuity, Article 373 specifies that any changes require approval of a two-thirds vote of all members of congress, by two legislatures in a row. Moreover, Article 374 indicates that some articles can never be changed, including Article 373, and the ones on the form of government, the national territory, the presidential period, the prohibition to run for president again after having occupied the office, and the ones referring to functionaries not eligible as president immediately after having occupied a certain office.
- *Extreme penalties.* In an effort to forestall any constitutional violations, highly punitive sanctions are established, in some cases quite disproportionate to the former. For example, alternation in the occupation of the office of the president is mandatory, and a violation is considered "a treason against the fatherland" (Art. 4). Taken to the limit, attempts to break this provision or to promote its

reform are sanctioned with a 10-year ban from the exercise of public offices (Art. 239), and any actions to encourage, promote or support the continuity or the re-election of the president leads to the loss of citizenship (Art. 42, para. 5). Members of parliament who unjustifiably miss a session of the legislature, causing the latter to lack a quorum, are to be expelled from congress, and are not eligible for public office for 10 years (Art. 197).

- *A unicameral congress prone to conflict with the executive.* The absence of a senate, or second legislative chamber, creates an in-built rivalry between the heads of the two leading branches of government, the executive and the legislative, the country's two highest-ranking elected officials. The constitution also bans the president of the congress from being a candidate for the presidency of the republic in the term immediately after heading the legislature (Art. 240).

- *A full-slate Supreme Court nomination process.* Most constitutions establish Supreme Courts (i.e. the apex body of the third government branch, the judiciary) whose members are appointed *seriatim*, and rotated in and out of the bench by various mechanisms, thus preserving over time a modicum of balance in its composition and judicial perspectives. Uniquely, the Honduran one is fully appointed at one fell swoop (Chapter XII of the constitution) for a fixed period of time, with the approval of two thirds of the members of congress. The highly partisan process means that, at least during the initial period following its appointment, the Supreme Court judges will reflect the particular majority obtaining in congress. This makes it difficult for it to mediate in disputes between the presidency and the latter. The odds are it will automatically align with congress, thus exacerbating intra-government tensions.

Zelaya's fuite en avance *and the "fourth ballot box"*

The immediate trigger of the Honduras crisis was President Zelaya's insistence on holding a referendum on 28 June 2009 on the subject of whether Honduras should set up, in the course of the presidential elections scheduled for 29 November of that year, a "fourth ballot box" to call for a constitutional assembly.[15] Other political actors, including head of congress Roberto Micheletti Baín, were at first receptive to the idea of constitutional reform, but wanted the consultation to be held after the 29 November 2009 elections. Some polls showed as much as 70 percent support for the initiative. Yet, in the end, there were suspicions about Zelaya's ulterior motives, namely that the new constitution might eventually allow for the re-election of the president. In addition, the association of the project with what was happening in other ALBA countries like Bolivia, Ecuador and Venezuela, where constitutional assemblies and new constitutions had gone hand in hand with progressive political and social reform, deprived it of support within the congress and the leadership of the National and the Liberal Parties. It was the increasingly determined opposition from different sectors of the Honduran state to this project that led to the clash between the president and his opponents.

The deepening rift between the executive, the legislature and the Supreme Court—ironically, all controlled by the Liberal Party, albeit by different factions—also had a personal component. Zelaya, although originally committed to back Roberto Micheletti to lead the parliament, had reneged on his commitment, and did not do so—though to no avail, as Micheletti was elected anyway. When it became time to appoint a new Supreme Court—a process with a strong partisan connotation—Zelaya tried to appoint several of his supporters, but was overruled by the congress, which imposed its own slate of judges. None of this bore great promise for a smooth and fluid relationship between the various powers of the Honduran state during the Zelaya presidency.

Thus, when on 23 March 2009 Zelaya signed an executive decree calling for the consultation, there was instant pushback. Zelaya's initiative was portrayed as inspired by the ALBA countries and denounced as aimed at bringing communism to Honduras. The attorney-general took the issue to the Supreme Court, which pronounced the decree null and void and in violation of a variety of articles of the constitution, including Article 2 (which specifies that any attempt at usurpation of popular sovereignty will constitute "treason to the fatherland"), and Articles 373 and 374, relative to constitutional reform. Zelaya withdrew the decree, but proceeded to issue another. This second, "softer" version, purported not to be a formal referendum or plebiscite (instruments that are contemplated and strictly regulated in the Honduran constitution) but more along the lines of a non-binding public opinion "poll," though still sticking to the procedures of an election, rather than those followed by pollsters. As Zelaya did not have the support of the congress for this, nor of the Supreme Electoral Tribunal (the legal entity especially set up to run Honduran elections), his first choice for running the consultation was the National Statistical Institute. Under pressure from a variety of quarters, the latter admitted it was not in a condition to do any such thing, at which point Zelaya turned to the armed forces to manage the 28 June "poll."

General Romeo Vásquez Velásquez, the head of the joint chiefs of staff, who was close to Zelaya and whose initial three-year term had been extended by the latter, originally went along with this. As the date of the consultation got closer, however, his legal advisors made clear to Vásquez that he could get himself in trouble by participating in an event that the Supreme Court had ruled as unconstitutional. When informing Zelaya that he was pulling back from his original commitment, Vásquez was sacked by the president, a decision that led to the resignation of the minister of defense, as well as of each of the heads of the three branches of the armed forces, precipitating a crisis in civil-military relations in a country where the military traditionally held great sway. Upon Vásquez's appeal of his dismissal to the Supreme Court, the latter promptly proceeded to reinstate him, arguing that his rights as a public employee had been violated by the president. Perhaps the culmination took place when, frustrated by the embargo of the voting materials for the 28 June consultation ordered by the attorney-general, Zelaya himself led a motley group of demonstrators to the air force base where the ballots were kept, confronted the general in charge, and prevailed in gaining access to this material and taking it with him, to be distributed throughout the country.

In this context, Zelaya's ousting on 28 June was nothing but the logical outcome of a breakdown of institutional comity and civility *ad limine* which by then was bursting at the seams and could no longer hold. A highly imperfect constitutional text, a polarized political situation and a political culture in which the strict following of established procedures is not a prominent feature thus aligned in Honduras in 2009.

The coup that dare not speak its name

Between five and six o'clock in the morning of 28 June 2009, a Sunday, a unit of balaclava-clad Honduras army soldiers arrived at the residence of President Zelaya in Tegucigalpa. Led by Lt Colonel René Antonio Hepburn, it carried arrest and search warrants, issued by the Supreme Court. The 15-strong presidential guard offered resistance, but was quickly overcome. Shots were fired, some to open the doors to the house. Still in his pajamas, Zelaya was detained, put into a car, and taken to the Hernán Acosta Mejía air force base. Once there, he was put into an air force plane and flown to another air base, known as Palmerola. There, the plane refueled, and flew to San José de Costa Rica, landing at the Juan Santamaría International Airport. Upon disembarking, Zelaya was driven into San José by someone waiting for him.

Back in Tegucigalpa, the congress, the armed forces, the judiciary, the Supreme Electoral Tribunal and other bodies that had joined forces to topple Zelaya, proceeded to replace him. At noon, the Supreme Electoral Tribunal announced that the forthcoming presidential elections of 29 November 2009 would be held as planned. In turn, the Supreme Court issued a statement specifying that Zelaya's arrest was backed by proper judicial orders emanating from a competent judge. The main action, however, took place at the congress, under the leadership of Roberto Micheletti, the man set to replace Zelaya and one of the main protagonists of events in Honduras in months to come.

Once in session, the congress listened to the report of the commission appointed the previous Thursday (25 June) to investigate Zelaya's behavior. The report's conclusions were that the actions of the president "had generated a climate of uncertainty, confrontation and division in Honduran society" and that these actions "had defied established authorities and constitutional and legal duties." It then listed a number of executive decrees, court sentences, and pieces of legislation to buttress those conclusions. Most of them are related to the "to-and-fro" between various entities on the "fourth ballot box." The vote to be held on that controversial issue on 28 June was the trigger of Zelaya's ouster.[16]

After the commission delivered its report, a document purporting to be Zelaya's letter of resignation was read to the congress, which unanimously voted to accept it (the members of parliament supporting Zelaya were not present). However, on the radio, from Costa Rica, Zelaya announced that he never wrote such a letter, which he alleged was a complete fabrication. Unable to go down that path, the congress backtracked, and, relying on the above mentioned commission's report and on the "absolute absence" of the president, determined that the presidency would be exercised by the then-leader of the legislature, Micheletti, until 27 January 2010, the date on which the newly elected president would take office. Once sworn in, Micheletti announced that he would devote himself to national reconciliation and a grand dialogue among all members of Honduran society. He committed to making the 29 November elections the cleanest and most transparent ever held in the country.[17]

A coup, albeit not an unprovoked one

Was the ouster of the head of state constitutional or not? Was the action of the armed forces within the limits of their role? Were the procedures followed to appoint a successor appropriate and according to the constitution? Does the fact that both the Honduran congress and the Supreme Court supported the ouster of President Zelaya mean that this ouster passes constitutional muster? In short, was the ouster of Zelaya on 28 June a coup, or not?

At the risk of compressing many complex developments that took place over a three-month period—from 23 March, when Zelaya signed the decree to have the consultation on the "fourth ballot box" on 28 June, and that very day—the answer to that question has to be disaggregated into two responses. The first relates to the actions on the part of Zelaya (and the reaction of the other government branches to them) in that period, and the degree to which they violated the constitution and the laws of Honduras. The second relates to what happened on 28 June itself. Much of the confusion in the ensuing public debate about the nature of the crisis arose from the conflation of these two rather different questions.

There is little doubt that relations between the Honduran presidency and the congress and the judiciary were not on a solid footing. Zelaya's seeming (and surprising) left turn, expressed in his decision to join ALBA and to increase the minimum wage, alienated the Honduran elite. That said, there is no reason to think that matters would have reached a breaking point, had it not been for the president's stubborn determination, come what may, to move forward on the 28 June consultation in order to facilitate a process leading to a constitutional assembly. The iterations between the various branches of government on this matter took an almost comic-opera character. Zelaya argued that all he wanted was to give Hondurans a chance to voice their opinion on the possibility of upgrading their constitution. Meanwhile, parliament, the Supreme Court, the Supreme Electoral Tribunal, the attorney-general, plus, in the end, the armed forces were determined to block the initiative. The Supreme Court declared presidential decrees null and void, the attorney-general stepped in with his own opinions, and parliament held forth on its own. The subtext of this was that this might eventually allow for presidential re-election, although it obviously would not apply to Zelaya in 2009.

Zelaya attempted to circumvent those objections through a variety of legalistic maneuvers. It is difficult to escape the conclusion that his actions stretched the limits of both the Honduran constitution and the rule of law. National referenda are contemplated in Article 2 and 5 of the constitution. Yet, they are strictly regulated. To be held, they require a special law approved in the congress by two thirds of all sitting members of parliament. They are also managed by the Supreme Electoral Tribunal. The 28 June consultation satisfied none of these requirements. Moreover, attempts to disguise this electoral exercise as some sort of non-binding public opinion poll were disingenuous. Public opinion polls, as run by companies like Gallup, do not use ballots, nor do they rely on the armed forces for their implementation. In public law, officials are only allowed to do what the law empowers them to do, and no such electoral exercises are foreseen in Honduran law.

In short, from March to June of 2009 the executive was on a steady course of collision with the law and with the constitution. The various attempts to find a compromise solution to the increasingly polarized situation were not bearing fruit, and the political elite, which had been through a number of crises in the eight elections in which it had been involved since the country's transition to democracy in 1981, found this one quite beyond its capabilities and skills. A case can thus be made that a firm response from the congress and from the judiciary to this untenable course of action was needed, perhaps even imperative. Taken to the limit, such a course of action might well end up with the removal of the president. Did what happened on 28 June, then, just simply reflect an orderly transfer of power from a president removed from office by the other two branches of government, to the next-in-line successor specified in the constitution? The answer to this question is no. It is true that the manner in which the president went about pushing for his ill-conceived and ill-fated popular consultation violated established norms and procedures, but the same goes for the way he was unceremoniously evicted from office and flown abroad.

The number of illegalities and irregularities in the events of 28 June are such that it is difficult to know where to begin. They start with the role of the armed forces. The Supreme Court's search and arrest warrants issued to detain President Zelaya for allegations of having broken the law should have been handled by the national police, not by the armed forces. The commander-in-chief of the armed forces in Honduras, as specified in the constitution (Art. 227), is the president. The Supreme Court has no authority over the armed forces whatsoever, let alone one empowering them to arrest their head. In deploying four units around the president's house and shooting their way into it that morning, the armed forces demonstrated insubordination and insurrection.[18]

A second violation of the constitution was the taking of Zelaya abroad. No Honduran citizen can be forcefully expelled from his own country. What the orders issued by the Supreme Court conveyed was that the president had to be arrested and brought before the magistrate responsible for that particular case. The decision to take him to Costa Rica was one made by the armed forces themselves, allegedly to avoid turmoil and confrontations with the president's supporters. While that may be a plausible, common-sense reason, it has no legal standing. It is also a logical consequence of enlisting the military in a venture in which they had no business to be in the first place.

The way the Honduran congress handled the sensitive matter of presidential succession was not a whole lot better. The production of a presidential resignation letter (by now demonstrated to be false) and a motion to accept such resignation as the first act of the congress that convened at 12:30 pm, on that very day, Sunday 28 June, introduced the first doubts about the seriousness and reliability of Zelaya's parliamentary opponents and their commitment to orderly procedures and the rule of law. The report delivered by the special committee appointed three days earlier to look into potential violations of the law by the president, a report made up of a few newspaper clippings and some generalities, was not very reassuring on these accounts either. When the congress proceeded to declare the presidency "vacant" because of the "overt absence" of the incumbent, and then voted to appoint its head, Roberto Micheletti, to the office, the unconstitutional ouster came full circle. The military, without legal standing to do so (supplanting the national police in these duties), detains the elected president of Honduras, and flies him out the country, thus violating one of his primordial constitutional rights. With the incumbent head of the executive thus out of the way, the congress, using as a justification the latter's absence from the country, proceeds to appoint its own head to the presidency. If this is not a coup, what is?[19]

Given the prominent role of the United States in the ultimate resolution of the Honduran crisis, the assessment of the US embassy in Tegucigalpa should be of special interest for these purposes. A detailed cable of 24 July 2009 to the US Department of State headquarters is emphatic: "no matter what the merits of the case against Zelaya, his forced removal was clearly illegal, and Micheletti's ascendance as 'interim president' was totally illegitimate."[20]

The regional reaction

In one of those extraordinary coincidences of history, the OAS General Assembly met in San Pedro Sula, Honduras, in early June 2009, only a few weeks before the ouster of President Zelaya. On that occasion, the local representative of the organization had reported on the growing political tension and polarization in the country, one which threatened to bring about a democratic breakdown. With the in-country presence of almost all foreign ministers from the hemisphere, and assorted other democratic leaders, one would have thought this an ideal opportunity for international mediation in the mounting Honduran crisis. This was not a pre-revolutionary situation nor a conflict fueled by deep social and ideological cleavages (pitting, say, a bourgeois versus a working-class coalition, or the landed aristocracy versus landless peasants), which would carry a forward momentum of its own and not lend itself to foreign mediation. Rather, it was very much an "inside Tegucigalpa" conflict within the political elite—in fact, mostly within a single political party, the Liberal Party, the oldest and most established within Honduras's somewhat sclerotic two-party system, and its different factions—and thus more amenable to mediation and resolution by outside parties.

The fact that it did not occur to anybody in the OAS Secretariat or in the participating delegations in its annual gathering, as they met with President Zelaya and the other protagonists of the unfolding Honduran tragedy, to do anything about it may have been due to the high-stakes game in which they were engaged on their own. It was at that General Assembly meeting in San Pedro Sula that the issue of lifting the resolution that suspended Cuba from the OAS in 1962 was mooted, and, in the end, unanimously approved—though not without extended backroom negotiations and compromises, due to a split between the US delegation headed by Secretary of State Hillary Clinton, and the vast majority of the Latin American and Caribbean ones on the merits, timing and conditions of such a measure. As we shall see below, this development would end up having its own, at the time quite unforeseen, consequences for the denouement of the Honduran crisis.

The OAS and other international organizations: unanimous repudiation

As political polarization within the country increased, the Zelaya government asked the OAS Permanent Council for assistance under Article 17 of the IADC.[21] A Permanent Council meeting to discuss the situation in Honduras was held on 25 and 26 June. Given that the events posed a threat to the democratic political process and the legitimate exercise of power, the Permanent Council adopted Resolution 952.[22] The SG immediately established a special commission, which was due to travel to Tegucigalpa on Monday 29 June.

Although ex post, rather than pre-emptive, on 28 June the OAS reaction was swift. In the very Sunday morning of Zelaya's ouster, the Permanent Council convened in the organization's headquarters building in Washington, DC. In Resolution 953, it invoked Article 20 IADC and unanimously condemned what it qualified as a *coup d'état* in Honduras. It demanded the immediate restoration of democracy in the country, and the return to power of Zelaya and rejected the recognition of the de facto government. A special session of the OAS General Assembly was convoked.[23] The Permanent Council mandated SG José Miguel Insulza "to urgently attend the meeting of the Central American Integration System (SICA) that will take place in Managua, Nicaragua, and in accordance with Article 20 of the IADC, to carry out the necessary consultations with the members of the Organization."[24] There was a sense of urgency and a sentiment that it was crucial to move quickly so as to prevent the new Honduras government from stabilizing and consolidating its hold on power. The SG travelled to Managua on 29 June and returned to Washington, DC, on the following day to attend the special session of the OAS General Assembly, which was held between 30 June and 4 July. The General Assembly issued Resolution 1 on 1 July, demanding the reinstatement of Zelaya within 72 hours. If within that time frame Zelaya was not reinstated, the organization would apply Article 21 of the IADC to suspend Honduras' membership.[25]

After a detour to the CARICOM summit in Georgetown, Guyana, where he discussed the Honduran situation, the SG traveled to Tegucigalpa on 3 July. While there, he held several rounds of meetings and conversations with Supreme Court justices, parliamentarians and party leaders from various groupings. Back in Washington, the SG reported that the new Honduras government had no intention of backtracking or of allowing the return of Zelaya to the country (let alone to the presidency). This had been confirmed to the SG personally by the president of the Supreme Court, who stood behind the notion that what happened on 28 June had been nothing but an orderly and fully constitutional transfer of power. The OAS General Assembly proceeded on 4 July unanimously to approve Resolution 2, which suspended Honduras from the organization, a first since the approval of the IADC.[26]

A large number of other regional and international organizations followed suit, condemning the ouster of President Zelaya. In the Americas, the Rio Group, MERCOSUR, UNASUR, ALBA, SICA, the Central American Parliament (PARLACEN) and the Latin American and Caribbean Economic System (SELA) joined the fray, expressing their concern and stressing the need to restore democracy and the rule of law. The representatives of the ALBA countries, with Venezuela and Nicaragua in the lead, were especially critical of what had happened, but so were the United States and Canada. The same goes for the UN and the EU. What had happened in Honduras seemed so much a throw-back to an earlier era in Latin American history, when the region was largely known as the one of "coups and earthquakes," that it resonated around the world. Many countries recalled their ambassadors for con-sultations. In due course, several of them would break diplomatic rela-tions altogether and close their missions in Tegucigalpa.[27]

Honduras is highly dependent on international cooperation—as much as a third of the central government budget came from it in 2009—and was thus especially vulnerable to cuts in it. Entities like the Inter-American Development Bank, the Spanish Agency of Interna-tional Cooperation (AECI), and various other European agencies have traditionally had programs in Honduras. To this we have to add the support provided by Petrocaribe and other ALBA programs after Honduras joined the latter. Although international financial institu-tions are famously reluctant to join in what they may consider to be politically motivated actions against member states, in the veritable tide of condemnation of what was widely described as the "Honduras military coup," even the IMF and the World Bank joined in, freezing a variety of programs and credit lines, much as the other entities listed above did.

The initial international pushback against the presidential ouster was thus considerable, on the bilateral and multilateral fronts, as well as on the political and economic ones. Seldom had there been as much of a seeming consensus on a political event in Latin America as on the breakdown of democracy in Honduras. This consensus cut across the political spectrum, across the hemisphere, and even across the Atlantic. As in many of the previous democratic crises in the region, the expec-tation was that a solution would emerge soon. This was reinforced by the perception that Honduras, as outlined above, was particularly vul-nerable to international pressures, and that the de facto government would be unable to withstand the latter for very long.

Yet, the OAS that took the lead in dealing with the crisis ended up as the victim of its own success. The assumption was that a quick, unan-imous response by the lead organization within the inter-American system, hand in hand with that of the broader international commu-nity, would soon bring the new Honduran government to the nego-tiating table—if not to give in, at least to search for a compromise solution and a way out of the crisis. The stronger and firmer the response, or so the reasoning went, the higher the chances of weakening the de facto regime's hold on power. The many moving parts of such a complex operation all fell into place, and the message sent to Hon-duras was loud and clear. Nonetheless, the effects of this unmistakable signal were not the ones anticipated. If anything, it only seemed to strengthen the determination of the new government to steer its own course, in overt defiance of the international community. Strongman Micheletti, offended by the OAS SG's refusal to meet him during his inspection visit to Tegucigalpa during the week of 29 June, and incensed about his country's suspension from the organization, announced he would no longer deal with the OAS. Micheletti and his followers, buttressed by the full support of the congress and the Supreme Court, as well as of the armed forces, "circled the wagons" and refused to budge. Popular demonstrations in Tegucigalpa demanding Zelaya's return were met with an iron fist. Attempts by Zelaya to return by himself were thwarted.

The OAS's mandate to defend and promote democracy in the Americas had placed it in the horns of a dilemma. Upon a democratic breakdown, the organization had immediately responded with its usual toolkit: an initial resolution by its Permanent Council condemning the coup, the convocation of a special session of the General Assembly, which issued an ultimatum, a field visit by the SG, and then the heaviest weapon in its arsenal—a membership suspension approved unanimously by the General Assembly, which gathered only for this purpose less than a week after the events in question. However, with Micheletti unwilling to play ball, the OAS found itself in a cul de sac. This was particularly so since the standard approach of the OAS to deal with such crises is centered on high-level conversations and negotiations between the relevant parties. As it takes two to tango, the unwillingness of one of these parties—in this case, the one holding the stronger hand of cards—to come to the table left the OAS in limbo.

With Zelaya in Costa Rica, the possibility of mediation led by former Costa Rican President and Nobel Peace Prize winner Oscar Arias, a widely respected statesman, was mooted, and taken up by both Zelaya and Micheletti. This had the advantage of giving a Central American, sub-regional imprimatur to the conflict resolution mechanism, one presumably closely attuned to realities on the ground in Honduras. Arias got to work with representatives of both camps—though not with the principals, as Micheletti refused to sit at the same table as Zelaya. An agreement going by the name of the San José Accord was presented by Arias on 22 July, giving rise to a renewed, albeit premature, set of expectations of an early resolution of the crisis. From July to November of 2009, Arias led mediation efforts, though often giving way to intercessions by various third parties—including the OAS, the US State Department, individual US senators, and Brazil's Itamaraty, among others. Brazil assumed its own significant role in the Honduran crisis by allowing Zelaya to take refuge in the country's Tegucigalpa mission in September 2009.[28] On 30 October, the "Tegucigalpa-San José Accord" was officially signed.[29]

Washington's one step forward, two steps backward

It is in this context that we must set the role of the United States in the Honduras crisis and its ultimate outcome.[30] The United States receives some 48 percent of Honduran exports, and originates 70 percent of FDI; US FDI in Honduras in 2008 reached US$700 million. A US military contingent of some 600 personnel under the name of Joint Task Force Bravo, and located at Soto Cano air force base, plays a key role in the interception of illegal drugs hailing from Colombia and destined for the United States, for which Honduras provides a convenient launching pad.[31] The US Agency for International Development (USAID) office in Honduras has a staff of 100, and it handles some 10 percent of all US aid to Latin America, a considerable amount given the size of the country. Historically, Honduras has been one of the Latin American countries most dependent on the United States. The military dictators who ruled Honduras for much of its history were closely aligned with the United States. As recently as in the 1980s, Honduras provided a base from which the United States supported the Nicaraguan Contras in their efforts to topple the Sandinista government. The Honduras crisis thus raised the question of whether Washington would side with the Honduran military, with which it had such close ties, or whether it would support democratic institutions and their continuity.

This question had an added twist because of its timing. The ouster of the Honduran president took place a little under six months into the Obama Administration, after a period during which Washington had made what seemed like a systematic effort to repair inter-American relations, in a bad state following the Bush Administration's selective and self-interested engagement with the region.[32] Perhaps to the surprise of many, the US government not only went along with the OAS and its decision to suspend Honduras, but also imposed sanctions on its own, stopped a number of aid programs, cancelled the US visas of prominent Honduran officials (including that of Micheletti) and otherwise indicated that it would not abide by the first full-fledged military coup in the region in 20 years. The high expectations generated in Latin America and the Caribbean by Obama's election seemed to have been vindicated. In an apparent bow to multilateralism, Washington seemed content to step aside and leave the OAS the initiative of dealing with Honduras.[33]

Yet, just at the moment when the sanctions were starting to kick in, and the pressure on the de facto government grew to implement the San José Accord—meaning a national unity government under Zelaya, a caretaker administration that would have seen the country through the 29 November elections, but which by restoring Zelaya to power would have undone the effects of the coup—Arias's finely calibrated solution began to unravel. In an unprecedented case of "parallel diplomacy," Senator Jim DeMint (Republican-South Carolina), not even a member of the Senate Foreign Affairs Committee, and who had put on hold two key US State Department appointments—those of Assistant Secretary of State for Western Hemisphere Affairs Arturo Valenzuela, and of the Ambassador to Brazil designate Thomas Shannon—flew to Tegucigalpa. Brushing off offers of assistance from the US embassy there, he met with Micheletti, encouraging him to stand firm and refuse Washington's entreaties to allow President Zelaya to return to office. Thus emboldened, Micheletti quickly realized it was just a question of running the clock towards the elections of 29 November, after which he would be home safe.

The actions of one senator from the opposition party thus single-handedly changed US policy towards the most critical issue in the Americas in the second half of 2009. However, even after Senator DeMint's initiative, Washington still had a last bargaining chip to reach a modicum of a compromise solution. This would have allowed a minimal concession to regional demands for standing up for democracy and not letting Honduras set a dangerous precedent for putschist forces in the hemisphere. The one outstanding problem for Micheletti and his followers was the need to have US recognition of the 29 November elections, something very much in doubt given the state of emergency being enforced, the human rights violations and the closing of media outlets supporting the Zelaya forces.[34]

To take care of that, incumbent Assistant Secretary of State for Western Hemisphere Affairs Thomas Shannon was dispatched to Honduras to broker a deal between the de facto government and the forces supporting Zelaya.[35] Ensconced in the Brazilian embassy in Tegucigalpa, Zelaya made the mistake of trusting this was a bona fide negotiation, and signed off on a deal by which he recognized the legitimacy of the presidential elections, in exchange for his restitution into power to serve the remainder of his term. This restitution was made contingent upon a vote of the Honduran parliament, on the not unreasonable assumption that having internationally recognized elections was a powerful incentive to doing so. Yet, the deal turned out to be a Faustian pact between the Democratic administration and the

Republican opposition. Back in Washington, Shannon promptly stated that Washington would recognize the 29 November elections no matter what happened with Zelaya, thus ending whatever leverage the United States might have had with Micheletti and his government.

From there on, the comedy turned into farce. The Honduras parliament did not even meet to vote on Zelaya's restitution before the presidential elections. When it did so, in early December, the vote started with a strident PowerPoint presentation on Zelaya's alleged misdeeds, and ended with a predictable vote against restoring him to office. Back in Washington, Senate Republicans lifted the hold on Valenzuela, who was quickly sworn in, and on Shannon. The de facto government of Honduras thus ran the table and got everything it wanted, leading it to boast how through Washington lobbyists and Republican senators they managed to humiliate the Obama Administration, the OAS and most Latin American governments, blocking the reinstatement of Zelaya and thus the undoing of the effects of the coup. In a fitting finale, strongman Roberto Micheletti was appointed a congressman for life.

Explaining the Honduras fiasco

As Casas-Zamora has pointed out, Honduras ended up being a lose-lose proposition for all parties involved, except for those behind the coup.[36] Why did we see this abject failure of the collective defense of democracy enshrined in the inter-American system, one that ended up having such an enormous cost, not least to inter-American relations, on a downward course ever since? This failure is particularly puzzling since Honduras, in the words of the US embassy in Honduras, was such an "open and shut case" that it should have been relatively easy to solve. A number of interpretations have been set forth for this.

The first is what we might call "OAS overzealousness." The argument here is that the hemisphere's premier organization overreacted to Zelaya's ouster on 28 June. By acting too fast, too soon, by suspending Honduras a scarce week after the coup, and by the SG's refusal to meet with Micheletti during his first inspection visit to Tegucigalpa, the OAS sidelined itself from any negotiations to resolve the crisis.[37] In general terms, this reflects one of the key challenges faced by those wanting to defend democracy in the Americas. On the one hand, being a neutral arbiter is important to reverse the situation on the ground once a breakdown of the democratic process has taken place. On the other hand, it is also necessary to send a signal to potential coup makers elsewhere that *golpes* will not be allowed. Sometimes, these dual objectives clash, and the compromises needed to achieve the former may be at odds with the latter.[38]

A second line of argumentation is that the OAS's failure was not so much in what it did after the events of 28 June 2009 in Honduras, but in what it failed to do before that day. The coup was months in the making, which raises the question why the IADC was not invoked much earlier. The OAS General Assembly in San Pedro Sula in early June 2009, and its obliviousness to the impending political crisis in the host nation was already mentioned. Executive sovereignty, a key building block within the OAS architecture, makes it impossible for the organization to intervene in any given country's affairs unless it is formally asked to do so by the government; and when Zelaya invoked the self-help clause of Article 17 IADC, it was too late to stop the escalation of the crisis.[39] Yet, the positive OAS response to Zelaya's request gave some legitimacy to his efforts to carry out the referendum. From the perspective of Zelaya's opponents, the Permanent Council resolution backing the "constitutional and democratic Government of Honduras"[40] was viewed as an instance of clear siding with the executive in its dispute with the congress and the judiciary. This show of support for the president seriously damaged the credibility of the OAS in the eyes of Zelaya's critics and diminished its leverage in dealing with the crisis after 28 June.[41]

A third interpretation relates to the particularities of the country at that specific moment in time. The timing of the crisis, with just five months to go till regular elections, emboldened the de facto government to employ delay tactics to hold out until the elections, counting on the international recognition of the election as a convenient exit from the crisis. Additionally, Honduras found itself at a unique historical moment of populist polarization in which established political institutions and political practices were thrown into upheaval and politics was turned into a battleground. Zelaya was facing a broad "coup coalition" comprising the armed forces, a bipartisan congressional consensus between his own Liberal Party and the National Party, the Supreme Court, the office of the attorney general, the Supreme Electoral Tribunal, and the national human rights ombudsman. The striking features of the crisis, which epitomize the emergence of a new type of coup, were that legislatures and judiciaries had emerged as destabilizing forces against democracy, and that some of the main players defined the events in Honduras as an orderly transfer of power, sanctioned by both the congress and the Supreme Court. Legler argues that the international community whose main concern was to avoid the precedent set by what was broadly seen as an old-fashioned coup did not sufficiently take into account this domestic constellation. International intervention in defense of democracy was unlikely to be successful in the context of an emotionally charged, confrontational atmosphere of populist polarization where the unconstitutional interruption of the democratic order was greeted by significant public approval and the de facto government was determined to run the clock towards the 29 November presidential elections.[42]

A fourth set of interpretations of the rather unsatisfactory outcome of the Honduras crisis focuses on the role of US foreign policy after the coup, i.e. the particular set of reasons for what can only be construed as Washington's erratic behavior and the mixed outcome to which it led. A standard interpretation is that of the "bureaucratic politics model," to which, to some extent, Casas-Zamora subscribes and which has also been used by Whitehead and Nolte to explain the failings of US policy towards Latin America under the Obama Administration.[43] In short, given the vast, sprawling, porous and open nature of the US government and the US political system more generally, and the relatively low priority that Latin America has within it, more often than not it is the case that perfectly legitimate regional policy objectives will fall prey to competing priorities and interests. Moreover, the underlying problem with Latin American policy issues is not so much that they lack significance within the larger scheme of US politics, but that they have *too much* significance, as long as they become absorbed within domestic politics, and thus acquire a different dynamic and imprint. The issue of immigration and that of illegal drugs, to mention but two critical hemispheric issues, are good examples of the degree to which US foreign policy becomes entangled with domestic concerns, which will then overshadow all others.

Another view, which we could call the "ideological politics model," holds that the Honduran crisis simply reflected the ideological blinders with which the United States looks at Latin America today.[44] These would show its obsession with the so-called two Lefts, and the ensuing need not to be seen cozying up to a leader like Zelaya, considered too close to the poster child of Latin America's "bad Left," Venezuela's Hugo Chávez. While this perspective was not predominant at the time of the initial repudiation of the coup, it slowly gained prominence in the course of the seven-month crisis—from 28 June 2009 to 27 January 2010, the date on which Zelaya was allowed to leave the Brazilian embassy in Tegucigalpa for the Dominican Republic. Over time, US policy toward Latin America was outsourced from the executive branch and taken over by the congressional opposition—in this case, the Republican Party. Although not in direct control, the latter set the parameters for it and kept tight reins on it, presumably in exchange for a "live-and-let-live" approach in other foreign policy areas.

Precisely at the moment when the vigorous application of international sanctions was having an effect in Honduras, and the OAS defense of democracy was showing some signs of success, there was a reaction from Republican senators and congressmen, who could not countenance the dislodging of an anti-Chávez regime, however illegitimate its origins. The visit of Senator DeMint to Tegucigalpa to instruct Micheletti not to give in was the first step in that direction. The seemingly inexplicable statement of Assistant Secretary of State for Western Hemisphere Affairs Thomas Shannon (whose appointment as ambassador to Brazil was being held up by DeMint) that Washington would recognize the outcome of the 29 November Honduras presidential elections even if the incumbent regime reneged on its deal to allow Zelaya back as president—thus giving up, with nothing in exchange, Washington's last bargaining chip—was the second, one that opened the doors for a resounding victory by the *golpista* forces.[45]

Three years later, by the time Paraguayan President Fernando Lugo was removed from office in a "soft coup" in June 2012, the State Department reacted with remarkable equanimity: "We call on all Paraguayans to act peacefully, with calm and responsibility, in the spirit of Paraguay's democratic principles [sic]." The boundaries by now had been established, and the defense of democracy had been relegated to the sidelines. The OAS itself, under fire for having acted too assertively in Honduras, was also very cautious in its reaction to the questionable ouster of President Lugo (see Chapter 4).

Conclusion

The Honduran crisis of 2009–10 brought to the fore, like few other instances in the past decade, some of the most significant forces at play in the hemisphere. Though it is tempting to dismiss it by now as an anecdotal occurrence in a small country of marginal significance, this would be a mistake. The state of the defense of democracy in the Americas, the condition of regional cooperation and the health of pan-American multilateralism were all tested and found wanting as the hemisphere grappled with the fallout of Honduran events. That this should have happened under the Obama Administration, the election of which had spurred such high expectations precisely on those fronts, after a difficult decade in US–Latin American relations, was surprising—if not downright disappointing—for many observers. In terms of US policy towards Latin America, the contrast many see between the promising first six months of President Obama's first term and the disappointing rest of his tenure in office is real enough. Strictly speaking, those first six months came to an end on 28 June, with the ouster of President Zelaya in Honduras, which was to unleash a complex chain of events whose consequences remain with us to this day.

One reason Honduras resonated so deeply in Latin America is because it touched two of the driving forces in the region since 1990: the defense of democracy and political cooperation and regionalization. By first coming forward in favor of a negotiated, multilateral solution to the Honduran imbroglio, only to retreat from that approach to impose a unilateral solution that sided fully with the *golpistas*, the Obama Administration broke the confidence that many Latin American governments were developing towards what had seemed a fresh start in Washington.

As Ruggie has pointed out, multilateralism is much more than just another tool in the foreign policy toolbox.[46] It is an expression of a willingness to work with others in the community of nations. It is a signal that one believes in collective action to promote public good, and that states are able to see beyond narrow Hobbesian perspectives. For many, one of President George W. Bush's failings was his unilateralism, which led him to waste the enormous sympathy the United States earned as a result of the 9/11 tragedy.[47] Part of the attractiveness of Obama's candidacy, a man who opposed the Iraq war from the very beginning, was his commitment to multilateralism. Yet, in Honduras, US policy ended up ignoring the multilateral majoritarian position and imposing its own solution.

Benítez Manaut has argued that the outcome of the Honduran crisis was the triumph of realism over principles.[48] We would argue that it was, rather, the triumph of expediency over consistency. At a critical juncture that put to the test what was supposed to be a fresh set of policy concepts on democracy and multilateralism, much more attuned to the new century, they were set aside to be replaced by the knee-jerk reactions of yesteryear, and thus provided a significant setback to the defense of democracy in the Americas.

Notes

1 Michael Shifter, "Obama's Honduras Problem," *Foreign Affairs* Snapshot, 24 August 2009; Peter Hakim, "The Meaning of Honduras," *Revista América Economía*, 27 August 2009.
2 Marcelo Raimundo da Silva, "El Tema de Honduras en Brasil," *Focus Brasil* 1, January 2010, Konrad Adenauer Stiftung; Jorge Heine, "Brasil y la Crisis de Honduras," *El País*, 30 September 2009; Peter Hakim,

"Relaciones EEUU-Brasil: se esperan mas conflictos," *Infolatam*, 21 October 2010.

3 Figures refer to 2009 and were retrieved from World Development Indicators, data.worldbank.org/data-catalog/world-development-indicators.

4 For the historical background in this, see Aníbal Pérez-Liñán, *Presidential Impeachment and the New Political Instability in Latin America* (New York: Cambridge University Press, 2007); see also Arturo Valenzuela, "Latin American Presidencies Interrupted," *Journal of Democracy* 15, no. 4 (2004): 5–19.

5 See Andrew F. Cooper and Thomas Legler, *Intervention Without Intervening? The OAS Defense and Promotion of Democracy in the Americas* (New York: Palgrave Macmillan, 2006); and Thomas Legler, Sharon F. Lean and Dexter S. Boniface, ed., *Promoting Democracy in the Americas* (Baltimore, Md.: Johns Hopkins University Press, 2007).

6 To put things in perspective, when Cuba was suspended from the OAS in 1962, at the height of the Cold War, the vote was split.

7 This is what Thomas Legler has referred to as the "Honduran paradox." See Thomas Legler, "Learning the Hard Way. Defending Democracy in Honduras," *International Journal* 65, no. 3 (2010): 601–18.

8 For a discussion of this arrested development within the broader Central American societal setting, see Edelberto Torres-Rivas, "Las democracias malas de centroamérica. Para entender lo de Honduras, una introducción a Centroamérica," *Nueva Sociedad* 226 (2010): 52–66. For an historical perspective on Honduran political development, see J. Mark Ruhl, "Honduras Unravels," *Journal of Democracy* 21, no. 2 (2010): 93–107, and his "Honduras: Militarism and Democratization in Troubled Waters," in *Repression, Resistance and Democratic Transition in Central America*, ed. Thomas W. Walker and Ariel C. Armony (Wilmington, Del.: Scholarly Resources, 2000), 47–66.

9 For a revealing, first-hand perspective on this polarization process, see Leticia Salomón, "Políticos, empresarios y militares: protagonistas de un golpe anunciado" (mimeo, 29 June 2009), and, by the same author, "El golpe de estado en Honduras: Caracterización, evolución y perspectivas" (mimeo, 3 July 2009).

10 The Liberal Party is a center-right liberal political party. The other main party is the National Party (Partido Nacional de Honduras), a right-wing conservative party.

11 For a profile on Zelaya, see "Manuel Zelaya: empresario conservador que transitó a la izquierda," *Agencia Mexicana de Noticias*, 29 June 2009.

12 For a survey of the crisis, see Peter J. Meyer, *Honduran Political Crisis, June 2009–January 2010*, CRS Report for Congress R41064, 1 February 2010 (Washington, DC: Congressional Research Service), www.fas.org/sgp/crs/row/R41064.pdf.

13 On the constitutional dimension of the Honduras crisis, see Antonio Franceschet and Pablo Policzer, "Constitutions and the Promotion of Democracy in Latin America: Lessons from the 2009 Honduran Crisis," Occasional Papers 1, no. 2 (Calgary: University of Calgary, Latin American Research Centre, 2011), larc.ucalgary.ca/sites/larc.ucalgary.ca/files/merica-Lessons_from_the_2009_Honduran_Crisis.pdf; Detlef Nolte, "Verfassungsänderungen und Verfassungskrise in Honduras in vergleichender Perspektive," *Verfassung und Recht in Übersee* 43, no. 1 (2010): 28–45.

128   *The OAS in action: the case of Honduras*

14 On ALBA, see Josette Altmann Borbón, ed., *ALBA: Una nueva forma de integración regional?* (Buenos Aires, Argentina: Teseo, 2011).

15 The fourth ballot box refers to the fact that in Honduran elections the first such box is for the presidential ballot, the second for the congressional one, and the third for the municipal elections one.

16 The report goes on to list a number of other extant situations in Honduras like a widespread grippe epidemic, the international financial crisis and the growing crime rate, whose neglect would be proof positive of a presidential behavior that would have endangered the rule of law, the country's governance and the democratic system more generally.

17 A comprehensive factual account of the evolution of the Honduran political crisis, the coup against Zelaya, and its aftermath is given in the report prepared by the Truth and Reconciliation Commission: Comisión de la Verdad y la Reconciliación, *Para que los hechos no se repitan: Informe de la Comisión de la Verdad y la Reconciliación* (Tegucigalpa, Honduras: Comisión de la Verdad y la Reconciliación, 2011). The reports by the IACHR and the Human Rights Foundation also provide useful background information on the genesis of the crisis: IACHR, *Honduras: Human Rights and the Coup d'état.* OEA/Ser.L/V/II. Doc. 55 (San José, Costa Rica: Inter-American Commission on Human Rights, 2009); Human Rights Foundation, *The Facts and the Law: Behind the Democratic Crisis of Honduras, 2009* (New York: Human Rights Foundation, 2009).

18 This was admitted by the anti-Zelaya forces in early 2010, upon the inauguration of the Porfirio Lobo administration, as they proceeded to a pro-forma filing of charges for it and a quick pardon, to bury the issue for good.

19 A similar assessment was made by Maxwell A. Cameron, "After the Democratic Charter's First Decade: Achievements, Limitations, and Next Steps," *Latin American Policy* 3, no. 1 (2012): 58–73 (61–62); Kevin Newmeyer, "The Honduran Coup of 2009: Application of the Inter-American Democratic Charter," *Security and Defense Studies Review* 12, no. 1–2 (2011): 177–87; Anika Oettler and Peter Peetz, "Putsch in Honduras: Störfall in der defekten Demokratie," *Internationale Politik und Gesellschaft* no. 1 (2010): 82–95. For a contrary view, see Marcus V. Freitas, "Honduras and the Emergence of a New Latin America," *Latin American Policy* 1, no. 1 (2010): 157–61. The divergent assessment of the Honduran crisis is also reflected in international coup datasets: Powell and Thyne count Honduras 2009 as a coup, whereas Marshall and Marshall classify it as "resignation of executive due to poor performance/loss of authority". See Jonathan M. Powell and Clayton L. Thyne, "Global Instances of Coups from 1950 to 2010: A New Dataset," *Journal of Peace Research* 48, no. 2 (2011): 249–59; Monty G. Marshall and Donna Ramsey Marshall, *Coup d'état Events, 1946–2012. Codebook*, Center for Systemic Peace, 9 April 2013, www.systemicpeace.org/inscr/CSPCoupsCodebook2012.pdf.

20 "TFHO1: Open and Shut: The Case of the Honduran Coup," WikiLeaks cable 09TEGUCIGALPA646, Embassy Tegucigalpa (Honduras), 24 July 2009.

21 This was the first time that Article 17 was explicitly mentioned in a Permanent Council resolution, although according to a report by the Secretariat for Political Affairs of the OAS and a report of the SG, Article 17 had already been invoked by the Bolivian government in 2008 and by the Guatemalan government in May 2009. See OAS, *Tenth Anniversary of the Inter-American*

Democratic Charter: A Hemispheric Commitment to Democracy (Washington, DC: Organization of American States, 2011); *Report of the Secretary General Concerning Compliance with Operative Paragraph 3 of Resolution AG/Res.2480 (XXXIX-O/09) "Promotion and Strengthening of Democracy: Follow-up to the Inter-American Democratic Charter"* (Permanent Council document OEA/Ser.G., CP/doc.4487/10), 4 May 2010.

22 "Situation in Honduras," OAS Permanent Council Resolution 952 (1699/09), 26 June 2009.

23 "Current Situation in Honduras," OAS Permanent Council Resolution 953 (1700/09), 28 June 2009.

24 Ibid.

25 "Resolution on the Political Crisis in Honduras", OAS General Assembly Resolution 1 (XXXVII-E/09), 1 July 2009.

26 "Suspension of the Right of Honduras to Participate in the Organization of American States," OAS General Assembly Resolution 2 (XXXVII-E/09), 4 July 2009.

27 For an initial assessment of the impact of the crisis on regional politics, see Raúl Benítez Manaut, "La crisis de Honduras y el sistema interamericano: el triunfo del realismo sobre los principios," *Foreign Affairs Latinoamérica* 9, no. 4 (2009): 75–84; for later ones, see Raúl Benítez Manaut and Rut Diamint, "La cuestión militar. El golpe de Estado en Honduras como desafío a la democracia y al sistema interamericano," *Nueva Sociedad* 226 (2010): 145–57; Carlos A. Romero, "Las secuelas regionales de la crisis de Honduras," *Nueva Sociedad* 226 (2010): 85–99; Orlando J. Pérez, "La crisis de Honduras y su repercusión regional," in *Anuario 2010 de la Seguridad Regional en América Latina y el Caribe*, ed. Hans Mathieu and Catalina Niño Guarnizo (Bogotá, Colombia: Friedrich Ebert Stiftung en Colombia (Fescol), 2010), 43–57.

28 See Heine, "Brasil y la Crisis de Honduras."

29 The accord envisaged recognizing the legitimacy of the 29 November elections, a congressional vote on Zelaya's return, a government of national unification, a verification commission and a truth commission. See *Acuerdo Tegucigalpa/San José para la reconciliación nacional y el fortalecimiento de la democracia en Honduras*. Diálogo Guaymuras, Tegucigalpa, Honduras, 30 October 2009.

30 For an overview of the bilateral relationship see Peter J. Meyer and Mark P. Sullivan, *Honduran-U.S. Relations*, CRS Report for Congress RL34027, 18 June 2010 (Washington, DC: Congressional Research Service), fpc.state.gov/documents/organization/145602.pdf. For an analysis of US policy towards the crisis, see Kevin Casas-Zamora, "The Honduran Crisis and the Obama Administration," in *Shifting the Balance: Obama and the Americas*, ed. Abraham F. Lowenthal, Theodore J. Piccone and Laurence Whitehead (Washington, DC: Brookings Institution Press, 2011), 114–31. For a more critical assessment, see Alexander Main, "'A New Chapter of Engagement': Obama and the Honduran Coup," *NACLA Report on the Americas* (January–February 2010), 15–21.

31 It is estimated that some 200 metric tons of cocaine went through Honduras in 2009.

32 See Abraham F. Lowenthal, Theodore J. Piccone and Laurence Whitehead, ed., *The Obama Administration and the Americas: Agenda for Change*

(Washington, DC: Brookings Institution Press, 2009); and, by the same editors, *Shifting the Balance: Obama and the Americas* (Washington, DC: Brookings Institution Press, 2011).

33 President Obama himself made a number of pointed comments alluding to the irony of Latin American governments pressing for Washington taking on a more assertive role in solving the Honduran crisis, given their past denunciations on undue US meddling in Latin American affairs.

34 Comisión de la Verdad y la Reconciliación, *Para que los hechos no se repitan.*

35 William Finnegan, "An Old-fashioned Coup: As Elections Loom, can a Deposed Leader Return?" *The New Yorker* 85, 30 November 2009, 38–45.

36 See Casas-Zamora, "The Honduran Crisis and the Obama Administration."

37 Thomas Legler, "The Democratic Charter in Action: Reflections on the Honduran Crisis," *Latin American Policy* 3, no. 1 (2012): 74–87.

38 Legler, "Learning the Hard Way."

39 Legler, "The Democratic Charter in Action."

40 "Situation in Honduras," OAS Permanent Council Resolution 952 (1699/09), 26 June 2009.

41 Legler, "The Democratic Charter in Action."

42 Legler, "Learning the Hard Way."

43 Casas-Zamora, "The Honduran Crisis and the Obama Administration"; Laurence Whitehead and Detlef Nolte, *The Obama Administration and Latin America: A Disappointing First Term?* GIGA Focus International Edition 6 (Hamburg: German Institute of Global and Area Studies, 2012), www.giga-hamburg.de/de/system/files/publications/gf_international_1206.pdf.

44 Main, "'A New Chapter of Engagement'."

45 If anyone thought that, given the questionable circumstances that surrounded the November 2009 elections, the 2013 elections would be much different, they were disappointed. Four activists of the Libre party, newly established by Zelaya, which ran Xiomara Castro, Zelaya's wife, as a presidential candidate, were murdered in the days before and after the 24 November 2013 elections. Although both the OAS and the EU gave the elections—won by Orlando Hernández, the candidate of the National party—the thumbs up, several international observers disagreed, noting many irregularities in the results that gave Hernández 36.9 percent of the vote versus 28.8 percent for Castro (see Nicholas Phillips and Elisabeth Malkin, "Honduras Election Results Challenged," *The New York Times*, 30 November 2013; Mark Weisbrot, "Why the World Should Care about Honduras' Recent Election," *The Guardian*, 3 December 2013). The elections deepened even further the profound cleavages that have marked Honduras since 2009, by no means a minor matter in a country with the dubious distinction of the highest murder rate in the world, 86 per 100,000, and the transit point for some 80 percent of the cocaine brought into the United States; see UNDP, *Informe Regional de Desarrollo Humano 2013–2014: Diagnóstico y Propuestas para América Latina* (New York: United Nations Development Programme, 2013).

46 John Gerard Ruggie, "Multilateralism: The Anatomy of an Institution," *International Organization* 46, no. 3 (1992): 561–98.

47 Key instances include Iraq, the Kyoto Protocol, Guantanamo and actions such as "un-signing" the Rome Statute that had given rise to the International Criminal Court.
48 Benítez Manaut, "La crisis de Honduras y el sistema interamericano."

6 The future of the OAS democratic paradigm

- **The new regional context**
- **Contestations about democracy promotion**
- **Reforming the Inter-American Democratic Charter?**
- **Conclusion**

One of the most significant trends in the Americas over the past three decades has been the reestablishment of democracy and the eradication of military coups. The Honduras coup of June 2009 broke that trend and set a dangerous precedent for the hemisphere. As Thomas Legler has stated, "Honduras presents a microcosm of the ongoing challenges confronting the Inter-American democracy promotion regime."[1] Truth is that the Americas are a very different setting, in terms of its politics and its dynamics, from what they were in 2001 when the IADC was approved. The Left has come to power in many countries in the region, including some of the biggest and most populated ones. After a decade of strong growth, the Latin American economies are in good shape, having paid off much of their debt, and stabilized their accounts. Many new regional entities have come to the fore, some of them excluding the United States and Canada.[2] All of this has meant a rearrangement of inter-American relations. A number of "wedge" issues, including Honduras, Cuba, the Falklands/Malvinas and drug legalization have caused an increased rift between Washington and some of the leading capitals in Latin America. The question of the defense and promotion of democracy is at the core of what these growing differences are all about. A first step in response to the changing regional context would be a reform of the IADC. It is often argued that the document's weaknesses stand in the way of more effective action by the OAS and/or its member states in preventive actions to forestall democratic breakdowns, in coping with authoritarian regressions and in considering different variants of democracy as it contends with a quickly changing hemisphere.[3]

This chapter analyzes the newly emerging situation in the Western hemisphere and assesses its implication for the defense of democracy regime. The first section examines the changes leading to a less hospitable environment for collective efforts to promote and defend democracy: the reshuffling of the regional structure of power characterized by a decreasing Latin American dependence on the United States and a rise of new regional actors; the surge of leftist governments in the region and ensuing alternative visions to market economy and representative democracy; the relative decline of US power and the changed attitude of the United States toward its Southern neighborhood; and the unraveling of hemispheric regionalism and the foundation of new regional projects. Against this backdrop, the second section highlights the contestations about democracy promotion that surfaced during the first attempts of using the IADC in reaction to democratic crises. How the challenges to the regional democratic consensus should be addressed is a subject currently under discussion in the OAS. The third section thus reviews the debates around the application and potential reform of the IADC.

The new regional context

What is taking place in the Americas is a complex interplay between foreign policy, regionalism and global presence. The process has torn asunder the old and somewhat frayed fabric of the inter-American system, built around the hub of a global superpower and a large number of weak, dependent states on the periphery. Hemispheric institutions had enjoyed a resurrection in the immediate post-Cold War period. The 1990s were characterized by multilateralism and a convergence of Latin American and US foreign policy preferences. Regional actors unanimously pushed for the renewal of the inter-American system, a revision of the concept of security towards a more cooperative version, and a commitment to the defense of democracy. A symbol of the new multilateral approach in the region was the First Summit of the Americas, convened in 1994 in Miami. As if in a seamless web, the objective of strengthening democracy fell neatly together with a new grand framework for economic governance in the Americas, the establishment of the FTAA, and with the new dogma of domestic governance, the Washington Consensus. Somewhat amazingly, all governments in the Americas, with the single exception of Cuba, found themselves on the same page on this.

Yet, this extraordinary convergence on so many fronts of the hemispheric agenda did not last long. The 9/11 terrorist attacks were a watershed event that impelled a shift in US foreign policy and directed its attention to other world regions. From the perspective of its OAS associates, Washington's new focus on the "War on Terror" was likened to its obsession with the fight against communism during the Cold War and was thus perceived as a reversion from multilateralism to unilateralism.[4] In the face of current challenges, the hemispheric scenario is shaped by the many more possibilities for autonomous international behavior afforded by the post-Cold War environment; the rise of the emerging economies like those of the BRICS countries (Brazil, Russia, India, China, South Africa); the much more assertive international role taken on by a newly empowered and economically stronger Latin America; the decline of US power, exemplified in the 2008–09 financial crisis, as well as ideological fragmentation within the hemisphere. Plagued by anachronisms like the Inter-American Treaty of Reciprocal Assistance of 1947, and affected by considerable organizational inertia, the OAS finds it difficult to adapt to such a new environment. One result of this has been the proliferation of a wide variety of regional and sub-regional bodies, often with seemingly overlapping mandates.

Latin America's new assertiveness

Latin America is shifting from a marginal towards an increasingly assertive role in international affairs. Latin American states have started to liberate themselves from traditional North American and European interference and to reinforce their Latin American or South American identity. Brazil as one of the BRICS is a regional power with global aspirations, while states like Argentina, Chile, Mexico and Venezuela become "secondary regional powers." As Gardini has observed, this new regionalism and the foreign policies it reflects are the product of a unique mix of rhetoric and pragmatism, of ideology and shrewd assessment of the national interest.[5] Though complex and multifaceted, they entail a proactive engagement in world affairs that is very different from the timidity of the past.[6]

The projection of Brazil within the concert of nations and its participation in international decision making is a main objective of Brazilian foreign policy. For a long time, Brazil portrayed itself as the dynamic "country of the future," but this rhetoric was not taken seriously by other major players. Only recently, in the face of Brazil's economic success and more assertive diplomacy, has the country been perceived as an emerging nation in the new international scenery.[7] During President Luiz Inácio Lula da Silva's mandate (2003–10) Brazil's foreign policy changed significantly towards a proactive role in its own neighborhood and beyond, based on two goals: regional integration and multilateralism.[8] The most important step was Brazil's proposal to create a Community of South American Nations, turned into the UNASUR in 2008, and to equip this organization with the South American Defense Council.[9]

Brazil has taken further steps to make its appearance on the global stage, such as its initiatives to found the G-20 and to strengthen South-South relations by the establishment of the IBSA Dialogue Forum (India, Brazil, South Africa) and the BRICS association. Other players in the region have also entered into extra-regional partnerships. China's influence in the region is growing. Chile, Peru and Costa Rica have signed bilateral free trade agreements with China, and Chile long ago established special links to Asia with its membership in the Asia-Pacific Economic Cooperation (APEC). The Pacific Alliance was founded in 2012 by Chile, Colombia, Peru and Mexico in order to advance free trade with a clear orientation toward Asia. In the new century, the region is adapting to a changing international environment, in which the balance of power shifts from North to South, from a unipolar to a multipolar system, and from a hegemonic to a post-hegemonic one.[10] This development not only results from economic growth in Latin America and the diminishing dependence on the United States. It is also an expression of a major breakdown in the political trust extant between Latin American governments and their US counterpart. For many, the Honduras crisis in 2009 is crucial as it left Latin American governments with the impression that the Obama Administration was defecting from the hemispheric consensus on what democracy is and how it should be defended.

A second reason for the weakening of pan-Americanism is the fact that left-wing parties and candidates have flourished in the region. During the 1990s, the Cold War and socialism were over and forgotten, and capitalism and liberal democracy were in. Yet, beginning in the late 1990s, things changed and the so-called "pink tide" swept Latin America. Some observers interpreted the pink tide as a swelling of the political "Left" (but in diluted form, hence the label "pink" instead of the more radical "red"), others disparaged it as a form of "populism."[11] It was an expression of discontent of large segments of Latin American society with neoliberalism, which had failed to fulfill its promise of enhancing mass prosperity and had exacerbated longstanding problems such as precarious employment.

Hugo Chávez, a military figure who had only years before taken part in an unsuccessful coup, won the Venezuelan presidential election of 1998. Thanks to rising petroleum prices and increasing oil revenues, he launched social programs designed to meet the needs of the poor. With the passage of time he asserted increasingly authoritarian control over the country's political apparatus and his discourse became more and more radical—anti-establishment, anti-globalization, and anti-American. He announced his intention to create "twenty-first-century socialism" and forged a close alliance with Cuba's Fidel Castro. In the following decade, presidents who identify themselves and are widely seen as part of the Left have been elected in Argentina, Bolivia, Brazil, Chile, Ecuador, El Salvador, Guatemala, Nicaragua, Paraguay, and Uruguay. The more radical of these leftist governments that were to become close allies of Chávez were those of Evo Morales, an indigenous leader of rural coca leaf farmers, elected president of Bolivia in 2005, Rafael Correa of Ecuador, a Left-wing economist, and Daniel Ortega, former leader of the revolutionary Sandinista regime in Nicaragua, both elected in 2006.

The pink tide had several implications for US–Latin American relations as well as for hemispheric democracy promotion. First, the depth and range of anti-American feeling showed that the United States had lost virtually all of its "soft power" in Latin America. Second, this trend demolished one of the implicit assumptions of US policy making, the idea that democratically elected leaders would automatically become allies of the United States. The pink tide meant that the United States had to face persistent criticism from leaders representing popular opinion in their countries—and because they were elected, Washington's hands were tied. Third, the pink tide mirrored profound political divisions between Left and Right in Latin America, meaning that the region would no longer unanimously follow US leadership. Fourth, the Left turn led to the emergence of conceptions of democracy that potentially undermine the hemispheric consensus achieved in the field of democracy promotion. Already in the preparatory phase of the IADC, the Chávez government expressed its reservations concerning the concept of representative democracy.[12] Thus, the pink tide reflects an increasing ideological distance of much of Latin America from the models of the 1990s. Liberal ideological content and discourses associated with free markets and representative democracy are challenged by alternative economic projects and direct, participatory and plebiscitary democratic experiments.[13] The continent-wide FTAA, scheduled to come into effect in 2005, was one casualty of these changes. It never managed to overcome the resistance it elicited in the changed environment of the new century.[14]

The United States and its Latin American policy

It is a commonly held view that following the 2001 terrorist attacks, the United States disengaged from Latin America. When George W. Bush's "War on Terror" gained ground, US foreign policy focused on the wars in Afghanistan and Iraq and there was thus a widespread perception of an attention deficit toward Latin America. Others see US passivity and disinterest in the region as beginning after Latin America rejected the US proposal for a continent-wide FTAA at the Fourth Summit of the Americas in Mar del Plata, Argentina, in 2005. During the George W. Bush Administration US–Latin American relations reached what many considered to be an all-time low.[15]

The election of President Barack Obama changed this for a time.[16] In 2007, only 39 percent of Latin Americans considered that the United States treated their countries with respect. By 2009, this figure was up to 63 percent. This new perception held up across the region, even in countries like Argentina, where positive responses to this question went up from 13 percent in 2007 to 43 percent in 2009.[17] Obama's program proposed re-engaging Latin American countries as partners and sovereign nations. New thinking on critical issues such as the illicit drug trade and Cuba was mooted. Support for the development—as opposed to the security—side of US policy as well as a restructuring of trade agreements were also promised. Obama's message of "Hope and Change" percolated not only to Latin American public opinion. It also reached the US foreign policy community. A flurry of reports from some of the leading US think tanks proffered advice on how to push the "reset" button in US–Latin American relations.[18]

Despite a promising start during the first six months of 2009, a case can be made that inter-American relations continued to slide on a steadily downhill path. Seldom have diplomatic relations between Washington and Latin America been so frayed.[19] Obama waited three years into his term before touring Latin America on a diplomatic mission, intentionally bypassing countries aligned with Venezuela's Chávez. Meanwhile, the position of US Assistant Secretary of State for Western Hemisphere Affairs was vacant for nearly eight months during 2011 and 2012. The Sixth Summit of the Americas, held in Cartagena, Colombia, in April 2012, was one of the least productive in the history of the Summit of the Americas.[20] It looked as if Obama, distracted by domestic concerns and other foreign policy issues, continued to ignore Latin America.

Yet, this perception betrays a misunderstanding of the dynamics of US policy. In fact, there is no withdrawal of the United States from the Americas. US Secretary of State Hillary Clinton visited more countries in the Western hemisphere than any of her predecessors. As Tokatlian has pointed out, in the midst of all of this Latin American growth, international assertiveness, diversification of markets and of diplomatic relations, the United States has continued to expand its presence in the region on many fronts.[21] This is particularly so for the region's "northern half" (i.e. Mexico, Central America and the Caribbean), but also holds for parts of South America. After the failure of the FTAA, smaller-scale free trade agreements such as the Dominican Republic-Central America-United States Free Trade Agreement (CAFTA-DR), plus bilateral agreements with Colombia, Panama and Peru have been signed, and in 2012, US transnational corporations accounted for 24 percent of FDI in Latin America.[22] Something similar can be said about the security front. A long list of initiatives like the Plan Colombia, the Plan Mérida and the Caribbean Basin Security Initiative, the 2008 re-launching of the US Fourth Fleet, and the massive US training programs of Latin American military personnel provide evidence that the United States renewed its military presence in Latin America.[23] Much of this is justified in terms of the so-called "new threats"—i.e. the drug trade, international organized crime, gang warfare, and illegal migration—which are more manifest and apparent to the United States in the region's northern tier than in South America.

The problem, then, is not one of lack of attention on the part of Washington towards Latin America and the Caribbean. The issue, rather, is one of a gap between Latin America's increased international role and autonomy in the conduct of its international affairs and Washington's incapacity to recognize the region as a partner.[24] With the rise of the Left in Latin America and the emergence of a new regionalism there in the last decade, the main obstacle for moving forward on a common hemispheric agenda is the unwillingness of Washington to take that regionalism seriously, thus contributing to what Julia Buxton has referred to as "a chasm in regional relations."[25] In substance, the idea that the policy perspectives emanating from the region deserve careful consideration, and even perhaps a revision of the established US policy stance on the matter, continues to be quite alien to the standard approach followed by the State Department and other agencies responsible for US policy toward Latin America.[26] This is a major obstacle to the development of a truly hemispheric agenda, including on items as sensitive as democracy promotion.

Towards a new regionalism

These changes in regional relations entail consequences for regional organizations, which, in Chapter 1 of this volume, were identified as a new actor in the external promotion and defense of democracy. In the Americas, the consequences were twofold. On the one hand, hemispheric meetings have developed into fields of contestation; on the other hand, disaffection with hemispheric institutions has triggered the foundation of new regional cooperation and integration schemes.

The clash between dwindling US influence on regional politics and Latin America's growing autonomy in the conduct of its international affairs has become manifest in the OAS, an entity known in the past for epitomizing the acquiescence and subordination of Latin American states to the dictates of Washington. Few issues illustrate the divergence between the OAS as an enforcer of US policy and as a stand-alone multilateral international organization as dramatically as Cuba's exclusion from the OAS. Ever since its suspension from the organization in 1962, this has been a sore point for a number of Latin American countries. After the end of the Cold War, the notion that Cuba could constitute any sort of threat to hemispheric peace became even more questionable than before. As a result of enormous pressures from a majority of member states, the lifting of Cuba's suspension was put on the agenda of the OAS General Assembly held in San Pedro Sula, Honduras, in early June 2009, only a few weeks before the coup that deposed Honduran President Zelaya.[27] While this proposal had the near-unanimous support of Latin American and Caribbean member states, the United States was adamantly opposed, for transparently domestic political reasons: i.e. the Miami Cubans. Finally, the compromise solution was to end Cuba's suspension from the OAS, but without an actual reinstatement. The understanding was that the latter would require a formal request on the part of the Cuban government, one that was unlikely to be forthcoming.

Although the issue was resolved more or less to the satisfaction of all parties, it left deep scars. On the one hand, it has meant that even the apex body of pan-Americanism, the OAS, has come to reflect this more autonomous and independent Latin America. It became very clear that the US government could no longer impose its will in the inter-American institutions. On the other hand, this generated adverse reactions within the United States from a variety of sectors used to having the OAS as an enforcer of US policy rather than as a stand-alone regional organization with its own dynamics.[28] Within the Obama Administration, there was a widespread feeling that an occasional Latin American majority had "hijacked" the OAS General Assembly for its own purposes, without giving due consideration to US interests. As a result, a decision was made to lower the profile of the OAS and of the US role within it. US legislators and high-ranking State Department officials complain that the OAS is useless because it is dominated by anti-American populist governments.[29] That OAS General Assembly was the first and last attended by Secretary of State Hillary Clinton and from that moment onwards the OAS would be dealt with only in a perfunctory manner. The failure of the 2012 Summit of the Americas, where Cuba's participation once again emerged as a bone of contention, highlighted the lack of support to the United States among leaders in the hemisphere and the diminishing leverage of the OAS. The net outcome of all this was that, paradoxically, while complaining about the emergence of new regional bodies that excluded the United States, Washington proceeded to weaken the most established and ancient pan-American body, the OAS, based in Washington, DC, largely funded by the US government and with a long tradition of being more than amenable to the priorities of US foreign policy.

At the same time, Latin American disaffection with hemispheric institutions led to the rise of a number of regional bodies that expressly exclude the United States. For a long time, the OAS and sub-regional organizations such as the CAN and MERCOSUR had clearly distinct tasks, with the first being the prime institution in the Western hemisphere to deal with security and other political matters, while the latter focused on trade. Yet, the more recently created organizations, such as ALBA, UNASUR, CELAC, and the Pacific Alliance were launched, among other reasons, to challenge the role of the OAS in the Americas. For Latin American leaders, regional and sub-regional advances in cooperation that assert their distinct Latin American or South American identity have become not the exception, but the rule.

Forming a new institution can be a means to balance against or exclude a dominant power from the region. As Acharya argues, power matters for the definition of regions, but local responses to power may matter even more in the construction of regional orders. How regions resist and/or socialize powers is at least as important as how powers create and manage regions.[30] Minor powers in a region tend to respond by resistance against the regional organization dominated by the powerful state, using strategies of exclusion (i.e. the formation of a new regional institution without the dominant power), or strategies of socialization and binding. The presence of a regional power allows for different responses, such as normative dissent (i.e. opposition to the dominant state's diplomacy), the creation of new spheres of influence by the regional power, and regional rivalry between the regional power and the existing dominant power. Creating an alternative sphere of influence does not necessarily require open opposition to the dominant power and the international organization supported by it, but could also be accomplished by establishing an organization perceived as subsidiary.[31]

Foreign policy leadership is built on individual initiative and on harnessing regional synergies. Brazil views the dominance of the United States in the inter-American system as well as the continuing US presence in some South American countries as an undue interference in the region. UNASUR and the South American Defense Council are therefore based on the idea that the region should emphasize its South American identity and develop a more autonomous agenda. Venezuela's regional project ALBA was founded in 2004. It is designed as the solidarity-based integration alternative to the FTAA, one to which it channels part of its petrodollars.[32] Mexico, frustrated by a stagnant North American Free Trade Agreement (NAFTA), proposed the creation of CELAC as the apex regional body.

These sub-regional organizations increasingly challenge the OAS in its traditional fields of activity. By now, almost all of them have issued a statement endorsing democracy; many have gone further by adopting a declaration or treaty stipulating full-fledged defense of democracy provisions (see Table 6.1). While the OAS had from the very beginning endorsed the principle of representative democracy, MERCOSUR was in its original design an economic integration scheme aiming at the creation of a common market.[33] Democracy was not even mentioned at the time that the founding Treaty of Asunción (1991) was signed, and only came back on the agenda in the face of the democratic crisis in Paraguay in 1996, when the presidents reacted swiftly by issuing a

Table 6.1 Documents on democracy by Latin American regional organizations

Organization	Date	Document
CAN	1998	Presidential Declaration on Democratic Commitment
	2000	Additional protocol to the Cartagena Agreement: "Commitment of the Andean Community to Democracy"
MERCOSUR	1996	Presidential Declaration on Democratic Commitment
	1998	Ushuaia Protocol
	2011	Montevideo Protocol ("Ushuaia II")
UNASUR	2010	Protocol on Commitment to Democracy
CELAC	2011	Special Declaration on the Defense of Democracy and the Constitutional Order

Source: Authors' elaboration.

"Presidential Declaration on Democratic Commitment" which stipulated a number of possibilities to sanction a state whose democratic order has been altered or interrupted by force. Two years later, the idea of defending democracy was turned into a legally binding document with the Protocol of Ushuaia. In 2011, MERCOSUR issued an updated and expanded version, the Protocol of Montevideo, also referred to as Ushuaia II.

The CAN adhered to democracy already in its founding treaty, the Cartagena Agreement of 1969, as well as in later agreements. However, only in 1998 did a "Presidential Declaration on Democratic Commitment" formulate for the first time the idea to establish democracy as a prerequisite for participation in the integration process and to create provisions to defend democracy in times of crisis. In 2000, an additional protocol to the Cartagena Agreement, "Commitment of the Andean Community to Democracy," adopted a number of instruments to react to interruptions of the democratic order in a member state.

The defense of democracy had been a priority of the initial South American summits that preceded the creation of UNASUR, but the issue lost salience in the mid-2000s. UNASUR's 2008 Constitutive Treaty includes only a very brief mention of strengthening democracy.[34] The main interest driving the creation of UNASUR at that time was sector cooperation, especially in the area of infrastructure and physical integration. A few months later, however, the Bolivian crisis—when calls for secession from the resource-rich eastern departments escalated into violence—forced UNASUR to take action on matters related to the defense of democracy. In September 2010, UNASUR was again compelled to react when a police mutiny in Ecuador appeared to threaten the incumbent President Rafael Correa. During the next UNASUR summit in November 2010, the "Additional Protocol to the Constitutive Treaty of UNASUR on Commitment to Democracy" was adopted. CELAC followed suit and issued a "Special Declaration on the Defense of Democracy and the Constitutional Order" in 2011, just one year after its foundation. These newly created provisions clearly adapt elements of the OAS defense of democracy regime. MERCOSUR and UNASUR partly go beyond the IADC, by setting up a more comprehensive toolkit of measures to sanction constitutional interruptions— such as closing the borders, interrupting trade relations, or promoting the suspension from other international organizations.[35] Yet, there is not much experience in using those provisions so far. In the case of Paraguay in 2012, the only case to date where MERCOSUR and UNASUR activated their most recent instruments, the sanction least costly for the adopters—suspension of the country from the activities of the organization—was used. In comparison to the OAS, the subregional organizations do not dispose of any organizational infrastructure to observe, monitor, follow up, and give recommendations during or after a democratic crisis.[36]

Contestations about democracy promotion

As has been discussed in earlier chapters, mechanisms for the defense and promotion of democracy in the Americas have been located primarily at the OAS.[37] For once, there was a convergence between Washington and the Latin American governments concerning the commitment to democracy in the hemisphere. The OAS was ideally placed to go about the task of standing up for the democratic cause and doing the needful when it was imperiled, undertaking "intervention without intervening," as Cooper and Legler put it.[38] These efforts culminated in the approval of the IADC in Lima in September 2001. Since then, however, the gap between regional priorities and those of the United States has steadily widened, and agreements on a wide range of questions, let alone one as sensitive as democracy promotion, have become problematic. US credibility in the region is in crisis, especially on the democracy front.[39] Political will for collective action in the promotion and defense of democracy in all but the most obvious cases of democratic rupture is waning.

The George W. Bush Administration on various occasions put into jeopardy the IADC consensus by withholding support from elected leaders it disliked. This became visible already during the first application of the IADC's Chapter IV provisions. In Venezuela, one of America's main oil suppliers, the Bush Administration in stark contrast to most of the rest of the Americas refused to treat the overthrow of Chávez during the April 2002 crisis as a *coup d'état*. While Latin American leaders almost unanimously condemned the coup (quickly reversed), US government representatives ruled that Chávez had provoked his own downfall. Senior officials had met several times with key Venezuelan opposition figures in the months prior to the coup. While the Bush Administration had many reasons for wanting to remove the Chávez government, the apparent US support for the coup was at odds with its stature as a promoter and signatory of the IADC.[40] According to Peter Hakim, the US refusal to recognize this as a clear violation of Venezuela's democratic order was one of the "important things that drove a nail into the heart of the democratic charter."[41]

Likewise, for the case of Aristide in Haiti in 2004, Washington did nothing to prevent his ouster when it allowed the opposition to take an inflexible position over the course of the internationally led mediation process that sought to resolve the political crisis. At the 2005 OAS General Assembly in Fort Lauderdale, tensions flared up when the US delegation proposed to establish a preventative mechanism for safeguarding democracy in Latin America, to be activated by the civil society of a threatened democracy. Against the backdrop of the Venezuelan experience, member states suspected this to be a move to grant the United States a tool to target governments it disliked.[42]

The Honduran *coup d'état* of 2009 was a point of culmination where, under pressure from a single opposition senator, the United States ended up supporting the coup makers against the overwhelming majority of Latin American governments (see Chapter 5). There are by now divergent assessments of the denouement to the Honduran drama. With hindsight, some say that the crisis was ultimately well managed and that the November 2009 elections presented a convenient exit in compliance with constitutional provisions. Others consider the US posture of unconditional acceptance of the elections (and hence the removal of Zelaya as *fait accompli*) a defection from the democratic consensus. In any case, the reneging of the Obama Administration on its commitment to support the return of Zelaya to the presidency led to disaffection among many Latin American leaders who were following the crisis.[43] Brazil, which had strongly defended the democratically elected Zelaya administration, was especially offended. US–Brazilian relations have since been characterized by multiple disagreements over global and regional issues.[44]

The strong demand to permit the unconditional return of Cuba as a member of the OAS—despite it not meeting the democratic criteria of the OAS Charter and the IADC—also had its implications for the regional democratic consensus. The gist of the Latin American position was that the United States' extreme policies of ostracizing Cuba for it being a communist threat to the region had become obsolete with the end of the Cold War. In turn, according to the dominant Washington perspective, if the illegal Micheletti government in Honduras, which replaced Zelaya's government after his ouster, was correctly suspended from the OAS, it stands to reason that the Cuban dictatorship would remain suspended from the OAS until it complies with the organization's principles. The exercise of democracy and protection of human rights are a precondition for participation in the inter-American system. If the IADC is ignored in the case of Cuba, it would be irremediably devalued and consigned to irrelevance.[45]

With the emergence of new regional actors that explicitly pursue a strategy of distancing from the OAS, there are also first indications of a competition between those new regional organizations and the OAS in the resolution of democratic crises. For example, it has been argued that UNASUR was much more successful than the OAS in acting as a crisis manager and mediator to prevent democratic breakdowns in Bolivia in 2008 and Ecuador in 2010.[46] When the Paraguayan congress impeached the leftist President Fernando Lugo on 16 June 2012, the OAS as a hemispheric organization and its South American counterparts came to divergent conclusions. UNASUR and MERCOSUR interpreted the express impeachment procedure as a rupture of the democratic order and decided to suspend Paraguay but without applying sanctions.[47] In turn, the OAS could not find a consistent position as to whether basic democratic principles and the Paraguayan constitution had been disregarded. Therefore, the IADC was not invoked. The US government backed this decision. Kevin Casas-Zamora suggests that a more cautious approach was pursued as a result of the lessons learnt from the Honduran crisis. The fact that the SG went to Paraguay shortly after the impeachment and delivered a report on the political events that was widely received as being very balanced was "a very conscious attempt not to burn bridges with some of the actors in the dispute."[48]

These examples indicate that the meaning of democracy and its defense in times of crisis are increasingly contested among OAS member states. As Schnably pointed out, assertions about the necessity of constitutional government cannot themselves tell us what the content of constitutionalism should be. Even the limited concern with maintaining continuity of constitutional government remains open to manipulation.[49] The promise of greater enforcement of democratic norms through the direct involvement of states in the diplomatic travails of the OAS Permanent Council and the General Assembly is jeopardized to some extent by governments' reluctance to protect elected incumbents they see as adversaries—and to be lenient towards democratic decline under like-minded governments. On the one hand, cases like Venezuela in 2002, Haiti in 2004, Honduras in 2009 and Paraguay in 2012 are cited as precedents for a US doctrine on failed elected leaders, whereby presidents whom Washington finds objectionable are allowed to fall with the hope that more amenable replacements will take their place.[50] On the other hand, due to the new strength of the Left in the region, Latin American leaders have likewise exhibited a biased assessment of democratic crises. Outright attacks on Left-wing governments are likely to be targeted within the defense of democracy framework, whereas slow-motion democratic decline under leftist regimes is widely tolerated.

Reforming the Inter-American Democratic Charter?

The flaws of OAS responses to the first crisis situations after its adoption underscored what many see as a longstanding OAS weakness to act decisively in such circumstances. Thus, suggestions for implementation of the IADC were mooted early on. The Carter Center began an initiative in 2004 to promote greater awareness and more constructive use of the IADC and formed a nongovernmental group of Friends of the Inter-American Democratic Charter.[51] Within the OAS proper, in the lead-up to the General Assembly session in Fort Lauderdale (2005) and on the fifth anniversary of signature of the IADC (2006), several member countries indicated the need for mechanisms for periodic evaluation of the status and quality of democracies in the hemisphere. As mentioned before, a reform proposal was brought forward during the 2005 General Assembly. The Bush Administration suggested establishing a preventative mechanism which could be activated on the initiative of the civil society of a threatened democracy and would thus allow for a more continuous monitoring of potential challenges to democracy.[52]

In the end, the member states rejected the US proposal and enjoined SG Insulza to submit a report to the Permanent Council on how the IADC had been implemented since its entry into force and to make suggestions concerning possible improvements.[53] The report was presented in April 2007,[54] and was followed by two updated reports in 2010 and 2011.[55] Still in 2007, the SG shared the main insights from his first report while delivering a lecture during a meeting of the IAJC.[56] His remarks prompted the IAJC to conduct its own investigation on the IADC. The outcome was a comprehensive document titled "Follow-up on the Application of the Inter-American Democratic Charter," which gives a summary of the evolution of the principle of democracy up to the IADC and discusses the legal status of the IADC and the role of the IAJC in protecting democracy in the Americas. Furthermore, the report analyzes the limitations of the IADC mentioned in the SG's 2007 report and comments on the solutions so far proposed.[57] On the occasion of the tenth anniversary of the IADC, the Permanent Council—mandated by the General Assembly to organize a dialogue on the effectiveness of the implementation of the IADC[58]—discussed the different sections of the democratic charter during a series of five meetings between May and September 2011, as documented by a final report.[59]

In the course of the discussion process it became clear that when the IADC has been put to a test in crisis situations, it has revealed limitations as to its legal, operational, and preventive scope. Most of the reports issued by the various OAS organs identified the following core problems:[60]

- The tension between the principle of non-intervention and the possibility of protecting democracy through collective mechanisms;
- The restricted access for those seeking to invoke the IADC when they consider democratic institutions to be threatened or to have been undermined;
- A lack of precision in the criteria for defining when and to what extent a country's democratic institutions have been altered, when the OAS is faced with an unconstitutional alteration or interruption of the democratic order; and
- The necessity to improve prevention in order to obtain information about potential democratic breakdowns and/or backsliding before they occur.

A number of solutions were proposed in order to address those limitations, some of which would require amendments to the text of the IADC, while for others a more effective usage of the given instruments would suffice.[61] The first problem—the obvious contradiction between the principle of non-intervention and the possibility of collective action in the face of a specific situation in a member country—reflects an inherent tension at the heart of the organization. To reconcile the language of non-intervention with Chapter IV of the IADC, which provides for means of collective action when a clearly "internal" matter threatens or interrupts the democratic process, the answer could be in Article 1 of the IADC, which declares that democracy is a right of the peoples and an obligation of governments. Hence, those who illegitimately alter the democratic order are those who threaten to subjugate the sovereignty of the people, not the OAS acting in defense of that right.[62] In order to enhance the authority of the IADC and to commit and compel member states to comply with its provisions, it has been suggested to convert the IADC into a legally binding document.[63]

The second major point of criticism is the fact that no branch of government other than the executive can activate the IADC to prevent a breakdown of democracy; much less can civil society organizations do so. The OAS is permitted to do only what the government of the interested member state consents to or requests. Especially if the executive itself is threatening democratic institutions (in the judgment of the other branches), it is unlikely to demand the IADC's application. Its actions can be blocked only by the Permanent Council once an unequivocal alteration of the democratic order has occurred. The solution proposed by the SG's reports was that "government" should be understood as referring to all the branches of state rather than only the executive. Permitting any branch of government to call attention to situations in their countries in which the democratic political institutional process might be imperiled would enable the General Secretariat to take preventive action before a crisis erupts. Under the impression of the failure of the OAS to intervene decisively in the course of events in the Honduran crisis, a more proactive role of the SG has additionally been advocated. Recent statements from OAS officials suggest giving the SG greater latitude to take action, activate preventive diplomacy mechanisms without prior consent of the government concerned, and find intermediate options to not have to resort to immediate suspension of the offending state.[64] Yet, during the dialogue process conducted by the Permanent Council in 2011 no consensus on these proposals could be reached.[65] While the state-centric multilateralism based on "executive sovereignty" practiced by the OAS is under pressure to become more inclusive and allow for non-state actors to play a role in the protection of democracy, the government representatives who form the Permanent Council and the General Assembly have refused to support any reforms that could undermine their authority.[66]

The problem of "vagueness" in determining when and to what extent a country's democratic institutions have been altered has sparked a number of initiatives outside the OAS—such as the attempts by the Carter Center to propose a definition of the concept of "unconstitutional alteration or interruption" of the democratic order (see Chapter 3). Certainly under the impression of this debate, the SG's 2007 report recommended to reach a formal political consensus, through a resolution of the General Assembly, on what situations may be identified as serious disruptions or interruptions of the democratic process.[67]

Having said that, a case was also made that the "graduated response" component makes it possible for the Secretariat and the Permanent Council to analyze politically the severity of the situation and develop responses consistent with the level of the crisis in order to restore the integrity of democratic institutions or prevent their breakdown. Following this point of view, the determination of whether there is an alteration that seriously impairs the democratic order requires political judgment and cannot be resolved *a priori* by establishing some arbitrary, supposedly objective criteria.[68] A juridical perspective emphasizes that Articles 3 and 4 of the IADC already offer a solution to the definitional problems. As the IAJC has argued, the situations described in Chapter IV of the IADC—risks to the democratic political institutional process or to the legitimate exercise of power (Art. 17), situations that might affect the development of the democratic political institutional process or the legitimate exercise of power (Art. 18), a breakdown of the democratic order (Art. 19 and 21), and an alteration to the constitutional regime that seriously affects democratic order (Art. 19 and 20)—must be assessed in terms of whether the essential elements of representative democracy (Art. 3) and the fundamental components of its exercise (Art. 4) are still intact and in force.[69] Yet, during the Permanent Council's deliberations in 2011, no common ground could be reached between those who demand a more precise definition of "alteration of the constitutional regime" and those who opt for an interpretation on a case-by-case basis.[70]

Another frequent query is that Chapter IV applies only in cases of democratic crisis or the immediate threat of a crisis and that it would be desirable to strengthen crisis-prevention mechanisms. A reform would entail the creation of semi-autonomous units designed to provide early-warning systems about potential democratic breakdowns and/or backsliding, as well as mechanisms to intervene to forestall any such occurrences. Yet, as the contention at the 2005 General Assembly showed, the political viability of including any such pillar in the IADC was tested and found wanting. In his 2007 report, the SG therefore emphasized the need to look beyond the democratic charter and outlined several alternative pathways to improve prevention without amending the IADC.[71] He suggested resorting to existing mechanisms such as the reports of the IACHR or the ex-post evaluations of electoral processes and systems conducted by the Secretariat for Political Affairs to evaluate the different traits of democracy covered in the IADC.

Given that a separate high-profile body modeled on the IACHR and tasked with a periodic evaluation of the quality of democracies did not seem feasible at the time, the SG decided to conduct an internal monitoring process and expand the institutional capacity of the General Secretariat to identify situations that could affect democratic processes in the region. Since then, the Secretariat for Political Affairs has developed a methodology for political analysis called the Political Analysis and Multiple Scenarios System,[72] which uses a combination of qualitative and quantitative tools to systematize political analysis and forecast different scenarios for the countries of the region. The Political Analysis and Scenarios Section[73] of the Department of Democratic Sustainability and Special Missions hires political analysts who follow the countries of the region. They identify potential risk factors for democratic stability and closely monitor the political situation in select countries whose democratic system passes through turbulence. The section has intentionally kept very low profile and does not disclose which countries' political trajectory is being monitored. The information produced is not widely disseminated, but destined for internal consumption by the authorities of the General Secretariat only.[74] Thus, a constant monitoring of states whose democratic stability is considered to be in danger is only possible unofficially. Nevertheless, the debate continues on whether to go further and establish an official monitoring body and early-warning system to produce periodic reports on the state of democracy in the region and to identify critical situations. Among the proposals considered is the idea to create a special designate—called special envoy, special rapporteur, high commissioner, or ombudsman—to perform preventive assignments.[75]

Apart from proposals designed to remedy the main weaknesses outlined above, additional desiderata in the defense of democracy regime were identified, such as the lack of mechanisms to support the normalization of the situation after an interruption of the democratic order has occurred.[76] The OAS has also responded to the shifting regional context, in particular to defy leftist governments' objections to the IADC. In his 2007 report, the SG emphasized that the IADC proclaims social citizenship whereby democracy and socio-economic development are interdependent and mutually reinforcing. He suggested adopting the Social Charter of the Americas—devised by Hugo Chávez as a complement to the democratic charter—as a way of promoting social citizenship and strengthening democracy.[77] With respect to the perceived discrepancies between representative and participatory democracy, he stressed that the wording of the IADC reflects the meaning of democracy to which the countries in the Americas had long adhered. Hence the OAS should not reopen the debate over the content of democracy. The Permanent Council's dialogue process emphasized that the IADC repeatedly refers to citizen participation as a fundament for the effective exercise of representative democracy and thus regards representative democracy and participatory democracy as complementing, not excluding, each other.[78]

There are divergent opinions as to whether a reform of the IADC should be undertaken or not. SG Insulza tends to be in favor of reform. His 2010 report states that the mechanisms for strengthening democracy and for its collective defense must be enhanced as democracy evolves. While Resolution 1080 was a milestone in the early 1990s (see Chapter 2), 10 years later, the IADC was addressing new threats to democracy. Another 10 years on, the scenario facing the OAS has changed yet again, and the IADC mechanisms should be updated accordingly.[79] Others contest the necessity for reforming or refining the IADC, arguing that it already disposes of all the necessary instruments to defend democracy.[80] Additionally, in the face of the ideological divide reigning in the hemisphere and the fundamental disagreement about the concept of democracy, any reform proposal on the table, as reasonable as it may sound, is unlikely to be adopted at this stage. If the IADC were reopened with the aim to redraft some of its articles, the end product would probably be very different and less auspicious than the current text.[81] The Permanent Council in its 2011 deliberation thus reached a consensus to avoid an amendment of the IADC and preserve its original text.

Conclusion

The Honduran events in 2009 acted both as a catalyst and as a syndrome of a wider rearranging of the underlying tectonic plates of the inter-American system.[82] This shift in what we might call the management of inter-American relations and of the key issues on the hemispheric agenda has significant implications for the defense and promotion of democracy in the Americas. For anything as sensitive as the evaluation of the ongoing democratic processes in any given country in the American continent, a minimum consensus and shared perspective on how democracy should be defined is needed. That is precisely what the IADC did so effectively in 2001, raising expectations about the sort of democratic bonanza it would bring about. More than a decade later, that consensus, and many of the ancillary premises and considerations that should inform such democracy promotion programs are no longer extant.

This is largely attributable to fundamental changes of the regional environment, such as the emergence of several Latin American countries as regional or secondary regional powers and the relative decline of US power. US hegemony appears to be an issue of the past. The liberal concepts of free markets and representative democracy have been challenged by solidarity-based economic projects and calls for participatory democracy. Hemispheric regionalism has entered into crisis and new sub-regional organizations play a more important role and attempt to displace the OAS as the leading regional organization.

Against this background, there is an ongoing discussion whether and in what manner the text or the application of the IADC could be improved. Suggested changes relate to the OAS's difficulty in dealing with different variants of authoritarian regression, the possibility of taking action in early stages of a democratic crisis and the concept of democracy that the organization is supposed to spread. Yet, the region currently finds itself at an impasse regarding the prospects of further evolution of the defense of democracy regime. This is attributable to an ancient obstacle, the adherence of certain governments to the principle of non-intervention, and a more recent one, the Left swing in Latin America and the resulting ideological division and divergence about the concept of representative democracy.

Notes

1 Thomas Legler, "Learning the Hard Way. Defending Democracy in Honduras," *International Journal* 65, no. 3 (2010): 601–18 (603).
2 See Jorge Heine, "Regional Integration and Political Cooperation in Latin America," *Latin American Research Review* 47, no. 3 (2012): 209–17; Brigitte Weiffen, Leslie Wehner and Detlef Nolte, "Overlapping Regional Security Institutions in South America: The Case of OAS and UNASUR," *International Area Studies Review* 16, no. 4 (2013): 370–89.
3 See, for example, "The Inter-American Democratic Charter: Charting a Course to Irrelevance," *The Economist*, 27 January 2011.
4 See for example, Brigitte Weiffen, "Persistence and Change in Regional Security Institutions: Does the OAS Still have a Project?" *Contemporary Security Policy* 33, no. 2 (2012): 360–83.
5 Gian Luca Gardini and Peter Lambert, ed., *Latin American Foreign Policies: Between Ideology and Pragmatism* (New York: Palgrave Macmillan, 2011).
6 See Jorge Heine "Latin America Goes Global," *Americas Quarterly* 7, no. 2 (2013): 38–44.
7 Andrew Hurrell, "Brazil and the New Global Order," *Current History* 109, no. 724 (2010): 60–68; Andrés Malamud, "A Leader Without Followers? The Growing Divergence Between the Regional and Global Performance of Brazilian Foreign Policy," *Latin American Politics and Society* 53, no. 3 (2011): 1–24.
8 Maria Regina Soares de Lima and Mónica Hirst, "Brazil as an Intermediate State and Regional Power: Action, Choice and Responsibilities," *International Affairs* 82, no. 1 (2006): 21–40; Wolf Grabendorff, "Brasil: de coloso regional a potencia global," *Nueva Sociedad* 226 (2010): 158–71; Rafael Duarte Villa and Manuela Trindade Viana, "Security Issues During Lula's Administration: From the Reactive to the Assertive Approach," *Revista Brasileira de Política Internacional* 53, special issue (2010): 91–114.
9 UNASUR represents all 12 sovereign South American countries: Argentina, Bolivia, Brazil, Chile, Colombia, Ecuador, Guyana, Paraguay, Peru, Suriname, Uruguay, and Venezuela.
10 Pía Riggirozzi and Diana Tussie, "The Rise of Post-Hegemonic Regionalism in Latin America," in *The Rise of Post-Hegemonic Regionalism: The Case of Latin America*, ed. Pía Riggirozzi and Diana Tussie (Dordrecht, Netherlands: Springer, 2012), 1–16.
11 See Peter H. Smith, *Talons of the Eagle: Latin America, the United States, and the World* (New York and Oxford: Oxford University Press, 2008),

342–46. The literature on the rise of the Left in Latin America is extensive. See, among other books, Rosario Queirolo, *The Success of the Left in Latin America: Untainted Parties, Market Reforms and Voting Behavior* (South Bend, Ind.: University of Notre Dame Press, 2013); Cynthia Arnson and Carlos de la Torre, eds, *Latin American Populism in the Twenty First Century* (Baltimore, Md.: Woodrow Wilson International Center Press with Johns Hopkins University Press, 2013); Evelyn Huber and John D. Stephens, *Democracy and the Left: Social Policy and Inequality in Latin America* (Chicago, Ill.: University of Chicago Press, 2012); Steven Levitsky and Kenneth Roberts, eds, *The Resurgence of the Latin American Left* (Baltimore, Md.: Johns Hopkins University Press, 2011); Maxwell A. Cameron and Eric Hershberg, eds, *Latin America's Left Turn: Politics, Policies and Trajectories of Change* (Boulder, Colo.: Lynne Rienner, 2010); Kurt Weyland, Raúl L. Madrid and Wendy Hunter, eds, *Leftist Governments in Latin America: Successes and Shortcomings* (New York: Cambridge University Press, 2010); Jorge G. Castañeda and Marco A. Morales, eds, *Leftovers: Tales of the Latin American Left* (London: Routledge, 2008).

12 See "Declaration of Quebec City," Third Summit of the Americas, 22 April 2001, www.iin.oea.org/tercera_cumbre_ingles.htm.

13 The characteristics of the leftist concept of democracy are described by Steve Ellner, "The Distinguishing Features of Latin America's New Left in Power: The Chávez, Morales, and Correa Governments," *Latin American Perspectives* 39, no. 1 (2012): 96–114; Jonas Wolff, "New Constitutions and the Transformation of Democracy in Bolivia and Ecuador," in *New Constitutionalism in Latin America: Promises and Practices*, ed. Detlef Nolte and Almut Schilling-Vacaflor (Farnham: Ashgate, 2012), 183–202; Jonas Wolff, "Towards Post-Liberal Democracy in Latin America? A Conceptual Framework Applied to Bolivia," *Journal of Latin American Studies* 45, no. 1 (2013): 31–59.

14 For the civil society coalition that opposed the FTAA, see Marisa von Bülow, *Building Transnational Networks: Civil Society and the Politics of Trade in the Americas* (New York: Cambridge University Press, 2010).

15 Whereas 33 percent of Latin Americans considered the United States to be the region's "best friend" in 1996, by 2006 that figure had dropped to 25 percent. Data from Corporación Latinobarómetro, *¿La era de Obama? La imagen de Estados Unidos en América Latina 1996–2010*, 17 March 2011, www4.ibope.com.br/download/110318_la_era_obama.pdf.

16 This section draws on Jorge Heine, "Les relations avec l'Amerique latine: une opportunité manqué?" in *Obama et le monde: Quel leadership pour les États-Unis?* ed. Isabelle Vagnoux (Paris: Editions l'Aube, 2013), 285–302.

17 Corporación Latinobarómetro, *¿La era de Obama?*

18 In addition to numerous reports from The Brookings Institution (www.brookings.edu), The Council on Foreign Relations (www.cfr.org) and the Inter-American Dialogue (www.thedialogue.org), see Abraham F. Lowenthal, Theodore J. Piccone and Laurence Whitehead, ed., *The Obama Administration and The Americas: An Agenda for Change* (Washington, DC: Brookings Institution Press, 2009).

19 There is no US ambassador in Caracas and no one in La Paz, and no prospects for this by now established situation to change. In 2011, Ecuador declared the US ambassador *persona non grata*, and Mexico, though not

formally, did so effectively as well. Both US envoys had to leave their posts in a hurry, as did the Ecuadorean one accredited in Washington, in a predictable tit for tat.

20 Jorge Heine, "A Tale of Two Very Different Summits", *The Hindu*, 24 April 2012, www.thehindu.com/opinion/lead/a-tale-of-two-very-different-summits/article3346328.ece.

21 Juan Gabriel Tokatlian, "Bye, Bye Monroe, Hello Troilo," *El País*, 29 November 2013.

22 Ibid.

23 Ibid.

24 A more positive interpretation reads that by ignoring Latin America, Obama has not necessarily done the region a disservice, but has allowed it to mature on its own, free from US foreign policy ambitions.

25 As Buxton put it, "There is nothing to demonstrate that the Obama administration, Congress, media or intellectual opinion has grasped the transformations in hemispheric ties of the last decade. The United States remains behind the curve on issues of high salience for Latin American countries such as poverty, insecurity and peace building, and is locked into a unilateralist mode that provides negligible space for renovation." See Statement by Julia Buxton, "What Does 2014 Hold for U.S.-Latin America Relations?" *Latin America Advisor*, 20 December 2013.

26 This was made especially clear in the matter of illegal drugs and the deliberations on it in Cartagena. The fact that the United States was unwilling to accommodate the more flexible approach advocated by a number of Latin American countries on such a critical issue on the inter-American agenda, despite a strong push in that direction within the United States itself (as shown in the subsequent legalization of cannabis in the states of Colorado and Washington) speaks volumes, and has been described as "comedic" (see Buxton, "What Does 2014 Hold for U.S.-Latin America Relations?"). The 2013 legalization of cannabis in Uruguay and indications that neighboring countries may follow suit reflects the degree to which this particular issue has resonated and found traction in the region (see "Uruguay Becomes First Country to Oversee Production and Sale of Marijuana," *Mercopress*, 11 December 2013).

27 As mentioned in Chapter 5, one reason the gathering political storm in Tegucigalpa received so little attention from the leaders and bureaucrats from throughout the Americas meeting in San Pedro Sula those days was because the "Cuba issue" monopolized their attention, almost to the exclusion of everything else.

28 A classic example of this was the 14 November 2012 letter sent to the president of the OAS Permanent Council by four members of the US Senate Foreign Relations Committee, John Kerry, Richard Lugar, Robert Menendez and Marco Rubio. The letter questioned the personnel policy and staff assignments made by OAS SG Insulza, a matter one would have thought to be beyond the purview of the US Senate. See "Why are U.S. Lawmakers Coming Down so Hard on the OAS?" *Latin America Advisor*, 30 November 2012.

29 As a leading observer has put it, "U.S. relations with the region are atomized. There is no Latin America or Latin American policy. The United States has largely disengaged from OAS operations—and is more distant

from the region's countries than ever." See statement by Peter Hakim, "What Does 2014 Hold for U.S.-Latin America Relations?" *Latin America Advisor*, 20 December 2013.

30 Amitav Acharya, "The Emerging Regional Architecture of World Politics," *World Politics* 59, no. 4 (2007): 629–52 (643).

31 Acharya introduces the concept of "norm subsidiarity," a process whereby local actors create rules with a view to preserve their autonomy from dominance, neglect, violation, or abuse by more powerful actors. At the same time, when a new institution is created, regional powers have an incentive to influence its design, as the institutional design will constrain or facilitate how a regional power can pursue and materialize its interests in the new organization. See Amitav Acharya, "Norm Subsidiarity and Regional Orders: Sovereignty, Regionalism, and Rule-Making in the Third World," *International Studies Quarterly* 55, no. 1 (2011): 95–123.

32 As of December 2013, ALBA member states in South America were Venezuela, Bolivia, and Ecuador; members from Central America and the Caribbean were Nicaragua, Cuba, Dominica, Antigua and Barbuda, Saint Lucia, and Saint Vincent and Grenadines.

33 However, the bilateral agreements between Argentina and Brazil which preceded the foundation of MERCOSUR were driven not only by the impulse to strengthen economic cooperation, but also to consolidate democracy. See Olivier Dabène, "Consistency and Resilience through Cycles of Repoliticization," in *The Rise of Post-hegemonic Regionalism: The Case of Latin America*, ed. Pía Riggirozzi and Diana Tussie (Dordrecht, Netherlands: Springer, 2012), 41–64.

34 South American Union of Nations Constitutive Treaty, Art. 2.

35 Protocolo Adicional al Tratado Constitutivo de UNASUR sobre Compromiso con la Democracia, Art. 4; Protocolo de Montevideo sobre Compromiso con la Democracia en el MERCOSUR (Ushuaia II), Art. 6.

36 Personal interview with Theodore Piccone, Washington, DC, 24 May 2013.

37 Also see Chapter 3, "The Democratic Paradigm," in Mônica Herz, *The Organization of American States (OAS)* (London and New York: Routledge, 2011).

38 Andrew F. Cooper and Thomas Legler, *Intervention Without Intervening? The OAS Defense and Promotion of Democracy in the Americas* (New York: Palgrave Macmillan, 2006).

39 Peter Hakim, "Is Washington Losing Latin America?" *Foreign Affairs* 85, no. 1 (2006): 39–53.

40 Andrew F. Cooper, "Renewing the OAS," in *Which Way Latin America? Hemispheric Politics Meets Globalization*, ed. Andrew F. Cooper and Jorge Heine (Tokyo: United Nations University Press, 2009), 159–81.

41 Personal interview with Peter Hakim, Washington, DC, 28 May 2013.

42 Analyses of US democracy promotion strategies in Latin America have shown that US policy toward Cuba and Venezuela was inclined to hard-line forms of incentives and instruments of persuasion, often aimed at the ultimate goal of regime change. See Susanne Gratius and Thomas Legler, "Latin America is Different: Transatlantic Discord on How to Promote Democracy in 'Problematic' Countries," in *Promoting Democracy and the Rule of Law: American and European Strategies*, ed. Amichai Magen, Thomas Risse and Michael A. McFaul (Basingstoke: Palgrave Macmillan,

2009), 185–215. In Bolivia, concerns of US officials about what they see as deviance from standards of liberal democracy and the rule of law have led to the suspension of development cooperation and democracy assistance programs. See Jonas Wolff, "Democracy Promotion, Empowerment, and Self-Determination: Conflicting Objectives in US and German Policies Towards Bolivia," *Democratization* 19, no. 3 (2012): 415–37.

43 On this denouement of the Honduras crisis, see Chapter 5 in this book, as well as William Finnegan, "An Old-fashioned Coup: As Elections Loom, can a Deposed Leader Return?" *The New Yorker*, 30 November 2009, 38–45.

44 US–Brazilian relations were brought to their lowest point in recent memory by revelations of the United States' massive surveillance in Brazil and worldwide. In 2013, the US-Brazil diplomatic spat led first to the unprecedented cancellation of a Brazilian presidential state visit to Washington, and the subsequent loss of a US\$4.5 billion fighter-jet contract for Boeing.

45 Personal interview with Theodore Piccone; also see Rubén M. Perina, "The Inter-American Democratic Charter: An Assessment and Ways to Strengthen It," in *The Road to Hemispheric Cooperation: Beyond the Cartagena Summit of the Americas*, ed. The Brookings Institution (Washington, DC: The Brookings Institution, Latin America Initiative, 2012), 77–87. Perina argues that to accept a non-democratic Cuba's participation in the activities of the hemispheric community of democracies would either require a change in the rules for participating in the OAS and the presidential summits, or the hemispheric community would have to accept the participation of any future government that emerges out of a coup.

46 Detlef Nolte and Leslie Wehner, "UNASUR and Regional Security Governance in the Americas," in *Regional Organisations and Security: Conceptions and Practices*, ed. Stephen Aris and Andreas Wenger (London: Routledge, 2014), 183–202.

47 The strong reactions were not driven solely by an impulse to defend democracy, but also by economic motives. The MERCOSUR countries took advantage of Paraguay's suspension to admit Venezuela, a major oil supplier, whose accession to MERCOSUR had been blocked by the Paraguayan senate since 2006.

48 Personal interview with Kevin Casas-Zamora, Washington, DC, 24 May 2013.

49 Stephen J. Schnably, "The Santiago Commitment as a Call to Democracy in the United States: Evaluating the OAS Role in Haiti, Peru, and Guatemala," *University of Miami Inter-American Law Review* 25, no. 3 (1994): 393–587.

50 Yasmine Shamsie, "Building 'Low-Intensity' Democracy in Haiti: The OAS Contribution," *Third World Quarterly* 25, no. 6 (2004): 1097–115; Carolyn M. Shaw, "The United States: Rhetoric and Reality," in *Promoting Democracy in the Americas*, ed. Thomas Legler, Sharon F. Lean and Dexter S. Boniface (Baltimore, Md.: Johns Hopkins University Press, 2007), 63–84.

51 The Carter Center made two concrete proposals to improve the IADC: first, a clear definition of "unconstitutional alteration" or "interruption" (for more details, see Chapter 3); second, the creation of a set of graduated, automatic responses to overcome the inertia of political will that results from uncertain standards and the need to reach a consensus *de novo* on each alleged violation. When a democratic threat is identified, the alleged offenders would be requested to explain their actions before the Permanent

Council. After a full evaluation, possible responses could be chosen from a prescribed menu of options. See Jimmy Carter, "The Promise and Peril of Democracy," *International Journal of Not-for-Profit Law* 7, no. 2 (2005): 4–9.

52 "Draft Declaration of Florida: Delivering the Benefits of Democracy," OAS General Assembly document AG/doc.4476/05, 1 June 2005. Other initiatives include that of Acting SG Luigi Einaudi who at a preparatory meeting of the 2005 Summit of the Americas in Buenos Aires proposed the creation of a multilateral evaluation mechanism on democracy to give content to definitions and develop cooperative support for democratic institutions (see www.oas.org/es/centro_noticias/discurso.asp?sCodigo=05-0043).

53 "Promotion of Regional Cooperation for Implementation of the Inter-American Democratic Charter," OAS General Assembly Resolution 2154 (XXXV-O/05), 7 June 2005; "Declaration of Florida: Delivering the Benefits of Democracy," OAS General Assembly Declaration 41 (XXXV-O/05), 7 June 2005.

54 The report examines the IADC "in action" along three dimensions: "(a) monitoring the situation of democracies; (b) promoting democracy; and (c) applying the Democratic Charter in crisis situations". See *The Inter-American Democratic Charter—Report of the Secretary General Pursuant to Resolutions AG/RES. 2154 (XXXV-O/05) and AG/RES. 2251 (XXXVI-O/06)* (Permanent Council document OEA/Ser.G., CP doc. 4184/07), 4 April 2007.

55 *Report of the Secretary General Concerning Compliance with Operative Paragraph 3 of Resolution AG/Res.2480 (XXXIX-O/09) "Promotion and Strengthening of Democracy: Follow-up to the Inter-American Democratic Charter"* (Permanent Council document OEA/Ser.G., CP/doc.4487/10), 4 May 2010; *Update of the Secretary General of the OAS Reports on the Inter-American Democratic Charter Submitted to the Permanent Council in April 2007 and May 2010* (Permanent Council document OEA/Ser.G., CP/INF. 6222/11 corr. 1), 12 April 2011.

56 José Miguel Insulza, "Palabras de inauguración del XXXIV Curso de Derecho Internacional," XXXIV Course on International Law of the Inter-American Juridical Committee, Rio de Janeiro, Brazil, 3 August 2007.

57 In its appendix, the report also compiles early assessments of the IADC by various academic experts. See Jean-Paul Hubert, *Follow-up on the Application of the Inter-American Democratic Charter* (Inter-American Juridical Committee document 317/09, corr. 1), 19 March 2009. Also in 2009, the IACJ adopted a resolution on essential elements of representative democracy that enumerates and summarizes OAS definitions of representative democracy, from the 1959 Santiago Declaration to the IADC; see "The Essential and Fundamental Elements of Representative Democracy and their Relation to Collective Action within the Framework of the Inter-American Democratic Charter," Inter-American Juridical Committee Resolution 159 (LXXV-O/09), 12 August 2009.

58 "Promotion and Strengthening of Democracy: Follow-up to the Inter-American Democratic Charter," General Assembly Resolution 2555 (XL-O/19), 8 June 2010; "Promotion and Strengthening of Democracy: Follow-up to the Inter-American Democratic Charter," General Assembly Resolution 2694 (XLI-O/11), 7 June 2011.

59 *Final Report on the Dialogue on the Effectiveness of the Implementation of the Inter-American Democratic Charter* (Permanent Council document

OEA/Ser.G. CP/doc.4669/11 rev. 3), 14 December 2011. The official dialogue needs to be distinguished from several additional events held during the year 2011 to commemorate the tenth anniversary of the IADC. These events took place in Costa Rica (May 2011), Trinidad and Tobago (June 2011), Chile (September 2011) and Peru (September 2011). For a detailed documentation, see the appendices of the *Final Report on the Dialogue on the Effectiveness of the Implementation of the Inter-American Democratic Charter.*

60 The first three problems were already identified early on, as shown in Chapter 3 of this book. For the ongoing debate on the IADC, see *The Inter-American Democratic Charter—Report of the Secretary General Pursuant to Resolutions AG/RES. 2154 (XXXV-O/05) and AG/RES. 2251 (XXXVI-O/06)*; *Report of the Secretary General Concerning Compliance with Operative Paragraph 3 of Resolution AG/Res.2480 (XXXIX-O/09) "Promotion and Strengthening of Democracy: Follow-up to the Inter-American Democratic Charter"*; Hubert, *Follow-up on the Application of the Inter-American Democratic Charter.*

61 To date, the most encompassing of all proposals on how to strengthen the IADC was compiled by former OAS official Rubén Perina. See Perina, "The Inter-American Democratic Charter"; Rubén M. Perina, "Los desafíos de la Carta Democrática Interamericana," *Estudios Internacionales* 173 (2012): 7–36.

62 *The Inter-American Democratic Charter—Report of the Secretary General Pursuant to Resolutions AG/RES. 2154 (XXXV-O/05) and AG/RES. 2251 (XXXVI-O/06).*

63 Perina, "The Inter-American Democratic Charter."

64 *Report of the Secretary General Concerning Compliance with Operative Paragraph 3 of Resolution AG/Res.2480 (XXXIX-O/09) "Promotion and Strengthening of Democracy: Follow-up to the Inter-American Democratic Charter"*; *Final Report on the Dialogue on the Effectiveness of the Implementation of the Inter-American Democratic Charter.*

65 Ibid.

66 Thomas Legler, "The Inter-American Democratic Charter: Rhetoric or Reality?" in *Governing the Americas. Assessing Multilateral Institutions*, ed. Gordon Mace, Jean-Philippe Thérien and Paul Haslam (Boulder, Colo.: Lynne Rienner, 2007), 113–30.

67 The SG also suggested producing periodic (annual) reports on the main issues defined as essential for democracy in the IADC. *The Inter-American Democratic Charter—Report of the Secretary General Pursuant to Resolutions AG/RES. 2154 (XXXV-O/05) and AG/RES. 2251 (XXXVI-O/06).*

68 Hubert, *Follow-up on the Application of the Inter-American Democratic Charter*; Maxwell A. Cameron, "Strengthening Checks and Balances: Democracy Defence and Promotion in the Americas," *Canadian Foreign Policy* 10, no. 3 (2003): 101–16.

69 "The Essential and Fundamental Elements of Representative Democracy and their Relation to Collective Action within the Framework of the Inter-American Democratic Charter," Inter-American Juridical Committee Resolution 159 (LXXV-O/09), 12 August 2009; also see Carlos Ayala Corao and Pedro Nikken Bellshaw-Hógg, *Collective Defense of Democracy:*

Concepts and Procedures (Lima, Peru: Andean Commission of Jurists, 2006).

70 *Final Report on the Dialogue on the Effectiveness of the Implementation of the Inter-American Democratic Charter.*

71 *The Inter-American Democratic Charter—Report of the Secretary General Pursuant to Resolutions AG/RES. 2154 (XXXV-O/05) and AG/RES. 2251 (XXXVI-O/06).*

72 Sistema de Análisis Político y Escenarios Múltiples (SAPEM) in its Spanish version.

73 Sección de Análisis Político y Prospectiva (SAPyP) in Spanish.

74 Personal interview with Maria Fernanda Trigo, Director of the Department for Effective Public Management, former Deputy Director of the Department of Democratic Sustainability and Special Missions, OAS General Secretariat, Washington, DC, 23 May 2013; personal interview with Kevin Casas-Zamora; personal communication via e-mail with Karen Bozicovic, Chief of Political Analysis, Department of Democratic Sustainability and Special Missions, OAS General Secretariat, 5 August 2013. Also see www.oas.org/en/spa/dsdsm/analisis_politico.asp.

75 *Final Report on the Dialogue on the Effectiveness of the Implementation of the Inter-American Democratic Charter*; also see Jorge Santistevan de Noriega, "Should the Office of Ombudsman for Democracy Be Created in the Inter-American System?" *Latin American Policy* 3, no. 1 (2012): 102–10.

76 Moreover, some thought has been devoted to threats to democracy not inherent in the malfunctioning of political institutions—for example, security challenges posed by transnational organized crime and drug trade. See Anthony T. Bryan, "Democracy and Security: Observations from Mexico, Central America, and the Caribbean," *Latin American Policy* 3, no. 1 (2012): 88–101.

77 *The Inter-American Democratic Charter—Report of the Secretary General Pursuant to Resolutions AG/RES. 2154 (XXXV-O/05) and AG/RES. 2251 (XXXVI-O/06).* On the question how the IADC accounts for the interdependence between democracy and socioeconomic development, see Kristen Sample and Santiago Mariani, "A Democracy Results Approach: The Present Debate and Growing Consensus Surrounding the Inter-American Democratic Charter," *Latin American Policy* 3, no. 1 (2012): 119–26.

78 *Final Report on the Dialogue on the Effectiveness of the Implementation of the Inter-American Democratic Charter.*

79 *Report of the Secretary General Concerning Compliance with Operative Paragraph 3 of Resolution AG/Res.2480 (XXXIX-O/09) "Promotion and Strengthening of Democracy: Follow-up to the Inter-American Democratic Charter"*; also see José Miguel Insulza, "Message from the Organization of American States Secretary General," *Latin American Policy* 3, no. 1 (2012): 13–17.

80 César Gaviria Trujillo, "The Inter-American Democratic Charter at Ten: A Commitment by the Americas to the Defense and Promotion of Democracy," *Latin American Policy* 3, no. 1 (2012): 18–25. Michael Shifter (personal communication, Washington, DC, 30 May 2013) emphasized that refining the instruments would not be of any help, as political will is the most crucial factor for the application of the IADC. It would thus be interesting to investigate in more detail the political motivations driving

decisions to take action (or to refrain from taking action) in defense of democracy.
81 Personal interview with Kevin Casas-Zamora.
82 See Jorge I. Dominguez and Rafael Fernández de Castro, eds, *Contemporary U.S.-Latin American Relations: Cooperation or Conflict in the 21st Century* (New York: Routledge, 2010).

7 Conclusion

- Hemispheric reactions to democratic crises
- Challenges to the inter-American system
- Implications and avenues for future research

The OAS democratic paradigm must be set against the background of a long and protracted struggle to construct and consolidate democracy in Latin America. Much progress has been made since the 1980s. Once OAS member states defined the future of democracy in the Americas as a collective concern, they began to build a regional regime to promote and defend it. Although the adoption of such regimes is a global trend, in no part of the world have these provisions been institutionalized as early as in Latin America. As shown in Chapters 2 and 3, this regime was built through a series of political and legal instruments. The "crown jewel" of the regime is the IADC, adopted in 2001. To that we should add the many regional and sub-regional cooperation schemes that include a democracy clause. Those instruments stipulate a series of democracy promotion and defense norms, such as democracy as an obligatory membership criterion, the condemnation of seizures of power as unacceptable, and the possibility of sanctioning members in the event of an illegal alteration or interruption of the constitutional order (see Table 3.1).

The prime evidence that such a regime exists is found in a series of collective interventions, mainly by the OAS, to defend democracy in a number of countries across the region. In countries such as Haiti (1991), Paraguay (1996, 1999), Venezuela (1992, 2002) and Honduras (2009), *coups d'état* or the threat of coups were the main challenge countered by the organization. Authoritarian backsliding became the focus of the OAS in the 1990s. In Peru (1992) and Guatemala (1993), *autogolpes* by elected leaders were the detonators of a democratic crisis, as was electoral fraud later on in Peru (2000). The OAS has also attempted to respond to forced presidential resignations after pressure in Bolivia (2003, 2005) and Ecuador (1997, 2000, 2005). Finally, conflict among different branches of government or between national and provincial governments has prompted the OAS to take action in Ecuador (1997, 2005), Nicaragua (2005), Bolivia (2008) and Paraguay (2012).

Hemispheric reactions to democratic crises

Our findings unveil key achievements and limitations of the OAS in the field. The emergence of the regime of democracy promotion and defense as such is an important achievement. The fact that state leaders in a region where the principle of state sovereignty is still paramount agree to adopt enforcement measures to be activated once democracy in any given member state is interrupted, is evidence of their commitment to democratic norms. The dynamic growth of the regime, including two legally binding amendments to the OAS Charter in 1985 and 1992, and two key political documents—Resolution 1080 of 1991 and the IADC—as well as numerous other resolutions and declarations, show that democracy promotion as one of the organization's essential purposes is no longer just rhetoric.

In accordance with earlier studies, the cases reviewed in Chapters 2, 4 and 5 present a mixed picture regarding the ability of the OAS to contain or reverse democratic crises.[1] The organization has been quite proficient in responding to unambiguous crises. The *autogolpe* remained a transitory phenomenon of the 1990s, thanks to the negative international reaction to the Peruvian and Guatemalan experiences. Several countries, such as Paraguay and Venezuela, witnessed coup attempts or coup threats, but quick OAS action made it possible for elected governments to endure. In spite of the ultimately unsatisfactory outcome, the initial powerful international reaction to the Honduran crisis of 2009 signaled that the countries of the Americas were willing to meet any coup with strength and determination. Some evidence for a deterrent effect exists as well. After the successful military coup in Haiti in 1991, the first instance where the OAS invoked its Resolution 1080, the Americas were free from military coups, a remarkable fact in a region where they once were commonplace.

Yet, there are challenges to the international defense of democracy regime. The OAS's capacity to enforce democratic norms has severe limitations. To begin with, the regime's authority remains weak with respect to the prevention of democratic crises. The nature of the problems confronting democracies in the region has evolved since the

IADC was adopted. The overt manifestations of these crises have become more ambiguous. Such emblematic events as the bombing of the Palacio de la Moneda, Chile's presidential palace, in 1973, are very much a thing of the past. There will often be constitutionally elected officials and unelected leaders or institutions involved in these crises, using both legal and semi-legal tools to achieve their purposes. Soft coups, like the one in Paraguay in June 2012, are now more likely— situations where endogenous agents such as the legislature or the judiciary instrumentalize the military or mass protests to interrupt normal democratic procedures. Thus, the very term of what a "coup" is has become contested—as happened in the democratic crises that befell Honduras in 2009, Ecuador in 2010 and Paraguay in 2012. With its present tools, the OAS has trouble in addressing such ambiguous threats. Clear-cut violations of the democratic order are more likely to trigger reactions from abroad than ambiguous ones.

By the same token, as shown in Chapter 4, acute crises are more likely to provoke international reactions than creeping processes of democratic decline. Rather than a one-off event, the breakdown of democratic rule can be a slow, encroaching process that strips away the system of checks and balances on which democracy is based. The concept of unconstitutional alteration stipulated by Articles 19 and 20 of the IADC suggests that the OAS should take into account both democratic crises and decline. Yet, in a number of cases of the latter, the OAS has done nothing. In practice, then, the actual implementation of the IADC has so far prioritized the more clearly defined and more immediate, tangible threats to democracy. The evidence indicates that cases of decline are unlikely to trigger an international reaction until they cross a certain critical threshold—generally what may be considered a point of no return in terms of democratic backsliding.

Another weakness is the focus on the immediate crisis situation and the lack of follow-up monitoring. In the aftermath of a crisis, the actual impact of the organization's activities can only be inferred from the further trajectory of the country and is often subject to biased interpretations. Thus, the question of whether an intervention failed or succeeded is often hotly contested, as the case of Honduras vividly illustrates.

Challenges to the inter-American system

Some of those limitations are attributable to design flaws of the democratic charter. As discussed in Chapters 3 and 6, the IADC does contain omissions, such as a lack of benchmarks and thresholds for authoritarian backsliding, the privileged access of executives to its application, and insufficient provisions to anticipate democratic crises and take preventive action in their early stages. Another issue needing clarification is the very concept of democracy for which the OAS stands. Does the IADC need more "teeth" to be deployed swiftly and effectively? Or, alternatively, is prompt and effective action by the OAS member states simply a matter of political will that has little to do with any kind of statute or internationally subscribed document? A key question is thus whether and in what manner the text of the IADC should be changed so as to facilitate its application.

Yet, textual improvements would not by themselves guarantee that member states will invoke the IADC when democracy is threatened. It might be wise not to expect too much from a mere political accord as long as states do not even generally comply with binding international treaties. The democratic charter is interpreted not only as a handbook on how to counter democratic crisis, but also as an agreement on objectives. According to the OAS SG, the IADC "like any political program ... is an objective we desire to achieve," and should be used "as a paradigm to see what progress our countries have made in that direction."[2]

Furthermore, no such discussion is feasible within the inter-American system today. There has been a dramatic shift in the regional context where the regime and its actors operate. While the OAS had always been hampered by the cleavage between the United States and Latin American countries, the 1990s were a period of friendly ties and multilateral policy making. There was also a consensus around the notion of representative democracy as the point of reference for building and consolidating new democracies in the region. The first decade of the new millennium saw key changes in the regional environment. The near-consensus of the 1990s gave way to division and fragmentation. Hemispheric regionalism no longer holds sway, and new regional and sub-regional organizations have arisen, calling into question the role of the OAS as the leading regional organization. The Western hemisphere has seen the rise of new regional powers. A number of Latin American countries started to engage with the rest of the world in a much more proactive and assertive manner. Relative prosperity and the diversification of their economic relations have made those countries less reliant than ever on the United States.

This went hand in hand with what is widely perceived as a decline in US power—signaled by the events of 9/11 first, and of the 2008–09 financial crisis later. The liberal, free-market ideology dominant in the 1990s suddenly started to be challenged by alternative economic paradigms. There is no longer a single project under the rubric of democracy that unites the countries of the region. Rather, at least two rival visions of democracy—representative versus participatory—vie for support. The lack of a shared understanding of what constitutes democracy makes the collective defense of democracy more problematic. A growing number of sub-regional organizations, including UNASUR and CELAC, but also MERCOSUR and the CAN, contest the OAS' authority with regard to how democracy should be promoted and defended. The defense of democracy regime, if not in tatters, has been seriously weakened by the broader tearing of the fabric of the pan-American idea that has taken place in the course of the new century.

A key problem is the seeming inability of US foreign policy to come to terms with this new reality, and treat the newly emerging Latin American regional powers, like Brazil, or the newly created regional entities, like CELAC, as partners to engage with rather than as client states to be dictated to. Many of the frictions in inter-American relations in this past decade can be traced back to this syndrome, and make it difficult to make progress on an issue as sensitive as the defense and promotion of democracy regime, by now in an almost critical condition. Regional fragmentation is hence an impediment to any consensus on amending the IADC.

The denouement of the crises in Honduras and Paraguay reflected the enormous differences in the hemisphere as to the meaning and import of the IADC and the ensuing regional defense of democracy regime. Another more recent example is what occurred at the OAS on 19 February 2014 in response to the week-long student demonstrations and mass mobilizations (which were heavily repressed, leading to a number of fatalities) taking place in the Venezuelan capital, Caracas. After a number of years of ignoring and sidelining the OAS, the Obama Administration finally decided to engage it as a forum to discuss the tense situation in Venezuela. At the request of the United States, the issue was brought up in "other business" at the meeting of the OAS Permanent Council. Through its Permanent Representative, Carmen Lomellín, the United States denounced the handling of the demonstrations by the Venezuelan government and intimated that civil liberties and freedom of expression were being curtailed by the *chavista* government led by President Nicolás Maduro, to the effect that democracy was under threat. Yet, the United States found itself quite isolated, being able to count only on the support of Canada and Panama. The response from fellow Latin American governments, from Left to Right, was underwhelming. The Venezuelan representative's reply to all this was to paint the demonstrations in Caracas as simply just another orchestrated attempt at a *coup d'état*, aimed at destabilizing the regime in Venezuela—something not altogether discounted by those who remember only too well what had happened in the short-lived, but initially successful coup against Hugo Chávez in 2002.

If a divided OAS did not issue any resolution on Venezuelan developments, the same cannot be said of other regional and sub-regional entities. Both MERCOSUR and UNASUR issued measured statements that called for government and opposition to cool things down and search for a compromise, while also making clear that (despite what some considered to be the excesses of the police against the demonstrators) they supported the constitutionally elected government of Maduro and did not abet any efforts at destabilizing it. The hemispheric division on this could not have been starker—the United States, Canada and tiny Panama on one side, and everybody else on the other.

Implications and avenues for future research

Yet, the debate around this issue also indicates that there is a continuing demand for regional governance in the area of democracy promotion and defense. On that score, this book has unveiled a number of policy implications as well as open questions for further research in its three central thematic areas: the role of regional organizations as promoters and defenders of democracy; democratic development and the nature of challenges to democracy in Latin America; and the status and perspectives of inter-American relations.

The IADC is so far the most significant hemispheric document on democratic rule and the ways of preserving it. The extant regional democracy promotion regime has helped democracy "find its feet" and make sure Latin America does not experience democratic breakdown. Yet, as the IADC enters its second decade, it is unclear whether it will remain the steady stalwart of democratic rule, or whether it needs an upgrade to make it conform to new realities. The "democracy promotion momentum" that gathered steam in the 1990s and the initial years of this century seems to have fizzled out. A core question to resolve is thus whether and by what means it is still possible to give new life to the democracy promotion regime in the making a decade ago, or whether that has by now become a futile, if not downright impossible, task.

To that end, some lessons can be drawn from the hitherto existing experiences in countering democratic crises. The nature of threats to democracy has changed since the IADC was adopted. The OAS must therefore adjust its responses to new circumstances. It must also strike a delicate balance between acting as a neutral arbiter and signaling resolve. The impossibility of influencing the course of events in Honduras once the country was suspended from the OAS in July 2009 showed that, perhaps, an automatic, by-the-book reaction might not always be helpful to overcome a crisis. On the other hand, the more cautious approach taken in reaction to the removal of the president of Paraguay in 2012 was interpreted by some as a sign of weakness and indeterminacy.

Monitoring of countries at risk could provide the information on the domestic setting that is needed to arrive at a well-informed decision. Before taking action, OAS decision makers need to know the origins of a crisis and untangle the various signals that aim to influence an intervention decision. The organization should strive to avoid ideologically biased actions when dealing with regimes disliked or favored by those countries that take the lead in the decision. Additionally, the OAS and the international community must be sensitive to the highly complex, transnational playing field upon which efforts to defend democracy unfold.

To learn more about regional democracy promotion, a stronger comparative perspective would be desirable. So far, most studies of regional organizations as democracy promoters have examined particular organizations at a particular point in time. It would be worthwhile to study the development of the defense of democracy regime across time and across various regional organizations to carve out processes of diffusion, emulation and organizational learning. More systematic research is also needed to analyze the effects of regional democracy promotion. When the outcome is democratic continuity, the explanatory power of instruments to defend democracy is difficult to isolate from other influential factors. So far, what we know about these organizations' capacity to put democratic norms into practice and to apply the defense of democracy mechanisms rests largely on anecdotal evidence. While case descriptions offer a nuanced account of different OAS reactions to various sorts of democratic crises, they do not tell us much about the concrete success of OAS responses and the impact of the organization's activities.

In light of the recent proliferation of provisions to defend democracy in Latin America (see Table 6.1), another interesting angle is institutional overlap.[3] Future research should address the motives of forming new sub-regional regimes for the defense of democracy when there is already one in place. The same goes for the features of those regimes, and their record in comparison to the OAS. The effects of such overlap should be explored in order to assess whether the coexistence of various regional democracy clauses leads to a beneficial effect of mutual reinforcement, or to competition or even contradiction and unhelpful interference between divergent approaches to the promotion and defense of democracy. This becomes particularly relevant when the different regimes diverge in their assessment of a crisis, as was the case in Paraguay in 2012.

Democracy has made much headway in the Americas, but also faces a number of significant challenges. The concept of democracy—and hence the understanding of what constitutes a democratic crisis—is a bone of contention. Even against the background of a regional consensus, there is a growing rift between blueprints of democracy fostered on the regional level and autochthonous trajectories of it. Whereas some thought has been devoted to democratic innovations in particular countries,[4] the regional implications have not received the same amount of attention. The IADC provides mechanisms to react to unconstitutional interruptions and alterations of the democratic order. Yet, the definition of what constitutes an unconstitutional interruption or alteration is increasingly contested. This is due to the morphing of democracy in a number of states from representative to participatory, from liberal to social and from exclusive to inclusive models. The Honduras crisis of 2009 underscored the very different perspectives extant in the United States and in the region on what democracy is all about and what should be done to defend it. It called into question the validity of the defense and promotion of democracy regime in the Americas. Increasingly, the regional democracy promotion regime collides with reformist governments' alternative political projects on the domestic level.

In the field of inter-American relations, as has been shown in Chapter 6, the Western hemisphere is changing from what used to be known as the United States' backyard toward a more autonomous and assertive stance of Latin American countries. Thus, new cleavages and ideological debates have emerged. This makes it imperative to produce a more nuanced picture of regional power dynamics. Future studies should connect research on regionalism to research on rising powers and investigate the strategies of emerging regional powers to cope with a longstanding dominant power, as well as the role of secondary regional powers. The latter is of particular relevance for regional organizations in the Americas, where the cause of promoting and defending democracy was advanced primarily by small and medium-sized states.

Notes

1 Earlier comparative studies of OAS reactions to democratic crises include Andrew F. Cooper and Thomas Legler, "A Tale of Two Mesas: The OAS

Defense of Democracy in Peru and Venezuela," *Global Governance* 11, no. 4 (2005): 425–44; Andrew F. Cooper and Thomas Legler, *Intervention Without Intervening? The OAS Defense and Promotion of Democracy in the Americas* (New York: Palgrave Macmillan, 2006); Barry S. Levitt, "A Desultory Defense of Democracy: OAS Resolution 1080 and the Inter-American Democratic Charter," *Latin American Politics and Society* 48, no. 3 (2006): 93–123; Craig Arceneaux and David Pion-Berlin, "Issues, Threats, and Institutions: Explaining OAS Responses to Democratic Dilemmas in Latin America," *Latin American Politics and Society* 49, no. 2 (2007): 1–31.

2 *Update of the Secretary General of the OAS Reports on the Inter-American Democratic Charter Submitted to the Permanent Council in April 2007 and May 2010* (Permanent Council document OEA/Ser.G., CP/INF. 6222/11 corr. 1), 12 April 2011.

3 In the Latin American context, this phenomenon has so far been examined for regional economic integration schemes and security cooperation. See Andrés Malamud and Gian Luca Gardini, "Has Regionalism Peaked? The Latin American Quagmire and its Lessons," *The International Spectator* 47, no. 1 (2012): 116–33; Pía Riggirozzi, "Region, Regionness and Regionalism in Latin America: Towards a New Synthesis," *New Political Economy* 17, no. 4 (2012): 421–43; Brigitte Weiffen, Leslie Wehner and Detlef Nolte, "Overlapping Regional Security Institutions in South America: The Case of OAS and UNASUR," *International Area Studies Review* 16, no. 4 (2013): 370–89.

4 See, for example Maxwell A. Cameron, Eric Hershberg and Kenneth E. Sharpe, eds, *New Institutions for Participatory Democracy in Latin America: Voice and Consequence* (New York: Palgrave Macmillan, 2012); Enrique Peruzzotti, "Broadening the Notion of Democratic Accountability: Participatory Innovation in Latin America," *Polity* 44, no. 4 (2012): 625–42; Thamy Pogrebinschi, "The Squared Circle of Participatory Democracy: Scaling up Deliberation to the National Level," *Critical Policy Studies* 7, no. 3 (2013): 219–41; Jonas Wolff, "Towards Post-Liberal Democracy in Latin America? A Conceptual Framework Applied to Bolivia," *Journal of Latin American Studies* 45, no. 1 (2013): 31–59.

Select bibliography

Regional organizations and democracy promotion

Daniela Donno, *Defending Democratic Norms: International Actors and the Politics of Electoral Misconduct* (New York: Oxford University Press, 2013).

Edward R. McMahon and Scott H. Baker, *Piecing a Democratic Quilt. Regional Organizations and Universal Norms* (Bloomfield, Conn.: Kumarian, 2006).

Jon C. Pevehouse, *Democracy from Above. Regional Organizations and Democratization* (Cambridge: Cambridge University Press, 2005).

OAS

Mônica Herz, *The Organization of American States (OAS)* (London and New York: Routledge, 2011).

Carolyn M. Shaw, *Cooperation, Conflict, and Consensus in the Organization of American States* (New York: Palgrave Macmillan, 2004).

Viron P. Vaky and Heraldo Muñoz, *The Future of the Organization of American States* (New York: Twentieth Century Fund, 1993).

Brigitte Weiffen, "Persistence and Change in Regional Security Institutions: Does the OAS still have a Project?" *Contemporary Security Policy* 33, no. 2 (2012): 360–83.

History of the democratic paradigm

Mauricio Alice, *La evaluación de la eficacia de la OEA en crisis democráticas en el continente. Las posiciones argentinas* (Buenos Aires, Argentina: Nuevohacer, 2002).

Tom Farer, ed., *Beyond Sovereignty. Collectively Defending Democracy in the Americas* (Baltimore, Md. and London: Johns Hopkins University Press, 1996).

Heraldo Muñoz, "The Right to Democracy in the Americas," *Journal of Interamerican Studies and World Affairs* 40, no. 1 (1998): 1–18.

The Inter-American Democratic Charter

Legal aspects

Carlos Ayala Corao and Pedro Nikken Bellshaw-Hógg, *Collective Defense of Democracy: Concepts and Procedures* (Lima, Peru: Andean Commission of Jurists, 2006), www.cartercenter.org/documents/collectivedefenseofdemocracy.pdf.

Enrique Lagos and Timothy D. Rudy, "In Defense of Democracy," *University of Miami Inter-American Law Review* 35, no. 2 (2004): 283–309.

Political aspects

Canadian Foreign Policy 10, no. 3 (2003) Special issue on the Inter-American Democratic Charter, with contributions by Maxwell A. Cameron, Lloyd Axworthy, Robert A. Pastor, Andrew F. Cooper, Lisa M. Sundstrom, Thomas Legler, Pablo Policzer, Geneviève Lessard.

Andrew F. Cooper, "The Making of the Inter-American Democratic Charter: A Case of Complex Multilateralism," *International Studies Perspectives* 5, no. 1 (2004): 92–113.

Latin American Policy 3, no. 1 (2012) Special issue on the tenth anniversary of the Inter-American Democratic Charter, with contributions by Thomas Legler, Riyad Insanally, Santiago Mariani, Timothy M. Shaw, José Miguel Insulza, César Gaviria Trujillo, Víctor Rico, Jennifer L. McCoy, Maxwell A. Cameron, Anthony T. Bryan, Jorge Santistevan de Noriega, Rafael Roncagliolo, Kristen Sample, Diego García-Sayán.

Thomas Legler, "The Inter-American Democratic Charter: Rhetoric or Reality?" in *Governing the Americas. Assessing Multilateral Institutions*, ed. Gordon Mace, Jean-Philippe Thérien and Paul Haslam (Boulder, Colo.: Lynne Rienner, 2007), 113–30.

——"The Shifting Sands of Regional Governance: The Case of Inter-American Democracy Promotion," *Politics & Policy* 40, no. 5 (2012): 848–70.

Documents

Humberto de la Calle, ed., *Carta Democrática Interamericana: documentos e interpretaciones* (Washington, DC: Organization of American States, 2003), www.oas.org/oaspage/esp/Publicaciones/CartaDemocratica_spa.pdf.

Jean-Paul Hubert, *Follow-up on the Application of the Inter-American Democratic Charter* (Inter-American Juridical Committee document CJI/doc.317/09 corr. 1), 19 March 2009, scm.oas.org/pdfs/2009/CP22837E-1.pdf.

OAS responses to democratic crises

Craig Arceneaux and David Pion-Berlin, "Issues, Threats, and Institutions: Explaining OAS Responses to Democratic Dilemmas in Latin America," *Latin American Politics and Society* 49, no. 2 (2007): 1–31.

Andrew F. Cooper and Thomas Legler, *Intervention Without Intervening? The OAS Defense and Promotion of Democracy in the Americas* (New York: Palgrave Macmillan, 2006).

Thomas Legler, Sharon F. Lean and Dexter S. Boniface, eds, *Promoting Democracy in the Americas* (Baltimore, Md.: Johns Hopkins University Press, 2007).

Barry S. Levitt, "A Desultory Defense of Democracy: OAS Resolution 1080 and the Inter-American Democratic Charter," *Latin American Politics and Society* 48, no. 3 (2006): 93–123.

The Honduran crisis

Comisión de la Verdad y la Reconciliación, *Para que los hechos no se repitan: Informe de la Comisión de la Verdad y la Reconciliación* (Tegucigalpa, Honduras: Comisión de la Verdad y la Reconciliación, 2011).

Human Rights Foundation, *The Facts and the Law: Behind the Democratic Crisis of Honduras, 2009* (New York: Human Rights Foundation, 2009).

Inter-American Commission on Human Rights, *Honduras: Human Rights and the Coup d'état*, OEA/Ser.L/V/II. Doc. 55 (San José, Costa Rica: Inter-American Commission on Human Rights, 2009).

Thomas Legler, "Learning the Hard Way. Defending Democracy in Honduras," *International Journal* 65, no. 3 (2010): 601–18.

Nueva Sociedad 226 (2010) Special issue on "Honduras, Status Quo," with contributions by Álvaro Cálix, Edelberto Torres Rivas, José Miguel Cruz, Carlos A. Romero, Manuel Rojas Bolaños, Pedro Páramo, José Antonio Sanahuja, Raúl Benítez Manaut, Rut Diamint, Wolf Grabendorff.

Multilateralism in the Americas

The Brookings Institution, *The Road to Hemispheric Cooperation: Beyond the Cartagena Summit of the Americas* (Washington, DC: The Brookings Institution, Latin America Initiative, 2012), www.brookings.edu/research/reports/2012/07/07-summit-of-the-americas.

Andrew F. Cooper and Jorge Heine, eds, *Which Way Latin America? Hemispheric Politics Meets Globalization* (Tokyo: United Nations University Press, 2009).

Olivier Dabène, *The Politics of Regional Integration in Latin America. Theoretical and Comparative Explorations* (New York: Palgrave Macmillan, 2009).

FOCAL, *Latin American Multilateralism: New Directions* (Ottawa: Canadian Foundation for the Americas, 2010), www.focal.ca/images/stories/Multilateralism_Compilation_Latin_American_Multilateralism_New_Directions_sm.pdf.

Jorge Heine, "Between a Rock and a Hard Place: Latin America and Multilateralism after 9/11," in *Multilateralism under Challenge? Power, International Order and Structural Change*, ed. Edward Newman, Ramesh Thakur and John Tirman (Tokyo: United Nations University Press, 2006), 481–503.

Pía Riggirozzi and Diana Tussie, ed., *The Rise of Post-hegemonic Regionalism. The Case of Latin America* (Dordrecht, Netherlands: Springer, 2012).

Peter H. Smith, *Talons of the Eagle. Latin America, the United States, and the World* (New York/Oxford: Oxford University Press, 2008).

Index

accountability 1, 75, 77; horizontal accountability 2–3, 52

ALBA (Bolivarian Alliance for the Peoples of Our America) 5, 140, 155; contender to OAS 140–41; Honduras 107–8, 113, 117–18; Venezuela 5, 107–8, 141

APEC (Asia-Pacific Economic Cooperation) 135

Argentina: 2001 democratic crisis 80, 89; De la Rúa, Fernando 89; defective democracy 3; dictatorship 35; mass mobilization and protests 80, 89; Menem, Carlos 52; OAS 89

ASEAN (Association of Southeast Asian Nations) 10

AU (African Union) 10

authoritarian regression 7, 51, 132, 151; Argentina 52; Brazil 52; *decretismo* 52; democratic backsliding 56, 57, 75–76, 163; IADC 53–54, 56–61, 65–67; Peru 52–54

autocracy 4, 16–17, 26, 32, 82, 100

Bolivia: 2003 democratic crisis 80, 89–91, 96, 162; 2005 democratic crisis 80, 91–92, 96, 162; 2008 democratic crisis 80, 94, 103–4, 142, 145, 162; ALBA 5, 107, 110, 155; constitutional reform 94, 110; defective democracy 3; democratic decline 91; leftist government 136; mass mobilization and protests 80, 89–91, 91–92, 94; Mesa, Carlos

90–91; Morales, Evo 91, 94, 136; OAS 90–92, 94, 96, 162; Sánchez de Lozada, Gonzalo 89–90; UNASUR 104, 152; US 89–90

Brazil 5, 134–35, 165; Collor de Mello, Fernando 52; democracy in consolidation 3; democratic commitment 99; foreign policy 134–35; Honduran crisis 119–20; IBSA Dialogue Forum 135; Lula da Silva, Luiz Inácio 134–35; Pericas, Bernardo 38; regional power 5, 99, 105, 134, 141, 165; Rousseff, Dilma 95; UNASUR 5, 135; US/Brazil relations 105, 141, 144, 156

BRICS (Brazil, Russia, India, China, South Africa) 134, 135

BTI (Bertelsmann Transformation Index) 3, 7–8

CAFTA-DR (Dominican Republic-Central America-United States Free Trade Agreement) 138

CAN (Andean Community, formerly Andean Pact) 4, 10, 37, 142, 165; democracy promotion and defense 21, 142

Canada 36, 53, 54, 106, 117, 132, 165–66; Honduran crisis 106, 117; role in the OAS 36, 53–54

CARICOM (Caribbean Community) 86, 117

Carter Center 73, 85, 146, 148, 156–57; Friends of the

threats to democracy 63–64, 65–67; democratic crisis 96–99 (invoking the IADC 83–86, 96–97); deterrent effect 60; distinction from Resolution 1080 64; distinction from Washington Protocol 61–62, 71; development 55; enforcement 57, 58–61; geopolitical context 67–69; key principles 54–56, 69; Honduras, 2009 coup 57–58, 60, 71, 87, 116–17, 123; human rights 55; leftist governments 68, 69, 150, 152; origins and antecedents 51–54, 56–57, 69; reform of 7, 64, 132, 133, 146–51, 156–57, 158, 159–60, 164 (legally binding document 147; OAS Permanent Council 148–51; OAS Secretary-General 146–51, 158); representative democracy 51, 55, 69, 71, 136, 149, 150, 153, 157 (representative/ participatory democracy discrepancies 150, 151); right to democracy 55, 56, 69, 147; sanctions 58–60; US 68, 69, 143–44; *see also* IADC, Articles and Chapters; IADC, limitations

IADC, Articles and Chapters 54–61, 69; Article 1: 55, 69, 147; Articles 3–4: 55, 66, 69, 148–49; Article 17: 57–58, 62, 63, 69, 84, 86, 87, 94, 96, 103–4, 116, 123, 128–29, 149; Article 18: 58, 62, 69, 84, 92–93, 93–94, 103, 149; Article 19: 58, 97, 149, 163; Article 20: 58–60, 69, 84, 86–87, 96, 116–17, 149, 163; Article 21: 58, 60, 62, 63, 71, 84, 87, 96, 117, 149; Chapter I 54, 55; Chapter II 55; Chapter III 55; Chapter IV 51, 54, 55–56, 57, 61, 63–64, 66, 69, 84, 87, 96–97, 143, 147, 148–49; Chapter V 55, 56; *see also* IADC

IADC, limitations 61–68, 69, 147, 162–64; concept of democracy 136, 151, 152, 164, 168; legal status of the document 61–62, 69, 147; non-intervention principle 54, 56, 57, 62, 69, 73, 147, 152; role of

the executive in IADC's application 61, 62–63, 69, 98, 123, 147–48, 164; state sovereignty 54, 56, 64, 69; vagueness in defining the antidemocratic scenario 63–64, 69, 98–99, 147–50, 162–64; *see also* IADC
IAJC (Inter-American Juridical Committee) 34, 146, 148–49
IMF (International Monetary Fund) 106, 118
inequality 2, 44, 55, 74–75
Insulza, José Miguel 58, 60, 66, 88, 93, 95, 103, 104, 116–17, 146, 150, 154, 164
inter-American relations: contestations about democracy promotion 143–45; defense of democracy 125–26, 132–60, 164–65, 166; Honduran crisis 6–7, 107, 135, 151 (precedent for military coup in the region 7, 106, 123–24, 132); IADC reform 64, 133, 146–51; Latin America's new assertiveness 133–36, 138, 164, 168 (Brazil 134–35, 141, 165; rise of new regional actors 133, 134, 151); Left, rise of 132, 133, 135–36, 138, 145, 152 (pink tide 135–36; populism 135); new regionalism 133, 134, 138, 139–43, 164 (new regional cooperation and integration schemes 139, 140, 144–45, 164; regional fragmentation 164, 165–66); pan-Americanism 125,135, 139–40, 165 (hemispheric meetings as fields of contestation 139–40); Summit of the Americas 4, 54, 133, 137, 140; *see also* US/Latin American relations
international relations 3, 5, 10–11, 14, 26
intervention: definition 82–83; military intervention 16, 18, 21; US unilateral intervention 33–34, 36, 37, 68, 126, 134, 154; *see also* enforcement; sanctions

Routledge Global Institutions Series

The International Monetary Fund (2nd edition)
Politics of conditional lending
by James Raymond Vreeland (Georgetown University)

The UN Global Compact
by Catia Gregoratti (Lund University)

Institutions for Women's Rights
*by Charlotte Patton (York College, CUNY) and
Carolyn Stephenson (University of Hawaii)*

International Aid
by Paul Mosley (University of Sheffield)

Global Consumer Policy
by Karsten Ronit (University of Copenhagen)

The Changing Political Map of Global Governance
*by Anthony Payne (University of Sheffield) and
Stephen Robert Buzdugan (Manchester Metropolitan University)*

Coping with Nuclear Weapons
by W. Pal Sidhu

EU Environmental Policy and Climate Change
*by Henrik Selin (Boston University) and
Stacy VanDeveer (University of New Hampshire)*

Global Governance and China
The dragon's learning curve
Edited by Scott Kennedy (Indiana University)

The Politics of Global Economic Surveillance
by Martin S. Edwards (Seton Hall University)

Mercy and Mercenaries
Humanitarian agencies and private security companies
by Peter Hoffman

Regional Organizations in the Middle East
by James Worrall (University of Leeds)

Governing Climate Change (2nd edition)
Peter Newell (University of East Anglia) and
Harriet A. Bulkeley (Durham University)

Contemporary Human Rights Ideas (2nd edition)
Betrand Ramcharan (Geneva Graduate Institute of International and
Development Studies)

Protecting the Internally Displaced
Rhetoric and reality
Phil Orchard (University of Queensland)

The Arctic Council
Within the far north
Douglas C. Nord (Umea University)

For further information regarding the series, please contact:
Craig Fowlie, Publisher, Politics & International Studies
Taylor & Francis
2 Park Square, Milton Park, Abingdon
Oxford OX14 4RN, UK
+44 (0)207 842 2057 Tel
+44 (0)207 842 2302 Fax
Craig.Fowlie@tandf.co.uk
www.routledge.com